Praise for Harold Sche[chter]
accounts, "well-documented nightmares
for anyone who dares to look."*

FIEND
The Shocking True Story of
America's Youngest Serial Killer

"A memorably gothic tale.... True-crime lovers will
not want to miss it."
—*Publishers Weekly*

"[Schechter] blends his research into a seamless story,
fascinating in its horror, as well as its ability to turn the
century-old characters into real people.... In *Fiend*,
Schechter succeeds at reminding us that modern times
don't have a monopoly on juvenile terror."
—*Amazon.com*

BESTIAL
The Savage Trail of a True American Monster

"[An] essential addition.... Deserves to be read and
pored over by the hard crime enthusiast as well as devo-
tees of social history."
—*The Boston Book Review*

"*Bestial* spare[s] no graphic detail.... Reads like fast-
paced fiction, complete with action, plot twists, suspense,
and eerie foreshadowing.... Provides chilling insights
into the motivations of a man who killed for killing's
sake."
—*Amazon.com*

"[A] deftly written, unflinching account."
—*Journal Star* (Peoria, IL)*

DEPRAVED
The Shocking True Story of
America's First Serial Killer

"Meticulously researched, brilliantly detailed, and above all riveting. . . . Schechter has done his usual sterling job in resurrecting this amazing tale."

—Caleb Carr, bestselling author of *The Alienist*

"Must reading for crime buffs. Gruesome, awesome, compelling reporting."

—Ann Rule

DERANGED
The Shocking True Story of
America's Most Fiendish Killer

"Reads like fiction but it's chillingly real. . . ."

—*The Philadelphia Inquirer*

DEVIANT
The Shocking True Story of Ed Gein,
the Original "Psycho"

"[A] grisly, wonderful book. . . . Scrupulously researched."

—*Film Quarterly*

THE A TO Z ENCYCLOPEDIA
OF SERIAL KILLERS
By Harold Schechter and David Everitt

"The scholarship is both genuine and fascinating."

—*The Boston Book Review*

"A grisly tome. . . . Schechter knows his subject matter."

—*Denver Rocky Mountain News*

And praise for Harold Schechter's historical crime fiction featuring Edgar Allan Poe

THE HUM BUG

A riveting excursion. . . . Poe and his times come across with wonderful credibility and vitality."

—*Booklist*

"Evocative. . . ."

—*Kirkus Reviews*

"Schechter effectively conveys the climate of New York at a time when people were easily suckered by Barnum's tricks."

—*Library Journal*

NEVERMORE

"In this gripping, suspenseful thriller, Harold Schechter does a splendid job of capturing the spirit of Edgar Allan Poe. I'm sure my late, great cousin would have loved *Nevermore!*"

—Anne Poe Lehr

"Schechter's entertaining premise is supported by rich period atmospherics. . . . Keeps the finger of suspicion wandering until the very end."

—*The New York Times Book Review*

"A literary confection. . . . A first-rate mystery."

—*Booklist*

"Authentic. . . . Engaging. . . . Schechter manages at once to be faithful to Poe's voice, and to poke gentle fun at it—to swing breezily between parody and homage."

—*The Baltimore Sun*

Pocket Books by Harold Schechter

NON-FICTION

The A-Z Encyclopedia of Serial Killers
   (with David Everitt)

Deranged

Depraved

Deviant

Fiend

Bestial

Fatal

FICTION

Nevermore

The Hum Bug

Outcry

HAROLD SCHECHTER

The Poisonous Life
of a Female Serial Killer

POCKET **STAR** BOOKS
New York   London   Toronto   Sydney   Singapore

The sale of this book without its cover is unauthorized. If you purchased this book without a cover, you should be aware that it was reported to the publisher as "unsold and destroyed." Neither the author nor the publisher has received payment for the sale of this "stripped book."

An *Original* Publication of POCKET BOOKS

 A Pocket Star Book published by
POCKET BOOKS, a division of Simon & Schuster, Inc.
1230 Avenue of the Americas, New York, NY 10020

Copyright © 2003 by Harold Schechter

All rights reserved, including the right to reproduce this book or portions thereof in any form whatsoever. For information address Pocket Books, 1230 Avenue of the Americas, New York, NY 10020

ISBN: 978-1-4391-8264-2

First Pocket Books printing July 2003

10 9 8 7 6 5 4 3 2 1

POCKET STAR BOOKS and colophon are registered trademarks of Simon & Schuster, Inc.

For information regarding special discounts for bulk purchases, please contact Simon & Schuster Special Sales at 1-800-456-6798 or business@simonandschuster.com

Cover design by Brigid Pearson
Photo by Misha Gravenor/Getty Images

Printed in the U.S.A.

For Kimiko
femme fatale

The cursed crimes of the secret poisoner
We must confess are the worst of all,
You bless the hand that smooths your pillow,
But by that hand you surely fall.
You put your trust in those about you,
When you lie sick upon your bed,
While you are blessing they are wishing
The very next moment would find you dead.

—Nineteenth-century broadside ballad

INTRODUCTION

FOR A PERIOD OF EXACTLY ONE YEAR, BEGINNING IN late 1989, a string of male motorists in central Florida ended up dead in the woods after picking up a roadside hooker named Aileen Wuornos. At the time of her arrest, Wuornos—who had led an extraordinarily brutalized life from childhood on—claimed that she had only been acting in self-defense. All seven of the victims, she insisted, had viciously attacked her. For the sake of her own self-preservation, she'd been forced to shoot each of them repeatedly with a .22-caliber semiautomatic, empty their pockets, steal their cars, and dump their corpses in various junkyards, vacant lots, and remote wooded areas.

Needless to say, prosecutors saw things very differently, portraying Wuornos as a cold-blooded predator who murdered partly for money but mostly for the sheer joy of it. The jury agreed, and Wuornos earned immediate infamy, not just as a homicidal maniac, but as something far more monstrous and alarming—the first woman serial killer in our nation's history.

Besides a death sentence (carried out, after much delay, in October 2002), this dubious distinction brought her the kind of celebrity we bestow on our most notorious criminals. Not long after her conviction, the first of several made-for-TV movies about her case hit the airwaves, and she has since been the subject of everything from a critically acclaimed documentary (Nick Broomfield's *Aileen Wuornos: The Selling of a Serial Killer*) to assorted Court TV specials. All of these works have treated her as a figure of considerable significance in the annals of crime: "America's First Female Serial Killer." There is, however, a serious problem with this label.

It's completely untrue.

In spite of the popular belief that sociopathic violence is a strictly male phenomenon, the fact is that women have always accounted for a sizable proportion of humanity's most prolific and reprehensible multiple-murderers. It is only in recent years, however, that serious attention has begun to be paid to the subject of female serial killers, in studies like Patricia Pearson's *When She was Bad* (1997) and Michael and C. L. Kelleher's *Murder Most Rare* (1998). The subject of my own book is a woman born in 1854—exactly a century before Aileen Wuornos was conceived—who conforms in every respect to the classic pattern of the psychopathic sex-killer. A true Jekyll-and-Hyde personality, she possessed a professional competence and affable charm that made her a valued companion to a large circle of people, who trusted her with their very lives. Beneath her jovial exterior, however, there lurked a being of genuinely monstrous drives and appetites—an implacable sadist who derived intense, sexual pleasure from watching a succession of innocent victims perish slowly at her hands. Jane Toppan was her name, and though degrees of evil are difficult to gauge, the sheer malignancy she embodied was, at the very least, equal to that of her better-known male counterparts.

The question, then, inevitably arises: How is it that when people hear the term "serial killer," they immediately think of men—John Wayne Gacy, Ted Bundy, Jeffrey Dahmer, et al.? And why are they surprised, if not incredulous, to learn that women have been among the most deadly of all serial killers?

As is often the case, the problem is largely one of semantics. The term "serial murder" itself is a relatively recent coinage, dating back only a few decades. Definitions vary, but the most useful comes from the National Institute of Justice, which describes it as a "series of two or more murders, committed as separate events, usually . . . by one offender acting alone. The crimes may occur over a period of time, ranging from hours to years. Quite often, the motive is psychological, and the offender's behavior and the physical evidence observed at the crime scenes will reflect sadistic, sexual overtones."

In other words, serial killers are, by and large, sexual psychopaths of a particularly depraved variety—deviants who can only achieve orgasmic release by making other people *die*. Once their morbid lust is satisfied, they experience an interval of calm—the equivalent of the sated lull that normally follows sex (the FBI calls this the "emotional cooling-off period"). Eventually, they grow ravenous again—horny for death—and go looking for someone new. This behavioral pattern explains the "serial" nature of the phenomenon. Every time one of these monsters is overwhelmed by an exigent sexual need, another person has to die.

Exactly who coined the term "serial killer" is a matter of some dispute (it is most often credited to former FBI agent Robert Ressler, though some criminologists trace its earliest use to a 1966 book, *The Meaning of Murder*, by the British writer John Brophy). In any case, it did not gain widespread currency until the 1970s—the decade that witnessed the depredations of Bundy, Gacy, Kenneth Bianchi, and Angelo Buono (the infamous "Hillside Strangler") and other savagely violent sociopaths. Since the term itself was brand-new at the time, it was easy to get the impression that a frighteningly new species of criminal—previously unheard-of in the long history of human iniquity—had suddenly appeared on the scene: the serial killer.

In point of fact, creatures like Gacy and his ilk have existed from time immemorial. Anyone who believes that viciously depraved sex-killers are unique to our age—a symptom of the "societal rot" that political demagogues are always blaming on things like Hollywood shoot-'em-ups, rap music, and the ban on classroom prayer—should take a look at *Psychopathia Sexualis* by Dr. Richard von Krafft-Ebing. Published in 1886, this pioneering work surveys a wide range of aberrant behavior, from foot fetishism to necrophilia, and includes capsule case studies of some of the most appalling sadists imaginable.

Among the monsters cited by Krafft-Ebing are "a certain Gruyo, aged forty-one," who strangled six women, then "tore out their intestines and kidneys through the vagina"; a fifty-five-year-old Hungarian named Tirsch, who "waylaid a wretched old woman" in the woods, choked her to death, then "cut off the dead woman's breasts and genitalia with a knife, cooked them at home, and, in the course of the next few days, ate them"; and a twenty-four-year-old

French vineyard worker named Leger, who—after wandering about the woods for eight days in search of a victim—"caught a girl twelve years old, violated her, mutilated her genitals, tore out her heart and ate of it, drank the blood, and buried the remains." There is also the case of "Alton, a clerk in England," who lured a little girl to a thicket, "cut her to pieces," then calmly returned to his office, were he made the following entry in his notebook: "Killed today a young girl; it was fine and hot."

These and other instances of hideously sadistic sex-killing are classified by Krafft-Ebing under an old-fashioned but highly expressive label: "lust-murder." The term nicely captures the particular combination of savage cruelty and frenzied sexual excitement that characterizes the crime and drives its perpetrators to such extremes of unspeakable behavior—to "strangling, cutting of the throat and ripping open of the abdomen, mutilation of the corpse, especially the genitals, [and] gratification of the sexual lust on the corpse" (in Krafft-Ebing's words).

Even today, *Psychopathia Sexualis* is a highly instructive (as well as morbidly titillating) work, whose enormous catalog of nineteenth-century perversion makes it abundantly clear that psychopathic sex-murder did not begin with Ted Bundy or Jeffrey Dahmer. Indeed, it did not even begin with Jack the Ripper, who is often regarded as the prototype of the modern-day psycho-killer. Krafft-Ebing himself makes reference to the infamous fifteenth-century monster Gilles de Rais, "who was executed in 1440, on account of mutilation and murder, which he had practiced for eight years on more than 800 children." And though their cases are not mentioned in *Psychopathia*

Sexualis, there are other medieval butchers whose atrocities might easily have earned them a place in Krafft-Ebing's encyclopedia of perversity: Gilles Garnier, for example, a sixteenth-century French maniac who savaged his victims with such bestial ferocity that he was thought to be a werewolf; and his German contemporary, Peter Stubbe, another ostensible lycanthrope who preyed primarily on young children and who was guilty—among other abominations—of cannibalizing his own son.

The history of sadistic mutilation-murder, of course, begins long before medieval times. Gilles de Rais himself claimed that he had derived inspiration from his reading of Suetonius, the Roman historian who chronicled the degenerate doings of Imperial madmen like Nero (who, we are told, enjoyed dressing up in the skins of a wild animal and dismembering young men and women with his bare hands).

Indeed, recent scientific evidence suggests that a taste for such savagery is encoded in our DNA, an evolutionary inheritance from our earliest primate ancestors. In his book *Demonic Males: Apes and the Origins of Human Violence,* Harvard anthropologist Richard Wrangham demonstrates that chimpanzees (who are "genetically closer to us than they are even to gorillas") routinely commit acts of torture and mayhem as appalling as anything recorded by Krafft-Ebing. Not only do they prey upon vulnerable members of their own species, but their assaults "are marked by a gratuitous cruelty—tearing off pieces of skin, for example, twisting limbs until they break, or drinking a victim's blood—reminiscent of acts that among humans are regarded as unspeakable crimes during peacetime and atrocities during war."

From African chimps to John Wayne Gacy, however, one fact is clear. As the title of Wrangham's book indicates, bestial, gratuitously cruel acts of lethal violence—the kind involving torture, rape, mutilation, dismemberment, cannibalism, etc.—are endemic to males. Indeed, there are unmistakable parallels between this kind of violence—phallic-aggressive, penetrative, rapacious, and (insofar as it commonly gratifies itself upon the bodies of strangers) undiscriminating—and the typical pattern of male sexual behavior. For this reason, it is possible to see sadistic mutilation-murder as a grotesque distortion (or "pathological intensification," in Krafft-Ebing's words) of normal male sexuality. Lust-murder, in short, is a specifically male phenomenon.

Lust-murder, however, is not synonymous with serial killing. Rather—and this is a point I want to stress—lust-murder is the *quintessential male form* of serial killing. When police discover a corpse with its throat slit, its torso cut open, its viscera removed, and its genitals excised, they are always justified in making one basic assumption: the perpetrator was a man. As culture-critic Camille Paglia puts it: "There is no female Jack the Ripper."

But if lust-murder is a form of serial killing exclusive to men—a monstrous expression of male sexuality—what, then, is the equivalent *female* form? Clearly, it must reflect female sexuality. Generally speaking, female serial killers differ from their male counterparts in roughly the same way that the sexual responses and behavior of woman typically differ from those of men.

A useful analogy here (and one that seems particularly apt to so lurid a subject) is pornography. It is a truth universally acknowledged that—while men are aroused by extremely raw depictions of abrupt, anonymous, anatomically explicit sex—women in general prefer their pornography to involve at least a suggestion of emotional intimacy and leisurely romance. Whether these differences in taste are a function of biology or culture is a question I'll leave to others. The indisputable fact is that the differences are real.

An analogous distinction holds true for serial killers. Female sociopaths are no less depraved than their male counterparts. As a rule, however, brutal penetration is not what turns them on. Their excitement comes not from violating the bodies of strangers with phallic objects, but from a grotesque, sadistic travesty of intimacy and love: from spooning poisoned medicine into the mouth of a trusting patient, for example, or smothering a sleeping child in its bed. In short, from tenderly turning a friend, family member, or dependent into a corpse.

To be sure, there may be other motives mixed up with the sadism—monetary gain, for example. Indeed, certain female serial killers may never admit, even to themselves, the true nature or extent of the gratification they deprive from their crimes. Their actions, however, speak for themselves. Whatever other benefits may accrue from their atrocities—a windfall of insurance money, for example, or a release from the burdens of motherhood—there is, at bottom, only one reason why a woman would, over the span of years, kill off the people closest to her, one by one, in ways that are to guaranteed make them undergo terrible suffering: because she gets pleasure from doing it.

There is no doubt that male serial sex-murder tends to be more lurid—more gruesomely violent—than the female variety. Whether it is more *evil* is another matter. After all, which is worse: to dismember a streetwalker after slitting her throat, or to cuddle in bed with a close friend you've just poisoned, and to climax repeatedly as you feel the body beside you subside into death? Ultimately, of course, it's an impossible question to answer. Still, there have been times when female serial killers have inspired a particular dread.

That was certainly the case in late-nineteenth-century America.

Every era is haunted by its own particular monsters—dark, unsettling figures who reflect the dominant anxieties of the time. During the Great Depression of the 1930s, for example, the mythic gangsters of the movies—the Scarfaces and Public Enemies and Little Caesars—were the brutal incarnations of a social system gone horribly awry: an America where only murderous ambition could propel a man to the top, and the old-fashioned virtues of hard work and honesty led to nowhere but the breadline. Two decades later, the juvenile delinquent—the switchblade-wielding punk with his sideburns and blue jeans and blaring rock 'n' roll—became a national bogeyman: the leather-jacketed symbol of a postwar teen culture that was shaking up the status quo. And the obsessive anxieties of today—our concerns about societal breakdown and sexual violence and the awful fragility of the flesh—are distilled into our own defining demon, the serial killer.

A hundred years ago, the figure that haunted America was the female serial poisoner. As Ann Jones points out in her seminal study *Women Who Kill* (1980), the feminist movement of the late 1800s—

when women first organized to demand social and political equality—triggered powerful anxieties in American men, who projected their fears into the nightmare-figure of the household murderess, the domestic angel of death. "As agitation for women's rights increased," Jones writes, "men shrilled that the traditional marriage relationship, established by God, would be destroyed. Women would no longer respect, serve, and obey their husbands. They might even turn against them. The rights of woman were at issue, but the fear of woman was never far from the surface of any debate. The poisoning wife became the specter of the century—the witch who lurked in woman's sphere."

According to Jones, the female murderer became a stock feature of late-nineteenth-century American popular culture, which spawned a whole genre of fictional crime stories devoted to the unspeakable doings of assorted "domestic fiends." The protagonists of works like *The Life and Confession of Ann Walters, the Female Murderess!* and *Ellen Irving, the Female Victimizer* reveled in depravity, taking "no delight whatever in anything but acts of the most bloodthirsty and inhuman nature"—in the most "cruel, heart-rending, atrocious, and horrible crimes and murders." The public never seemed to tire of reading about the lethal doings of these and other female "multi-murderers" (as serial killers were sometimes referred to back then).

Far more unnerving, of course, were the real-life cases of women who gleefully wiped out large numbers of their nearest and dearest. Jane Toppan—a matronly New England sociopath whose tally of victims was more than five times higher than Jack the

Ripper's—was, in the view of her contemporaries, the worst of these creatures. But she was by no means the first. In post–Civil War America, a string of "domestic fiends" cropped up in New England: homicidal maniacs in the garb of housewives, mothers, and loving caregivers—the living incarnations of the culture's worst fears.

PART ONE

AMERICAN BORGIA

1

Then my little daughter Ann Eliza took the chills and fever, and was continually sick. This made me downhearted and discouraged again. I had some arsenic in the house which I purchased in Harlem, and I put it in the medicine I bought for her to cure the chills. I gave it to her twice, then she was taken sick as the others were, and died about noon four days afterward. She was the happiest child I ever saw.

—FROM THE CONFESSION OF LYDIA SHERMAN

EXACTLY WHAT TRANSPIRED ON THAT LONG-AGO DAY when Edward Struck lost his job in disgrace will never be fully known. Certain facts, however, are beyond dispute.

It happened on a late fall afternoon in 1863, when a knife-wielding drunkard—described in existing accounts as "deranged"—attacked the bartender at Stratton's Hotel on Bloomingdale Road and 125th Street in Manhattan. Shouts of "Murder!" and frantic cries for help erupted from the barroom. Struck, a member of the Metropolitan Police force working in Manhattanville, appeared a few minutes later. By the time he showed up, however, the assailant was already dead—shot down by a detective who, by happenstance, had been riding past the hotel when he'd heard the commotion.

That much is certain. The great, unresolved question is: Why didn't Officer Struck get there sooner?

Several hotel employees testified that Struck had, in fact, been right outside the hotel when the fracas broke out, but refused to intervene. The enraged drunk, he believed, was brandishing a pistol, while Struck—like all New York City policemen at the time—was armed with nothing but a billy club. Turning on his heels, he had dashed off in the opposite direction—ostensibly to get help.

When Struck's superiors at the Manhattanville station learned of these accusations of cowardice, they took immediate action. Without so much as a hearing, Officer Struck was summarily discharged from the force.

Struck's account of these events was considerably different. According to the story he told his wife, Lydia, he was blocks away from the hotel, walking his beat, when he heard that someone had just gone berserk in the Stratton barroom. He'd immediately hopped on a streetcar and hurried to the scene, only to find that the disturbance was already over.

He had been dismissed, he insisted, not because he was a coward but, on the contrary, because he was a man of principle. The Manhattanville precinct was rife with corruption, and Struck—so he claimed—was simply too honest for his own good. He knew things that made his superiors extremely nervous. His supposedly craven conduct in the Stratton barroom affair had been nothing more than a convenient pretext for getting rid of him.

Lydia chose to believe her husband's version. She was, after all, an utterly devoted wife and mother. At least, that was how she thought of herself. This wildly deluded self-image, in fact, was a mark of her utter derangement. For Lydia Struck belonged to that terrifying species of sociopaths who commit the most hideous atrocities imaginable, while telling themselves that they are only acting for the good of their victims.

Whatever the truth behind Struck's dismissal, it was a devastating blow to the man. He had worked hard all his adult life to earn an honest wage, sustained in his struggles by his deep religious faith. Both he and his wife were devout Christians. They had first gotten to know each other, in fact, while attending the same Methodist church in New Brunswick, New Jersey, twenty years earlier.

Struck was nearly forty at the time, a widower with six young children. Lydia, a tailoress by trade, was only seventeen: a fetching young woman with rich chestnut hair, large blue eyes, and a milky complexion. Despite the disparity in their ages, she readily accepted when Struck proposed marriage to her not long after they met. The ceremony took place at the home of her brother, Ellsworth. Within a year of the nuptials, Lydia had given birth to a healthy girl. Six more babies followed in rapid succession.

With a wife and thirteen children to support— seven by Lydia, six from his earlier marriage—Struck, a carriage blacksmith, toiled away at his trade, first in Yorkville, then on Elizabeth Street in lower Manhattan, just north of the infamous Five Points slum district. Eventually, he moved his family uptown, where they rented the first floor of a small house on 125th Street. It was then that a golden opportunity presented itself.

After years of political wrangling, the city of New York was in the process of reorganizing its police force. In January 1857, Struck applied for and obtained an appointment to the newly created Metroplitan Police.

For six years, he patrolled the streets of the Manhattanville ward, proud to wear the uniform: blue frock coat, dark vest, blue pantaloons, star-shaped copper badge. He was, he believed, a credit to the force.

Then came the Stratton barroom fiasco, and Struck found himself not only unemployed but branded a coward.

By this time, there had been a significant reduction in the size of the Struck household. All six of Edward's children by his first marriage had grown up and left home. And little Josephine—the daughter Lydia had given birth to less than two years before—had died after a painful bout of intestinal illness. In light of later events, it is reasonable to speculate that the little girl did not perish of natural causes. The doctor who attended her, however, had no cause to suspect foul play and attributed her death to "inflammation of the bowels."

Even with seven fewer mouths to feed, the Strucks still had six sons and daughters to care for. With the whole family crowded into a few dreary rooms and not a penny coming in to feed them, Edward plunged into a state of extreme despondency that had all the earmarks of what we now call clinical depression. He wouldn't look for work or see his old friends. After a while, he wouldn't leave the house at all. He was ashamed to show himself in public, convinced that he was an object of universal contempt. His behavior grew increasingly erratic. He would lie awake at night, certain that he was about to be arrested. On one occasion, he took a pistol from a bureau drawer, stuck it in his mouth, and threatened to blow his head off. Eventually, he stopped getting out of bed.

Lydia suffered terribly to see her husband sink into

such a hopeless condition. With every passing day, he was becoming an increasingly onerous burden. "He caused me at this time a great deal of trouble" was the way Lydia later put it. She sought advice from Captain Hart, her husband's immediate superior at the Manhattanville station. Hart—a decent fellow who had tried in vain to get Struck reinstated—shook his head at Lydia's shocking account of her husband's behavior. The man was clearly out of his mind. As far as Hart could see, there was only one thing to be done. Her husband must be "put out of the way," Hart gently told her—advice that was seconded by several other people she consulted.

Exactly what was intended by this suggestion is somewhat unclear, though Hart apparently meant that Struck should be committed to an insane asylum before he did harm to himself or his loved ones. Lydia, however, chose to place a different construction on the words.

Scraping together ten cents from her meager household funds, she repaired to a drugstore in Harlem and purchased an ounce of powdered arsenic.

The druggist who dispensed the poison would not have raised an eyebrow at Lydia's request. Arsenic was a popular over-the-counter item at the time, sold in various forms and used—bizarrely enough—as both a pesticide and a beauty product. A homeowner whose premises were infested with rodents might deal with the problem by sprinkling his floorboards with an arsenic compound called "Rough on Rats." At the same time, his adolescent daughter might hope to improve her complexion by dosing herself with "Bellavita Arsenic Beauty Tablets"—absolutely guaranteed (according to the newspaper ads) to eliminate "Pimples,

Blotches, Freckles, Sunburn, Discolorations, Eczema, Blackheads, Roughness, Redness, and to Restore the Bloom of Youth to Faded Faces!"

That American women would eagerly ingest rat poison for its supposedly cosmetic properties seems flatly incredible to us—equivalent to treating a bad case of acne by swallowing a few shots of Raid. But it was typical of those wildly unregulated, pre-FDA days, when the marketplace was flooded with medicinal cure-alls concocted of everything from cocaine and chloroform to morphine and mercury.

And so the druggist would have sold Lydia all the poison she wanted, no questions asked. Lydia requested an ounce, but she probably came away with even more, since arsenic was so cheap that most druggists rarely measured it out with any precision, scooping a mound of it onto a paper, then either transferring it into a bottle or wrapping it up into a neat little package.

Two to four grains of white arsenic—a fraction of a teaspoonful—is enough to kill an adult human being. For ten pennies, Lydia Struck—one of the most remorseless sociopaths ever produced in this country—purchased enough of the poison to murder every member of her household several times over.

By this time, the fifty-nine-year-old Struck had ceased performing the most basic functions. He no longer seemed capable of washing, dressing, or feeding himself. Back at home, Lydia fixed her husband a nice bowl of oatmeal gruel, then—using one of her sewing thimbles as a measure—sprinkled in a small but deadly portion of the powdered arsenic and stirred it into the porridge. Seated at his bedside, she helped him drink the noxious mixture down. As the afternoon wore on, she fed him several additional servings. There is no evidence to suggest that, as she killed her husband of eighteen years, Lydia experienced anything other than a sense of the fullest satisfaction. It was, she felt, the merciful thing to do. After all—as she later put it—it was clear that he "would never be any good to me or to himself again."

There is a quaint, *Arsenic and Old Lace* quality that we tend to associate with the crimes committed by female poisoners, as though disposing of a few people by feeding them arsenic-laced oatmeal or hot chocolate were a rather genteel form of murder. The truth is that, compared to the agonies suffered by the average poisoning victim, the deaths meted out by male serial killers like Jack the Ripper, "Son of Sam," or the Boston Strangler—the sudden executions by knife blade, bullet, or garrote—seem positively humane.

In most cases of arsenic ingestion, the commencement of symptoms occurs within the hour. The first sign is an acrid sensation in the throat. Nausea sets in, growing more unbearable by the moment. Then the vomiting begins. It continues long after the stomach is empty, until the victim is heaving up a foul whitish fluid streaked with blood. The mouth is parched, the tongue thickly coated, the throat constricted. The victim is seized with a terrible thirst. Anything he drinks, however—even a few sips of ice water—only makes the vomiting worse.

Uncontrollable diarrhea—often bloody, and invariably accompanied by racking abdominal pain—follows the vomiting. Some victims experience a violent burning from mouth to anus. Urine is scanty and red in color. As the hours pass, the victim's face—deathly pale to begin with—takes on a bluish tint. The eyes grow hollow. The skin is slick with perspiration that gives off an unusually thick, fetid odor. The victim's breathing becomes harsh and irregular, his extremities cold, his heartbeat feeble. There may be convulsions of the limbs and excruciating cramps in the muscles of the legs. Depending on the amount of poison consumed, this torment may last anywhere from five or six hours to several days.

In Struck's case, it lasted until early the next morning. Lydia sat up with him throughout the night, while her husband underwent his harrowing disintegration before her vaguely curious eyes.

His death, when it finally came at around eight o'clock on the morning of May 24, 1864 was—just as Lydia had intended—a mercy.

The attending physician, Dr. N. Hustead, decided that Edward Struck had perished of natural causes. On the official certificate, he filled in the cause of death as "consumption."

Lydia Struck was now a forty-two-year-old widow with no means of support and six children to care for. She would not, however, remain in those circumstances for very long. Within a few years of Struck's death, she would no longer be a widow.

Or a mother.

In our own time, the case of Susan Smith—"The Modern Medea," as the media dubbed her—transfixed our country with horror. In October 1994, the twenty-three-year-old mother drove her Mazda Protegé to the shore of John D. Long Lake in Union, South Carolina, and sent the car rolling down a boat ramp with her two little boys, ages one and three, strapped into the backseat. Smith watched for more than five minutes as the car bobbed on the surface, then slowly filled with water, then sank with her babies inside. So unthinkable was the crime that—in the perversely paradoxical way of such atrocities—it became a national obsession, impossible to stop thinking about. How could a mother do such a thing—set the deaths of her own babies in motion, then stand idly by while their helpless lives were extinguished before her eyes?

One hundred and thirty years before Susan Smith committed the filicide that made her (in the judgment of the tabloids) "America's Most Hated Woman," Lydia Struck perpetrated a similar horror. She did not, however, murder her own two children.

She murdered all six.

By the end of June, just a month after disposing of her husband, Lydia was feeling "much discouraged and downhearted" by the difficulty of supporting the children on her own. The three youngest—six-year-old Martha Ann, four-year-old Edward Jr., and baby William, aged nine months and fifteen days—were a particular burden, since they "could [do] nothing for me or for themselves." Of course, she did not want to act rashly. She therefore "thought the matter over for several days" before coming to the inevitable conclusion "that it would be better for them if they were out of the way."

In the first week of July, she poisoned all three of them with arsenic. Their deaths are described in the confession that Lydia ultimately supplied to the authorities. It is a remarkable document, offering hair-raising insight into the workings of a profoundly diseased mind. In it, Lydia reveals herself to be a quintessential psychopath, an utterly self-gratifying monster who contemplates and carries out the most unimaginable horrors without displaying the slightest trace of normal human emotion.

Martha Ann was the first to go. "She was taken with vomiting soon after I gave her the arsenic," Lydia writes, "and was afflicted in that way until she died. The doctors said nothing to indicate that they knew what was the matter."

Edward went later that same day. "He was sick to the stomach, and vomited frequently," Lydia reports in her chillingly off-handed tone.

In the evening, Edward died. He was a beautiful boy, and did not complain during his illness. He was very patient. The afternoon before he died, my stepdaughter, Gertrude Thompson, came in to see my children, and spoke to him and said,

"Eddy, are you sick?"

He said, "Yes,"

Then she said, "You will get better," and he said, "No, I shall never get well."

The doctors had no suspicions in this case either, and I did not hear of any one having any.

Shortly after Edward emitted his last, tormented breath, baby William also expired in great agony. In the official records of the Bureau of Vital Statistics, their deaths were attributed to "remittant fever" and "bronchitis," respectively.

From our present vantage point, it seems inconceivable that three healthy young children could suffer horrible deaths within a twenty-four-hour span without arousing medical suspicion. But in the Civil War era—when applying a bunch of live leeches to a patient's body was still a common practice—medicine had not yet emerged from the dark ages. Diseases now easily treatable could decimate entire families (particularly poor ones) in frighteningly short order. In the meantime, family doctors could do little more than dispense learned, if largely useless, advice, along with drugs that, at best, would not make the patient sicker.

As she repeatedly stressed, Lydia's three youngest children had been a considerable burden to her—a constant drain on her resources. Now that they were permanently "out of the way," her situation was much improved, particularly since her fourteen-year-old son, George Whitfield, had gotten a job as a painter's assistant and was bringing in a steady $2.50 a week. As long as George was contributing to the household, his existence was secure. Unfortunately for him, he soon developed a condition known as "painter's colic" and was forced to quit work. His mother gave him some time to recuperate, but when a full week passed and he showed no signs of improvement, she "got discouraged"—a frame of mind that always boded very ill for her loved ones.

"I thought he would become a burden upon me," Lydia would later explain, "so I mixed up some arsenic in his tea. I think he died the next morning."

By this time, Lydia had become well acquainted with a neighborhood physician named L. Rosenstein, who had been called in to treat several of her dying children. For unexplained reasons—perhaps because of the exceptional care she had lavished on the little ones, never leaving their bedsides until they had suffered their last, agonized convulsions and subsided into death—Rosenstein was sufficiently impressed with Lydia to offer her a job. And so, in the fall of 1864, Lydia Struck—whose experience in the health care field consisted entirely of having induced mortal sickness in a half-dozen members of her immediate family—became a full-time nurse.

In light of what her contemporaries would later describe as her "mania for life-taking," it is entirely possible that an indeterminate number of the patients who died in Dr. Rosenstein's care during this period were hastened to the grave by the ministrations of his kindly new nurse, Mrs. Struck. This part of Lydia's career, however, remains shrouded in obscurity, since she said almost nothing about her professional life in her published confession.

Four of Lydia's children now lay alongside their father in the sod of Trinity graveyard. Two still remained aboveground: her eighteen-year-old daughter, also named Lydia, and little Ann Eliza, aged twelve, described by her mother as "the happiest child I ever saw."

The younger Lydia—by all accounts a lovely girl, who was being assiduously courted by a suitor named John Smith—clerked at a dry-goods store in Harlem. She was often forced to miss work, however. The winter was unusually harsh, and little Ann Eliza was frequently sick with fever and chills. With their mother assisting Dr. Rosenstein all day, it fell to the eighteen-year-old girl to stay home and take care of her ailing sister. This happened so often that, as the winter wore on, the younger Lydia had to give up her clerking job entirely, and bring in whatever pittance she could by sewing bonnet frames at home.

Once again, Lydia Struck, as she reports in her confession, grew "downhearted and much discouraged." Her little daughter's fragile health was having a serious effect on the family income. As far as she could see, there was only one solution to the dilemma: "I thought if I got rid of her that Lydia and myself could make a living."

The bottle of arsenic she had bought in Harlem the previous spring was still more than half full. On March 2, 1864, Lydia returned to the same drugstore and purchased one of the countless patent medicines that promised to cure everything from catarrh to cancer. Back home, she mixed a few grains of the arsenic into the medicine and fed it to her daughter. When the little girl was seized with a violent bout of vomiting, Lydia gave her a second dose of the poisoned nostrum. And then some more.

It took twelve-year-old Ann Eliza four days to die. Dr. Rosenstein, who attended the agonized child, diagnosed the cause as "typhoid fever."

For the next six or seven weeks, the two Lydias, mother and daughter, lived together in a small apartment on upper Broadway. In early May, after paying an overnight visit to her stepsister in lower Manhattan, young Lydia returned home with a fever and took to her bed. Her mother—according to her confession—immediately repaired to the local druggist and bought "some medicine to give her." Somehow, the medication only made her daughter sicker, and Lydia "had to sit up with her all night."

The following morning, she sent for Dr. Rosenstein, who—as he had in the case of little Ann Eliza—diagnosed the illness as "typhoid fever." By the afternoon, young Lydia was in a state of such acute distress that she felt the need for spiritual succor and asked to see the pastor of her church, the Reverend Mr. Payson.

Nothing, however—not the ministrations of Dr. Rosenstein, not the prayers of Reverend Payson, and certainly not the bitter-tasting powders her mother kept feeding her—could save the young woman. She suffered her final throes on the morning of May 19, 1866, and was buried later that same day in Trinity graveyard, beside the bodies of her father and five siblings.

In her confession, Lydia Struck—who freely admitted to all the other murders—insisted that her oldest daughter and namesake died of natural causes. And perhaps she did. Even at the time, however, there were those who suspected otherwise. One of these was the Reverend Mr. Payson. As the long-time pastor of the First Presbyterian Church, he had been called to many deathbeds, including those of several suicides—poor, despairing souls who had turned to arsenic for deliverance. The ghastly last moments of eighteen-year-old Lydia bore a disconcerting resemblance to the convulsive death agonies of those unfortunates.

Payson's darkest suspicions were strengthened several weeks later when he received an unexpected visit from Cornelius Struck, Lydia's adult stepson. As it happened, Cornelius had long harbored his own doubts about his stepmother. Now—after conferring with Payson and hearing the pastor's appalling account of the torments young Lydia had suffered in extremis—Cornelius decided to take action. Shortly afterward, he paid a visit to District Attorney Garvin and urged him to exhume all seven corpses in the Struck family plot. Though reluctant to take such a drastic step, Garvin promised to launch an investigation. For the first time, Lydia Struck had fallen under the notice of the law.

By then, however, she was no longer living in New

York City. Indeed, by then, she was no longer Lydia
Struck.

In her own grotesque way, the forty-two-year-
old ex-wife-and-mother was authentically American: a
true believer in the possibility of endless self-renewal,
of leaving the past behind and reinventing her life. In
the months following her oldest daughter's death, she
was seized with an unaccustomed sense of well-being.
For the first time in years (as she declared in her confession) she "felt good. . . . I had nothing to fret or
trouble me." Now that her husband and six children
had been turned into carrion, she felt wonderfully
unburdened.

For a while, she worked as a general helper and
clerk at Cochran's, a sewing machine store on Canal
Street. One of her customers, a gentleman named
James Curtiss, was much taken with Lydia, who—like
other celebrated sociopaths (Ted Bundy, for example)—possessed an ingratiating charm that completely
masked her monstrous degeneracy. When the store
went out of business, Curtiss offered Lydia a job as a
companion nurse to his mother, an elderly invalid living in Stratford, Connecticut. The salary was eight
dollars per month, in addition to room and board.
Lydia leaped at the offer. After all, she had no other
prospects. And with her family in the ground, there
was nothing to keep her shackled to the city.

Lydia's stint as Mrs. Curtiss's live-in companion
did not last very long. Within weeks of arriving in
Stratford, she heard about an old man named Dennis
Hurlburt, a local farmer of considerable means and a
reputation as a notorious miser. "Old Hurlburt," as
he was known around town, had recently lost his wife
of many years and was looking to hire a dependable

housekeeper. Before long, Lydia had not only secured the position but somehow managed to win the old skinflint's heart as well.

"I was there only a few days," she reports in her confession, "when he wanted me to marry him." Lydia acted suitably coy until Hurlburt promised "that if I would marry him, all that he was worth should be mine." The wedding took place the following day at the home of the Reverend Mr. Morton.

Shortly afterward, Lydia saw to it that Old Hurlburt made good on his promise and signed a new will, leaving his entire estate to her.

For slightly over a year, the old man and his new bride enjoyed a seemingly idyllic existence. Neighbors saw her greet him at the door with a kiss whenever he returned home from an errand. She did all the housekeeping and mending, cooked his meals, even shaved him. Hurlburt's palsied hands trembled too badly for him to handle a razor, so Lydia performed the operation herself, carefully scraping the bristles from her husband's wattled chin three times a week.

Indeed, it was while being shaved one Sunday morning before leaving for church that the old man first began to die.

Lydia had just lathered up his face and put the razor to his jaw, when—as she would later write—"he was taken with dizziness." He decided that he needed fresh air, and went outside to feed his horse. He returned about ten minutes later, seemingly recovered, but when she began to shave him again, he was hit with another dizzy spell. They decided to skip church. It was clear that the old man was having what his wife called a "sick turn." And indeed, as the day progressed, he "continued quite feeble."

The next afternoon, hearing that Hurlburt was ill, a neighbor brought over a bucket of freshly dug clams. Lydia proceeded to fix her husband a nice pot of chowder, spiced with a special ingredient. With her coaxing, he managed to consume a full bowl of it for supper, washing it down with a glass of hard cider, which had also been doctored with the special powder Lydia kept secreted in her bureau.

That night, Hurlburt was dreadfully sick with nausea and vomiting, racking bowel pains, bloody diarrhea, a violent headache, high fever, and a torturous thirst. There was a powerful burning in the pit of his stomach and a ghastly lividity to his skin. In the morning—though his throat was so swollen he could barely speak—he managed to plead for a dose of his favorite patent medicine, Hostetter's Stomach Bitters.

The old man was not alone in swearing by Hostetter's. Throughout the mid-nineteenth century, Americans consumed so much of the stuff that the quack who concocted it died a multimillionaire. And indeed—though its medicinal value was nil—people *did* tend to feel more chipper after taking a few slugs of Hostetter's, mainly because its alcoholic content was approximately ninety proof.

Before giving her husband a drink of his beloved bitters, Lydia rendered it even more potent by stirring in a small measure of her secret white powder.

The tainted nostrum merely redoubled the old man's torments. On Tuesday, he begged his wife to send for a doctor. When a physician named Shelton finally arrived, it was clear at a glance that Old Hurlburt was beyond help. Lydia stayed by her husband's bedside, stroking his sweat-drenched brow until he was "taken with a sinking turn," as she put it. He died the way her other victims had, after undergoing several days of uttermost agony. Though Shelton couldn't say exactly what had killed the old man, he attributed the death to "cholera morbus."

The forty-six-year-old widow came into a considerable inheritance by 1868 standards—$20,000 in real estate and another $10,000 in cash. For the first time in her life, she was free of financial cares. If her motives had been entirely mercenary, she could have tossed away her arsenic and never killed again. But—though Lydia was happy to profit from her crimes—money was not, in the end, what drove her. Like others of her breed, she was a confirmed predator, addicted to cruelty and death. Making other people die—and deriving sadistic delight from their torments—was a pleasure she couldn't easily do without.

Within months of Hurlburt's death, Lydia found herself being wooed by one Horatio N. Sherman, a hard-living factory mechanic with a boisterous personality and a fondness for the bottle. Sherman's first wife had died the previous year, leaving him with four children and a live-in mother-in-law who—in the time-honored way of such relationships—was driving him crazy. He urgently needed a new wife to care for his household. Though something of a ne'er-do-well, Sherman was a popular local character renowned for his exuberant charm. Not only did Lydia accept his proposal, she agreed to bail him out of his debts to the tune of $300. They were married on September 2, 1870 at the home of Sherman's sister in Bridgeport.

The woman who had been born Lydia Danbury, then became Lydia Struck upon her first marriage and Lydia Hurlburt upon her second, now took the name by which she would achieve everlasting infamy in the annals of American crime: Lydia Sherman.

In mid-November 1870—just two months after the wedding—Lydia put some arsenic in the milk of Sherman's youngest child, a four-month-old baby named Frankie. The infant, sickly from birth, required just a single dose of the poison. After a savage bout of stomach pains and vomiting, he died that same night.

The following month, fourteen-year-old Ada—an exceptionally pretty, sweet-tempered girl, much beloved in the village—was stricken with nausea while helping to put up the Christmas decorations at church. Back home, Lydia fixed her some poisoned tea and watched to make sure that her stepdaughter drank it all down. Later that day, after Ada grew worse, Lydia made her swallow a second cup. Unlike her congenitally frail infant brother, Ada was a strong girl. She did not die until New Year's Eve, after several days of harrowing illness.

The sudden death of his two children—and particularly of his cherished daughter, Ada—devastated Sherman. Always a heavy drinker, he began to hit the bottle harder than ever, going on benders that sometimes lasted for days. At the tail end of April, he and several cronies took off for New Haven. A week later, he still hadn't returned home. His seventeen-year-old son, Nelson, decided to go look for his wayward father.

Lydia—whose relationship to Sherman had deteriorated so drastically that they were no longer sharing the same bed—agreed to pay her stepson's way. Nelson found his father in a "den of low people" and fetched him home. Unsurprisingly, Sherman wasn't feeling very well. He took to bed for several days before returning to work on Monday, May 8. When he came home from the factory that evening, Lydia was waiting with a nice cup of hot chocolate.

That night, Sherman was very sick with severe nausea, racking bowel pains, and diarrhea. The next morning, at her husband's urging, Lydia sent for Dr. Beardsley, the family physician. Beardsley—who had been called to Sherman's bedside before when the latter was suffering from a particularly brutal hangover—was puzzled by the symptoms, which bore little resemblance to the patient's previous alcohol-induced "turns." He prescribed one-eighth grain of morphine and a "blue pill" consisting mostly of mercury to be taken every two hours. Lydia dutifully administered the medication, helping her husband get it down with a few sips of one of her "soothing drinks."

Beardsley returned early the next morning to find Sherman in a worse state than before. His breathing was terribly labored, his throat so constricted that he could barely speak. He was afflicted with a savage thirst and a burning pain in the pit of his stomach. He could not keep anything down. Beardsley prescribed brandy and water, then departed on his daily rounds, leaving Sherman in the care of the ever-attentive Lydia.

When the doctor showed up the following morning, it was clear that Sherman would not survive much longer. His pulse was almost imperceptible, his extremities cold, his skin a ghastly gray, particularly under the eyes. Beardsley examined the dying man with a growing sense of alarm. As he would later testify, neither an alcoholic "debauch" nor an "ordinary disease" could account for Sherman's condition. To the physician's great dismay, Sherman's symptoms bore an unmistakable resemblance to "those originating from poisoning by arsenic"—several cases of which Beardsley had witnessed in his professional career.

As the doctor sat at the failing man's bedside that Thursday morning, Sherman opened his eyes and—mustering what little strength he had—managed to gasp out a question: Was he dying?

"I fear that you are in your last sickness," Beardsley said gently.

"I fear so, too," Sherman said in a barely audible voice.

Beardsley slowly shook his head. "I do not understand this," he said. "Tell me, have you taken anything other than what I prescribed?"

"Only what my wife has given me," Sherman answered. They were his last documented words. Emitting an anguished groan, he closed his eyes and subsided onto his sweat-drenched pillow.

He died at approximately eight o'clock the next morning, Friday, May 12, 1871.

As a general rule, serial killers will continue to commit their atrocities until they are forcibly stopped. The reason is simple: killing and torture are their highest forms of pleasure. For nearly a decade, Lydia Sherman had been able to get away with almost a dozen hideous murders—three husbands, eight children—thanks in large part to the blind incompetence of the various physicians who attended her victims without ever suspecting foul play. In Beardsley, however, a doctor had come along who would finally bring the horror to an end.

After sharing his suspicions with a colleague named Kinney, Beardsley secured permission to conduct a postmortem on Sherman. On Saturday, May 20, the two doctors dissected the cadaver, removing the stomach and liver and shipping the organs to a toxicology professor at Yale for analysis. Three weeks later, they received the results. Sherman's liver was absolutely saturated with arsenic. There was enough poison in his system to have killed three men.

A warrant was promptly issued for the arrest of Lydia Sherman.

By then, however, she was no longer in Connecticut. Realizing that the law was closing in on her, she had decamped for New Brunswick. Several officers were immediately dispatched to New Jersey to keep her under surveillance. In the meantime, the bodies of Frankie and Ada Sherman were exhumed. So was the corpse of Dennis Hurlburt. All were found to contain significant traces of arsenic. Inquiring at the local pharmacies, police discovered that, in the spring of 1870, Lydia had purchased an ounce of white arsenic from a druggist named Peck, explaining that she needed the poison because her house was "overrun with rats." They also learned about the bizarre string of tragedies that had befallen Edward Struck and his six children several years earlier when the ill-fated ex-policeman was married to Lydia.

On June 7, 1871, authorities decided that the time had come to put the warrant into action. Lydia, shadowed by a pair of detectives, had gone off to New York City on a shopping expedition. When she returned to New Brunswick that evening, she was greeted at the train station by a detective and a deputy sheriff who took her into custody and transported her back to New Haven, where she was charged with the murder of Horatio Sherman.

Her trial was a sensation, generating headlines in papers from the *New Haven Register* to the *New York*

Times. According to the press, her crimes were unparalleled; the world hadn't witnessed such horrors since the days of Lucretia Borgia, the infamous Italian noblewoman and reputed serial poisoner whose name was a byword for lethal treachery. When the trial opened in New Haven on April 16, 1872, spectators traveled great distances for a glimpse of this prodigy of evil—"the arch murderess of Connecticut." What they saw was not the ogre they were expecting but a prim, proper, perfectly ordinary-looking woman in a black alpaca dress, black-and-white shawl, white straw hat, and black kid gloves.

The sight of the forty-eight-year-old Lydia, looking calm, even somewhat cheerful, beneath her thin lace veil, had them shaking their heads in confusion. How could this utterly nondescript woman be guilty of such atrocities? The answer, of course, was simple. As with most serial killers, there was a terrifying disparity in Lydia between her mundane appearance and the monstrous abnormality of her mind. But back then, people were unfamiliar with the grotesque operations of the sociopathic personality. The term "serial killer" wouldn't even be invented for another hundred years.

The trial lasted eight days. The defense tried to persuade the jury that Horatio Sherman's death was accidental, possibly caused when he had swallowed tainted water, drawn from a well in which a poisoned rat had drowned. Or perhaps he had taken his own life, driven to suicide by depression over his money problems, marital woes, and the recent deaths of his two children.

The evidence against Lydia, however, was overwhelming. In the end, she was found guilty of second-degree murder and sentenced to life imprisonment in the state prison at Wethersfield.

Public fascination with Lydia's case did not end with her conviction. Quite the contrary. Then as now, people had a powerful appetite for true-crime sensationalism, and instant books like *The Poison Fiend: Life, Crimes, and Conviction of Lydia Sherman (The Modern Lucretia Borgia)* were rushed into print. Lydia's confession—composed in jail while she awaited sentencing and immediately issued in pamphlet form—also became a popular seller. She even became immortalized in a ballad:

> Lydia Sherman is plagued with rats.
> Lydia has no faith in cats.
> So Lydia buys some arsenic,
> And then her husband gets sick;
> And then her husband, he does die,
> And Lydia's neighbors wonder why.
>
> Lydia moves, but still has rats;
> And still she puts no faith in cats;
> So again she buys some arsenic,
> This time her children, they get sick,
> This time her children, they do die,
> And Lydia's neighbors wonder why.
>
> Lydia lies in Wethersfield jail,
> And loudly does she moan and wail.
> She blames her fate on a plague of rats;
> She blames the laziness of cats.
> But her neighbors' questions she can't deny—
> So Lydia now in prison must lie.

To her contemporaries, the Sherman case was uniquely appalling—"the horror of the century," as one newspaper called it. In the hundred-year history of the republic, nothing like the "American Borgia" had ever been seen, and her countrymen felt certain that they would never witness such a monster again.

But they were wrong

2

You may ask yourselves the question, how is it possible for a woman like this to commit such a crime? The answer is, from the depravity that is sometimes found to exist in the human heart—in the heart of a woman as well as in that of a man. As the female sex ordinarily rise above men in morality and kindness and gentleness, so they sometimes sink to lower depths of cruelty and malignity.

—FROM THE TRIAL OF SARAH JANE ROBINSON

ONLY THE SENTIMENTAL ATTITUDES OF THE DAY SAVED Lydia Sherman from the gallows. The idea of hanging any woman, even a certified fiend, was repugnant to Victorian sensibilities. Still, there were many New Englanders who felt strongly that her sentence was a miscarriage of justice. A monster like Lydia, they proclaimed, should not be suffered to live.

They got their wish soon enough. In May 1878—just five years after she was locked away in Wethersfield—Lydia Sherman died after a brief illness. America's "Queen Poisoner," as she had come to be known, was gone. But her throne wouldn't remain empty for long.

According to the cliché, every woman dreams of marrying a prince. For Annie McCormick, a young widow living in South Boston, that wish came true—in a manner of speaking. After several lonely years, she was rescued from widowhood by a man with the unlikely name of Prince Arthur Freeman. They were wed in 1879.

The life he offered her, however, was anything but regal. An unskilled laborer who spent his days slaving in an iron foundry, Prince Arthur had never earned more than a few dollars per week in his life. To make ends meet, Annie continued to ply her trade as a seamstress. Even with the extra money she brought in, they barely managed to scrape by. Food was scant, their tenement flat dismal and underheated. It is little wonder that in February 1885—just a few weeks after their second child was born—the overworked woman contracted pneumonia.

It was Prince Arthur's mother, Mrs. Freeman, who took care of the medical bills. In addition to paying the family doctor, Archibald Davidson, she hired an elderly woman named Mrs. Randall to help nurse her bedridden daughter-in-law. After ten days in bed, Annie—to the great relief of her family—began to show definite signs of improvement. By the second week of February, Dr. Davidson confidently predicted that, "with proper nourishment," the patient would almost certainly make a complete recovery.

And then Annie's sister showed up.

Her name was Sarah Jane Robinson. Like Annie, she was a skilled seamstress, though she had also done her share of nursing. To be sure, her patients had an unfortunate habit of dying. Just a few years earlier, for example, she had cared for her landlord, Oliver Sleeper, during what turned out to be his final illness. His death had taken his friends by surprise. Until he was stricken with a sudden intestinal ailment, the seventy-year-old

Sleeper had appeared in perfectly sound health. Still, he was an old man. Certainly Mrs. Robinson had given him assiduous attention, remaining at his bedside day and night and making sure that he swallowed every last dose of his medication. For her services, she had charged his estate fifty dollars following the old man's intensely unpleasant death—a bill that Sleeper's survivors ultimately settled by remitting Mrs. Robinson's overdue rent.

A few years later, her own husband, Moses Robinson, died of an illness whose symptoms bore a remarkable similarity to those manifested by old Mr. Sleeper during his final, agonized days—violent nausea and vomiting, bloody diarrhea, burning pains in the stomach. She had also lost three of her eight children to the same devastating disease, including both of her twin sons, who died within a week of one another when they were barely eight months old.

Now, she had come to take care of her sister, Annie.

Taking care of Annie was nothing new for Sarah. She'd been doing it ever since they were children in Ireland. When their parents, a poor farming couple named Tennent, died within a few months of each other in 1853, it was fourteen-year-old Sarah, all by herself, who took her nine-year-old sister across the ocean to America. Later—after Annie's first husband sliced his hand on a saw blade and succumbed to blood poisoning—it was Sarah who opened her home to the grieving young widow.

To those who knew her, therefore, it came as no surprise that Sarah had hurried to her sister's sickbed the moment she got word of Annie's illness. Of course, in a very real sense, no one knew Sarah Jane

Robinson. Even her nearest acquaintances had been deceived by her apparent normality. Several years would pass before she stood revealed to the world as the kind of virulent personality we now describe as a criminal psychopath. Though capable of counterfeiting ordinary human emotions, such beings lack every trace of fellow feeling. Like Sarah Jane Robinson, they may be adept at putting on convincing shows of sympathy and concern. At bottom, however, they care about nothing but their own monstrous needs. And they will happily sacrifice anyone—a husband, a child, or an ailing younger sister—to make sure those needs are gratified.

When Sarah arrived at the Freeman's tenement, she found a family friend, a woman named Susan Marshall, seated at Annie's bedside. Annie herself was much improved. Her coloring was better than it had been in many days, and her coughing had let up significantly. Propped up on her pillow, she greeted her sister with a fond smile.

Sarah, however, seemed strangely dismayed at the sight of her sister. After spending a few minutes quizzing Annie about her health, she asked to speak to Mrs. Marshall in private.

Retreating to the kitchen, Sarah told Mrs. Marshall about a terrible dream she'd had the night before. In it, Annie had gotten sicker and sicker, until she had wasted into a skeleton.

"I just know she'll never get any better," Sarah exclaimed as she finished describing the nightmare.

"But she *is* getting better," Mrs. Marshall replied, seeking to reassure the obviously distraught older woman.

But Sarah would not be consoled. "Whenever I

have a dream like that," she said, "there is always one of the family who dies."

Later that day, after Prince Arthur returned home from work, Sarah persuaded him to dismiss Mrs. Randall. Why waste good money to pay for a nurse when she herself could tend to Annie? To demonstrate the point, she proceeded to fix her sister a nice bowl of oatmeal gruel and a cup of freshly brewed tea. Both appeared to have a strangely bitter quality to Annie, though her sense of taste had been so impaired by her illness that she could not really be sure.

That night, Annie took a sudden and devastating turn for the worse. She was overcome with nausea, and seized with savage stomach pains. She lay awake all night, alternately retching into the chamber pot and writhing on her mattress in agony. When Dr. Davidson arrived for his morning visit, he was completely bewildered by her altered condition. Only one day earlier, his patient had been well on the way to recovery. Now, she had not merely suffered a setback; she had begun to display an entirely new set of symptoms. Davidson prescribed a common nineteenth-century remedy for acute gastric distress: bismuth phosphate, each dose to be dissolved in three parts water and taken at regular intervals.

In spite of the medicine—faithfully administered by Sarah, who made sure that her sister swallowed every sip of the doctored water—Annie continued to grow worse. In addition to her other symptoms, she was stricken with a ferocious burning in the pit of her stomach. She begged for anything to soothe the pain. Sarah bought her some ice cream, and fed it to her a few spoonfuls at a time. But the ice cream only made Annie's nausea worse, and intensified the vomiting until she was bringing up nothing but a thin, blood-streaked fluid.

When Susan Marshall came by several days later, she was shocked at her friend's transformation. The last time she'd visited, Annie had clearly been on the mend, her strength returning, her appearance improved. Now—as Mrs. Marshall would later testify—her "features were very much bloated," and her complexion was of a ghastly "discolored" hue. It was clear to Mrs. Marshall that her friend wasn't suffering from "any ordinary sickness." Her throat was so constricted that she could barely speak, though she did manage to voice a desperate plea for something cold to drink, to ease the dreadful burning in her stomach. She was afflicted with a blinding headache, overwhelming nausea, and another, deeply puzzling, symptom—terrible cramps in the calves of her legs. Even with the opium that Dr. Davidson had prescribed to alleviate the poor woman's suffering, she remained in an almost constant state of agony, groaning miserably and rolling back and forth on her mattress.

Utterly aghast, Mrs. Marshall questioned Sarah about this sudden, inexplicable reversal in Annie's condition. "We have been doing all we can for her," Sarah replied, shaking her head mournfully. "But I do not expect that she will ever leave her bed." Then, after a brief pause, she gave a heavy sigh and added: "It is happening just as in my dream."

On February 27, 1885—slightly more than a week after Sarah came to care for her sister—Annie Freeman died in the presence of her weeping husband, several grief-stricken friends, and her dry-eyed older sister.

Sarah Jane Robinson's dream had come true.

No sooner had Annie emitted her last, tortured

breath than Sarah asked to speak to Mrs. Marshall and another family friend, Mrs. Mary L. Moore. Much to the consternation of the two sorrowing women, Sarah—who seemed bizarrely unaffected by her sister's death—wanted to discuss a matter of obviously paramount importance to her. She wanted them to use whatever influence they possessed to persuade Prince Arthur to come live with her, along with his two children. It was, she declared, her sister's last wish. To be sure, no one had heard Annie express such a desire in her final days. But then, no one had spent as much time in the dying woman's company as Sarah, who had remained at her sister's side night and day, refusing to allow anyone else to feed her or to administer her medication.

Mrs. Marshall and Mrs. Moore promised to do everything in their power to see that Annie's last wish was honored.

The last shovelful of dirt had barely been tossed onto Annie Freeman's grave when Sarah herself spoke to Prince Arthur, telling him the same flagrant lie that she had told Mrs. Moore and Mrs. Marshall: that Annie had expressly wanted him and the two children to come live in Sarah's home. The stricken man—who had just seen his beloved wife vanish forever into the ground—seemed too stunned to think clearly about the subject, though he did permit Sarah to take his two small children home with her to Boylston Street that night. He himself followed a few weeks later, taking up residence at the home of Sarah Jane Robinson in early April 1885.

Three weeks later, Prince Arthur suffered a second devastating blow when his one-year-old daughter, Elizabeth, developed a sudden case of "intestinal ca-

tarrh." Sarah gave little Elizabeth the same watchful
care that she had lavished on the baby's mother, and
with the same results. In the last week of April, Elizabeth died in great distress and was laid in the ground
beside her mother.

Immediately after the child's funeral, Sarah sat her
brother-in-law down at the kitchen table and explained what must be done. Like other laboring men
of the time, Prince Arthur belonged to a "mutual assessment and cooperative society"—the United Order
of Pilgrim Fathers of Boston—whose main function
was to provide low-cost life insurance to its working-
class members. He owned a policy worth $2,000.
Annie, of course, had been the beneficiary. Now that
she was gone and Prince Arthur and his remaining
child—a six-year-old boy named Thomas—were residing with Sarah, it was only reasonable that *she* be made
the beneficiary. That way, little Thomas was sure to be
well taken care of. Just in case anything unfortunate
should happen to Prince Arthur.

One month later, on May 31, 1885, Prince
Arthur's $2,000 life insurance policy was made over
to his sister-in-law, Mrs. Sarah Jane Robinson.

Almost immediately, people around Sarah began to
notice a dramatic shift in her attitude toward Prince
Arthur. Ever since the deaths of his wife and infant
daughter, she had treated him with utmost kindness
and consideration. Suddenly, he became a constant
source of annoyance to her. It was as though she no
longer had the slightest use for him. And she didn't
hesitate to let others know exactly how she felt.

During the first week of June, for example, a friend
named Belle Clough dropped by Sarah's apartment for
a cup of chamomile tea and some neighborly gossip. As

they sat at the kitchen table, Sarah suddenly burst into a bitter denunciation of her brother-in-law. He was "worthless"—"good-for-nothing"—"too lazy to earn a living." His wages amounted to only six dollars a week, half of which he spent on trolley fare. She ended her harangue with a comment whose sheer vehemence caused Mrs. Clough to raise her eyebrows in surprise.

"I wish," said Sarah, virtually spitting out the words, "that *he* had died instead of my poor sister."

Just a few days later, Sarah was seated at the same table, this time with her twenty-five-year-old daughter, Lizzie. They were eating a modest supper of boiled beets and codfish. All of a sudden, Sarah gave a violent shudder and went deathly pale.

"Mama, what's wrong?" Lizzie cried in alarm.

Sarah passed a hand across her eyes. "I felt a ghost tap me on the shoulder," she replied.

Though Lizzie herself had never experienced such supernatural visitations, she knew that her mother was particularly prone to them. Sarah was often possessed by dark forebodings regarding family members, and her premonitions had an uncanny way of coming true.

"Did he say anything?" asked Lizzie.

Sarah nodded. "He said he would be coming for someone in the family." Here, she emitted a theatrical sigh before adding sadly: "I shouldn't wonder if something happened to your uncle very soon."

The ghost proved remarkably prescient. Just a few days later, on June 17, 1885, Prince Arthur and Sarah were seated in the parlor, when—apropos of nothing—she announced that it would be a good idea if he paid an immediate visit to his mother. Given the precarious nature of human existence, it might be his last chance to see her.

Prince Arthur was inclined to take his sister-in-law's words to heart. He, too, believed that she possessed a strange, prophetic gift. After all, hadn't she foreseen the death of his wife, when everyone else, even Dr. Davidson, had been so optimistic? Now, she appeared to have been visited by some dark apprehension regarding his mother. And it was certainly true that the old lady had been in a bad way since taking a fall the previous winter and fracturing her left hip. Early the following day, he set out for Charlestown.

When he arrived at his mother's home, he was relieved to find her in generally sound health and good spirits. Though still hobbling around with a cane and unable to travel, she seemed more energetic than she'd been in months. When he explained the reason for the unexpected visit, she pooh-poohed Sarah's grim premonition.

"Why, I'm fit as a fiddle," she declared. She planned to be around for a good many years to come. Prince Arthur stayed long enough to share a meal with his mother—ham simmered in milk, boiled potatoes, sweet pickles—before kissing her good-bye and heading back to Cambridge.

It turned out to be their final farewell—just as Sarah Jane Robinson had intended.

On the morning of June 22, 1885, after finishing the bowl of oatmeal and molasses Sarah had prepared for his breakfast, Prince Arthur set off for his job at the Norwegian Steel and Iron Company in South Boston. He hadn't gotten very far when he was suddenly overcome with nausea. Staggering into an alleyway, he threw up his breakfast. Feeling slightly better, he continued on his way. It wasn't long, however, before the sickness returned.

Just then, an acquaintance named F. J. Hayes happened by. At his first glimpse of Prince Arthur, Hayes could see that something was wrong.

"Are you all right, Mr. Freeman?" he asked. "You do not look at all well."

"I'm feeling awfully queer in the stomach," Prince Arthur admitted.

"Well, if I was you," said Hayes, "I'd turn right around and go home."

"I can't," said Prince Arthur, wincing at the spasms in his bowels. "I've already missed a considerable number of days on account of sickness, and I am only getting paid six dollars a week. I have to look out for my family."

He continued on his way to the foundry, but by the time he arrived, he was feeling so wretched that his boss insisted he go home.

A short time later, he arrived back at his sister-in-law's flat on Boylston Street. Strangely, she seemed unsurprised to see him—almost as if she'd been expecting him to return. She put him to bed and fixed him a cup of tea, which he was unable to keep down. Throughout the day, she fed him small amounts of strange-tasting water, telling him that it was mixed with bismuth phosphate.

"Here," she said, holding the glass to his lips. "It will make you feel better."

But the nausea and stomach pains only grew worse.

That evening, Sarah told her daughter, Lizzie, that the message she had received from her dead husband's ghost appeared to be coming true. "I fear your uncle will never get out of bed again," she said, arranging her features into a suitably somber expression.

The following afternoon, Prince Arthur received a

visit from Dr. John T. G. Nichols, a physician who resided on the same block as Sarah. Nichols—as he would later testify—found the patient suffering from "headache, vomiting, pain in the stomach, thirst, quick pulse, and low elevation in temperature." He prescribed the usual remedies—mustard and milk, lime water, soda water, opium. In spite of these measures, however, the symptoms grew worse over the next several days. By Wednesday, June 24, the baffled physician summoned a colleague, Dr. Driver of Cambridge, who—like Nichols—could find no sign of organic disease.

It was Driver who first raised the possibility that the patient might have been exposed to some sort of "irritant poison." Questioning Mrs. Robinson, they discovered that Prince Arthur spent his days at the foundry immersing iron bars in an acid bath, a process known as "pickling." The doctors, however, were inclined to doubt that even prolonged exposure to the fumes of sulfuric acid could produce such a devastating sickness.

Was it possible, they inquired, that her brother-in-law had inadvertently ingested arsenic? Such accidents were not uncommon. People who used it as rat poison were often surprisingly careless in handling the stuff, using household utensils to sprinkle it around the floorboards, then neglecting to wash the implements with sufficient care.

Mrs. Robinson dismissed the notion out of hand. She never kept arsenic around the house. If the doctors wished, they were welcome to examine her cupboards and utensils. Nichols and Driver declined her offer. After all, Mrs. Robinson was clearly such a nice person—so frank and natural in her responses—that there was no reason to doubt her. As Nichols would later put it, "there was nothing in her behavior to warrant the slightest suspicion."

Two days later, Prince Arthur's last hope for survival arrived in the form of his older sister, Mrs. Catherine Melvin, who had just gotten word of his desperate condition. At her first glimpse of her brother, she let out an involuntary gasp. She had heard that he was very sick, but she was unprepared for the sheer ghastliness of his suffering. Face contorted, frame shockingly wasted, he thrashed back and forth on the mattress, while begging for something—*anything*—to ease the terrible pain in his stomach.

Over her sister-in-law's protests, Mrs. Melvin immediately assumed the role of nurse. She sat at Prince Arthur's bedside throughout the night, soothing his forehead with a moist compress and feeding him small sips of brandy, along with the medication prescribed by Dr. Nichols: tincture of nux vomica, two drops every hour.

When Nichols arrived early the next day for his morning visit, he was relieved to find that Prince Arthur's condition had grown no worse. He was even more gratified when he returned that afternoon. For the first time since the onset of his mysterious sickness, the patient actually seemed slightly improved.

That night, Sarah urged her sister-in-law to get some sleep. *She* would resume the care of Prince Arthur. Mrs. Melvin, however, insisted on staying up with her brother again. The next morning, he felt so much better that, for the first time in days, he expressed a desire for food.

Believing that her brother had turned a corner, Mrs. Melvin—who had her own family to take care of—departed that morning, physically exhausted but feeling hopeful about his recovery. She had no way of knowing that she had returned him to the malevolent care of a madwoman, who was more determined than ever to have him hurry up and die.

That same night—after drinking a cup of the odd-tasting tea prepared by his sister-in-law—Prince Arthur took a violent turn for the worse. Shortly before midnight—Saturday, June 27—he went into convulsions and died, while Sarah Jane Robinson stood at his bedside and looked on with vague, detached interest.

Dr. Nichols, who still could not guess what had killed Prince Arthur Freeman, certified the cause of death as "disease of the stomach."

As dreadful as his suffering had been, Prince Arthur at least had the comfort of knowing that his six-year-old son, Tommy, was well provided for. Two months after the funeral, the Order of Pilgrim Fathers made good on his life insurance policy, paying $2,000 to his beneficiary, Sarah Jane Robinson. She immediately paid off her creditors, moved into a larger flat, purchased new furniture and clothing, and took a trip to Wisconsin to visit her brother. When she returned, she used the remainder of the money to take out an insurance policy on the life of her twenty-five-year-old daughter, Lizzie.

Six months later, in February 1886, Lizzie was stricken with a catastrophic illness and died after several weeks of acute suffering.

In the meantime, little Tommy Freeman had received no benefits at all from the money left by his father. His aunt Sarah—who had been so nice to him while his father was alive—now acted as though she could barely stand the sight of him, treating him like a particularly onerous burden she'd unfairly been saddled with. Visitors to the Robinson household were taken aback by how pale, skinny, and utterly forlorn the little boy looked. When they questioned Sarah about the child, she explained with a sigh that the poor boy missed his parents dreadfully. "Sometimes," she remarked to one of her neighbors, "I think he would be better off following in their footsteps."

On July 19, 1886, a year and three weeks after the death of his father, Tommy fell ill with uncontrolled vomiting and diarrhea. Sarah had one of her premonitions, telling several acquaintances that the boy would never recover. He died four days later, on July 23.

The terrible fragility of life—the possibility that anyone, no matter how young and healthy, could be struck down at any moment—was a lesson that the inhabitants of the Robinson household could hardly fail to learn. Perhaps for that reason, Sarah's oldest son, twenty-three-year old William, insured his life with the Order of Pilgrim Fathers shortly after the death of his beloved sister, Lizzie.

One month later, in August 1886, William—who was employed at a commercial warehouse—suffered a minor accident when a wooden crate toppled from a shelf and struck him between the shoulder blades. He shrugged off the mishap: the box was empty, and though the breath had been knocked out of him, he hadn't been seriously injured. Not long afterward, however, he felt suddenly nauseous and threw up the breakfast his mother had prepared for him that morning.

That evening at dinner, his mother fixed him a cup of her special tea. William took a sip and wrinkled his nose. It tasted very strange to him. Still, at his mother's urging, he drank it all down. No sooner had he finished his meal than the nausea returned, worse than ever. He took to his bed and was up all night with racking cramps and constant vomiting.

The next morning, his mother sent for Dr. Emory White, a local physician affiliated with the Order of Pilgrim Fathers. White knew about the strange series of tragedies that had befallen the Robinson household—most of them involving family members insured by the Order—and resolved to keep a close eye on William. When the young man continued to deteriorate, White shipped a sample of his vomit to a Harvard toxicologist named Edward Wood. He also informed Police Chief Parkhurst of his suspicions regarding Sarah Jane Robinson. Parkhurst dispatched a couple of his men to keep watch over Mrs. Robinson. Two days later, word arrived from Dr. Wood: William Robinson's stomach was saturated with arsenic. By then, however, the young man was beyond saving. He died that same afternoon. "The old lady dosed me" were the last words anyone heard him say.

Sarah Jane Robinson was immediately arrested for the murder of her son.

In the weeks that followed, authorities exhumed the bodies of six more of her victims: her daughter, Lizzie; her sister, Annie; her brother-in-law, Prince Arthur Freeman; her nephew, Tommy; her husband, Moses; and her former landlord, Oliver Sleeper. Arsenic was found in all of the corpses.

For the second time in living memory, New England had produced a homegrown "Borgia," a female "poison fiend" in the monstrous mold of Lydia Sherman. Public excitement over the case was intense, and the newspapers showed little restraint in their sensationalistic coverage. The *New York Times* placed the number of her victims at an even dozen, while one widely circulated story claimed that she'd once poisoned more than a hundred people at a picnic.

Largely as a result of prosecutorial incompetence, her first trial ended with a hung jury. She was immediately indicted again, this time for the murder of Prince Arthur Freeman. During her second trial in February 1886, the government argued that Prince Arthur's killing had been part of an elaborate plot to obtain his $2,000 life insurance policy, a scheme that also necessitated the murder of both Annie Freeman and seven-year-old Tommy.

Interestingly, it was the defense attorney, John B. Goodrich, who did a better job of identifying Sarah Jane Robinson as the homicidal maniac she so clearly was. In his closing argument, Goodrich argued that money couldn't possibly explain the horrors of which his client stood accused. "The idea is repellent; it is unnatural; it is unreasonable to suppose that that would be a sufficient motive," he insisted. The crimes allegedly perpetrated by his client could have only one cause: "uncontrolled depravity." If "such be the case," he told the jury, "you must pity her. You cannot condemn her." After all, it took a "monster" to commit such atrocities, said Goodrich, and "I do not know that the law hangs monsters."

In the end, the jury required less than one day to side with the prosecution. Sarah Jane Robinson was found guilty of first-degree murder and condemned to hang, though her sentence was later commuted to life in prison. She lived out the remainder of her days in a narrow cell decorated with engraved portraits of her victims, clipped from local newspapers.

As in the case of Lydia Sherman, one of the most striking features of the Sarah Jane Robinson affair was the harsh light it shed on the state of nineteenth-century medicine. Though various medical men had been called in to examine her victims throughout the years, none of them had seriously suspected foul play until Dr. White came along—by which time there were virtually no members of Mrs. Robinson's family left for her to murder.

To be sure, this failure was partly a function of her own plausibility—of the "mask of sanity" that she, like other psychopaths, was so skillful in presenting to the world. But it was also a reflection of the inadequacies of horse-and-buggy physicians like Drs. Driver and John T. G. Nichols.

For Dr. Nichols, at least, there was some consolation to be taken from the experience. It had taught him several valuable lessons. For one thing, he was now completely conversant with the symptoms of arsenical poisoning and would, he felt, have no trouble identifying them in the future, should the occasion arise.

Even more important, he had discovered that human depravity can come in many different forms—even in the guise of a perfectly ordinary-looking Boston matron. In the exceedingly unlikely event that he ever encountered another creature like Sarah Jane Robinson, he would not be fooled again.

Or so he believed.

3

And girls defenseless, wretched, poor,
Snatched from the haunts of vice and care,
From ill examples here secure,
Instruction and protection share.

Train'd soon in Wisdom's pleasant ways,
And taught to be discreet and good,
Virtue will be through all their days
From habit and from choice pursued.

—HYMN, SUNG BY THE ORPHANS
OF THE BOSTON FEMALE ASYLUM,
THIRTEENTH ANNIVERSARY CELEBRATION

BESIDES THE ALMSHOUSE, ONLY THREE MUNICIPAL charities existed in Boston prior to 1800: the Boston Dispensary, the Boston Humane Society, and—oldest of all—the Boston Maritime Society, founded in 1742 for "the relief of distressed mariners, their widows, and their children." It was not until 1799 that the idea for a public orphanage for destitute young girls was first proposed by Mrs. Hannah Stillman, wife of the Reverend Samuel Stillman of the First Baptist Church of Boston, one of the most beloved clergymen of his day.

In September 1800, Mrs. Stillman's pet project came to fruition when the Boston Female Asylum accepted its first orphan, a young girl identified in later histories only as "Betsey D." The circumstances of her admission became part of the official lore of the society, a kind of sacred myth clearly meant to show that the Deity Himself had taken a direct hand in the founding of the institution. As recounted in an 1844 pamphlet issued by the society, the story went as follows:

> Having lost her parents when about five years of age, [Betsey] was received by an aunt, affectionate but poor, who adopted her as her own. Soon after, disease attacked this aunt and she expected to die. Her principal anxiety now was what would become of this destitute child. In the moment of her distress, she was visited by a friend, who told her that a place was just established under the management of the ladies of Boston for female orphan children, and that they would certainly receive the child on application being made to them.
>
> Overjoyed at this unexpected information, she exclaimed: "Thank God for providing that place for my little girl!"

The asylum had been in existence for just a few months when the Board of Managers was confronted with an unforeseen dilemma. At its fourth meeting, in December 1800, a young mother "in a very distressed situation" appeared before the board. Unable to provide for her little girl, the distraught woman made a tearful plea to the managers, beseeching them to accept her child "in the name of humanity." Since the asylum had initially been conceived strictly as a place for "those who had neither father nor mother," this appeal set off a spirited debate among the board members.

In the end, by a vote of eight to six, they agreed to accept the little girl. From that day forth, the Boston Female Asylum was open not only to orphans, but to any suffering child, even if her parents were still alive. Anyone who placed a girl in the institution—whether parent, guardian, or next of kin—was required to sign an official "form of surrender," relinquishing "all right and claim to her and her services," and promising "not to interfere with the management of her in any respect whatsoever."

In the following decades, the asylum continued to expand its operations. By the middle of the century, the society was able to purchase a plot of land in the southerly part of the city and erect a handsome new building. Nearly 100 girls between the ages of three and ten resided there at any given time.

Their breakfasts consisted of hasty pudding, boiled rice with molasses, or milk porridge thickened with flour, depending on the season. Their dinner menus remained the same from week to week: soup on Monday and Wednesday, boiled meat on Tuesday, pork and beans on Thursday, lamb broth on Friday, fish on Saturday, and roast meat and pudding on Sunday.

Their education was restricted to "those useful things suitable to their age, sex, and station." Since their sex was female and their station distinctly lower class, this meant that (according to official reports of the asylum) they were taught to read, spell, and cipher only "so far as necessary." Mostly, they were instructed in domestic skills: sewing, knitting, cooking, and housekeeping.

When a girl reached the age of eleven, she was "placed out" with a private family. Only a relative handful were actually adopted. Most became indentured servants, legally bound—usually for a term of six or seven years—to the families who took them in. Indeed, the Boston Female Asylum served a dual purpose, functioning as both a refuge for indigent children and a source of cheap domestic labor.

In exchange for room, board, and the promise of "kind treatment," the overburdened mistress of a large New England household could receive her own personal house-servant—a well-trained menial, contractually bound to perform whatever drudgery was demanded of her. It is clear that many Boston-area women regarded this as an exceptionally good bargain—a way "of obtaining the most service at the least price for which it can be procured," as one historian of the institution noted. It was largely for this reason that "applications for the children always greatly exceeded the number to be placed out."

The indenture lasted until the girl reached the age of eighteen, at which time she was entitled to receive her freedom from servitude, along with "two suits of clothes, one proper for Sunday, the other for domestic business." In later years, this stipulation was revised. Instead of clothing, the girl was to be given fifty dollars upon her release. In theory, at least, the arrangement was advantageous for everyone. The indentured girls obtained the "incalculable benefits" of a "permanent home," "thorough instruction in domestic affairs," and the sort of moral guidance "that youth requires." In return, their mistresses received dutiful "apprentices" to help around the house.

In reality, of course, things didn't always work out quite so well. Many "apprentices" suffered from abusive treatment at the hands of tyrannical mistresses. And some of the girls gave their adoptive families legitimate cause for complaint. In spite of years of instruction, there were girls who remained hopelessly recalcitrant, causing their new families "much trouble and anxiety." According to the regulations, no child could be given back to the orphanage once an indenture was signed. In later years, however, this rule appears to have been relaxed, and dissatisfied families were permitted to return the girls after a brief trial period, as though each orphan came with a thirty-day, money-back guarantee. The official records of the asylum (preserved at the Massachusetts State Library) contain numerous entries like the following:

> The Committee reported that Agnes Alexander, who had been living on trial with Mrs. Josephson in Newton, had been returned to the Asylum during the month, Mrs. Josephson having found it impossible to bear with her any longer.

> The Committee reported that Louise Ostman had been returned to the Asylum by Mrs. Bartlett, who made complaints of her temper.

> Agnes Parker was returned to the Asylum by Dr. and Mrs. Mill with complaints of her stupidity and untruthfulness.

On balance, however, it was generally acknowledged that the asylum had fulfilled its mission with admirable success. "It is unquestionable," wrote its official historian, "that much wretchedness has been relieved, and much suffering and exposure to vice prevented." If a certain percentage of the girls remained "unworthy," that was only to be expected. After all, "what human means have ever produced all the good results which the sanguine have anticipated?" Besides, the historian added, if all the effort expended on them had failed to improve their character, it was legitimate to wonder how much worse they would have been without it—what kind of viciously depraved creatures they would have turned into without the elevating influences of the Boston Female Asylum.

The asylum had been performing its charitable mission for more than half-a-century when, in early February 1863, a hard-luck case named Peter Kelley showed up at the institution with his two youngest daughters in tow: eight-year-old Delia Josephine and her six-year-old sister, Honora. The shabbily dressed Kelley—who gave off a powerful whiff of rotgut—was looking to dispose of the children, his wife, Bridget, having died of consumption several years earlier.

Though certifiable facts about him are sparse, it is clear from existing records that Kelley was a chronic drunk, prone to violent outbursts and so wildly eccentric that his neighborhood nickname was "Kelley the Crack" (as in "crackpot"). In later years, he would become the subject of bizarre legends. According to the most colorful of these, he eventually went insane, and—while working in a tailor shop—sewed his own eyelids shut.

The story is undoubtedly apocryphal, though it apparently reflected the prevailing perception of him as a frighteningly unstable individual. One fact about him, however, was undoubtedly true: he was a sorry excuse for a father. The managers needed just a single glimpse of the two little girls to see how wretched their home life had been. By a unanimous vote, the board approved their admission to the asylum. That very day, Kelley signed the standard form of surrender—or, more accurately, endorsed it with his mark, a laboriously inscribed cross. He never saw the children again.

Of their experience as inmates of the Boston Female Asylum no record exists, though a check of existing documents shows that neither Delia nor Honora was ever awarded one of the prizes periodically handed out for industry, obedience, truthfulness, or improvement. But, then, Honora's stay at the asylum was relatively brief—less than two years. In November 1864, she was indentured to Mrs. Ann C. Toppan of Lowell, Massachusetts, who impressed the Board as "a very respectable woman" with "a home that appeared to possess many advantages" for Honora. Delia would remain in the institution for another four years, until she reached the stipulated age of twelve and was bound out to a couple in Athol.

From a clinical point of view, it would be illuminating to know precisely how Peter Kelley mistreated his children. Though no specific details have come down to us, it seems safe to assume that they were subjected to some severe form of abuse. Modern research has conclusively shown that such brutalization is always a factor in the development of adult psychopatholgy. Sometimes the abuse takes the form of extreme corporal punishment, even to the point of torture. At other times, it is sexual. Or it may even be verbal. (One recent study lists the kind of parental taunts that female sociopaths were constantly subjected to as children. "You're a worthless fat piece of shit" and "Why don't you go somewhere and die?" were typical remarks.)

Though we cannot say exactly what happened to Delia and Honora, it is certain that—as noted in the offial records of the Boston Female Asylum—they "were rescued from a very miserable home." Unfortunately, they were rescued too late. In spite of the moral instruction they received at the asylum, as well as the many advantages of the homes in which they were placed, the lives of both girls ended up badly. Delia would eventually become an outcast, sink into a life of drink and prostitution, and die in squalid circumstances.

As for Honora, though she was never formally adopted, she assumed the name of the family that took her in. She became known as Jane Toppan. And in an era that had already produced some of the most remorseless female sociopaths in American history, little Jane Toppan would grow up to be the worst of them all.

PART TWO

—⁕—

JOLLY JANE

JOLLY JANE

4

Unrelieved, unremitting self-contempt is virtually unbearable. To survive both psychologically and physically, the sufferer must somehow cast off the terrible
feelings of self-hate. Some sufferers try bravado, performing risky or heroic deeds in order to restore self-
esteem. If this course fails, shamelessness is likely to
follow . . . the sufferer will lash out, becoming the
perpetrator of malevolence.

—CARL GOLDBERG, *Speaking with the Devil*

WITH HER BIG DARK EYES, THICK BLACK HAIR, STRONG
nose, and somewhat olive complexion, little Jane
could have hailed from Naples. And indeed, there
were people in Lowell who believed that she was Italian—an orphan whose parents had died of ship fever
while emigrating to America.

At home, of course, she was never allowed to forget
the truth of her heritage. "You can't help being Irish,"
she would often be told by the widow Toppan, the
woman she referred to as "Auntie." "But that doesn't
mean you have to act like a 'Paddy.' "

Italian, Irish—it made little difference. In the Wasp
world she inhabited, Jane was constantly being put in
her place—reminded of her outsider status.

To win the world's favor, she developed a vivacious,
ingratiating personality. She was renowned as a "clever
and amusing" storyteller. At picnics—as one of her

childhood acquaintances would later recall—"if Jane Toppan were there, it wasn't necessary to provide any other entertainment." Of course, such verbal facility was common among "her kind." After all, even the lowest-born "Paddy" was known to possess an innate "gift of gab."

Recent criminological research teaches that shame and humiliation are common factors in the genesis of malevolent personalities. Children instilled with self-loathing—a sense that they are worthless, the lowest of the low—may grow up to be adults fueled by baleful impulses. Besides a lust for revenge—for getting back at a world that has treated them so contemptuously—they are filled with a pernicious need to prove their superiority over the rest of humankind. They are possessed, in the words of one criminal psychologist, "by a demoniac compulsion," driven to show that they are people to be reckoned with—beings endowed with formidable, even terrifying, powers. And what power is more fearsome, more godlike, than that of holding a human life in your hands—of dispensing death on a whim?

For the first six years of her life, Jane Toppan had been subjected to shocking mistreatment at the hands of her deplorable father. Rescued from his custody, she was taken into a home in which she was continually reminded of her social inferiority. That Jane was made to feel profoundly ashamed of her heritage is clear from her later behavior. As she grew older, she displayed the classic symptoms of ethnic and religious self-hatred, lying about her origins to new acquaintances, and voicing anti-Irish and anti-Catholic sentiments more derogatory than the most bigoted remarks bandied in the polite, Protestant circles in which she moved.

And then, of course, there was her position as a
bond servant. In the end, Jane would live with the
Toppan family until she was twenty-eight without ever
being adopted. To be sure, her material circumstances
were infinitely preferable to the misery she had suffered in her early years. At the same time, she was
never allowed to forget her subordinate position. It
was her foster sister, Elizabeth, who was unmistakably
the beloved and pampered daughter of the household.
Jane, though sharing the Toppan name, was never
more than a relatively well-treated menial.

In the final analysis, of course, there is no way of
telling what childhood influences will turn someone
into a sociopath. The sources of criminal malevolence
are, in their way, as mysterious as those of creative ge-
nius. Still, it is significant that an examination of Jane
Toppan's background reveals two of the factors commonly found in the early lives of serial killers: severe
childhood mistreatment by an egregious parent and
unremitting humiliation throughout her formative
years. And in Jane's case, there was a third factor as
well—an apparent hereditary predisposition toward
mental derangement. Not only was her father notoriously unstable but another of her siblings, an older sister named Nellie, went insane and spent her adult life
confined to a series of asylums.

At no point in her life did Jane appear criminally
deranged. On the contrary, she struck most of her acquaintances as an exceptionally amiable and outgoing
person. Certainly, she was able to win the confidence
of many sound and sensible people, who welcomed
her into their homes without ever suspecting that they
were entrusting their lives to a monster.

Like others of her ilk, however, Jane had a hidden

self that was hopelessly diseased and that revealed itself in particular, symptomatic ways. "Despite a superficial bonhomie and apparently plausible disposition," writes Edward Glover in his study *The Roots of Crime*, "the psychopath is outstandingly selfish, egotistical, stubborn and deceitful, with an insatiable need for prestige." All the traits that Glover mentions—the deceit, the egotism, the desperate craving for prestige—were present in Jane Toppan from the start. Though her lively personality made her popular among some of her schoolmates, others despised her as an incorrigible liar, prone to wild fabrications that she doggedly stuck to even when they were proven to be flagrantly false. Her father, she claimed, had sailed around the world and lived for many years in China. Her brother had fought with such heroism at Gettysburg that President Lincoln himself had given him a medal. Her sister was a legendary beauty who had won the heart of an English lord.

If some of her lies were the pathetically self-aggrandizing claims of a young girl desperate for distinction, others had a more insidious aim: to prove her superiority by making other people look bad. In high school, Jane was a notorious gossip, spreading nasty rumors about classmates she envied or bore grudges against. She became a schoolroom snitch, ingratiating herself with her teachers by tattling on her misbehaving peers. Not that Jane herself was a model of behavior. On the contrary, she was an inveterate troublemaker. But more often than not, she contrived to escape punishment by pinning her misdeeds on others.

Of course, she didn't always escape punishment, particularly at home. Jane's foster mother believed in old-fashioned notions of discipline, and Jane was not spared the rod. But the beatings she endured did not have the desired, uplifting effect. On the contrary, every stroke of the switch only intensified the bitter sense of grievance and injustice she bore against the world.

Her deepest feelings of envy were reserved for her foster sister, Elizabeth, who—from Jane's jaundiced point of view—enjoyed everything that she herself had been so unfairly deprived of: social position, familial love, and—as Elizabeth matured into a handsome young woman—the ardent attentions of an exemplary suitor, a young deacon named Oramel A. Brigham. Jane's own love life would remain forever thwarted. According to unsubstantiated stories, she was courted at one point in her early twenties by a Lowell office worker, who went so far as to give her an engagement ring engraved with the image of a bird. The relationship ended badly, however, when the young man moved to Holyoke, took a room in a boardinghouse, and fell in love with the landlady's daughter, whom he eventually wed.

Whatever the truth of this story, it is hardly surprising that Jane Toppan never married. Possessed of a monstrous egotism—committed to nothing except absolute self-gratification—the psychopathic personality is, as Edward Glover writes, "incapable of deep attachments." As Jane settled into permanent spinsterhood, she allowed her youthful figure to balloon. By the time she reached her late twenties, the five-foot-three-inch woman weighed nearly 170 pounds—unattractively plump even by the generous standards of her age, when, according to one guidebook, the "recognized perfection for a woman's stature" was five-feet-five-inches tall and 138 pounds ("If she be well formed," advises the book, "she can stand another ten pounds without greatly showing it").

Her frustrated erotic longings found a partial outlet in the sentimental fiction of the day. Throughout her adult life, Jane was addicted to the cloying romantic fantasies peddled in popular bestsellers like *The House of Dreams-Come-True*, *Miss Marjorie of Silvermead*, and *The Princess of the Purple Palace*. Even a constant diet of these sugarcoated daydreams, however, could not satisfy the strongest of her cravings; for—as events would prove—there was another, far darker side to her warped erotic nature. But many years would pass before the full extent of her depravity was revealed to a stunned and disbelieving world.

When Jane reached the age of eighteen, she received a payment of fifty dollars, as stipulated in her indenture. History does not record what she did with the money. We do know, however, that it was the largest amount she would ever receive from her foster mother. When Ann Toppan died a few years later, Jane was not included in the will. Everything went to Elizabeth. Shortly after her mother's death, Elizabeth became Mrs. O. A. Brigham, and the deacon settled into his new bride's handsome Georgian-style house.

Though Jane was now legally emancipated from her servitude, she continued to live at home for another decade, functioning in the same capacity as always. Now, however, she was working for Elizabeth—a situation that could only have exacerbated Jane's already acute feelings of resentment toward her foster sister. Inevitably, relations between the two women became impossibly strained. The precise circumstances of Jane's ultimate departure—whether she was expelled from the house or left voluntarily—are unknown. What we do know for certain is that she moved out in 1885. Elizabeth—a good-natured young woman who, by and large, had always treated Jane considerately—assured her that she "was welcome to visit her old home whenever she wished. There would always be a room waiting for her."

For twenty-two years, Jane had lived with people who—however well-meaning—had never let her forget that she was not one of them. Now, pushing thirty, she was out in the world on her own. She had no inherited money, no social position, no family to fall back on. Nor, aside from her domestic skills, did she have any definite occupation.

At a time when females were taught that their "proper sphere" was in the home, career opportunities for respectable young women were severely restricted in America. Aside from teaching—either as schoolmarms or as private governesses—they might become seamstresses, servants, or workers in a textile mill. None of those occupations appealed to Jane. She wanted what most people do: a job that would bring in a living wage, while offering opportunities for personal fulfillment. For many years, her deepest appetites had gone largely unsatisfied. Now, she was tired of acting out her desires entirely in fantasy. At twenty-nine years old, she hungered to taste the exquisite pleasures she had spent so much time imagining.

And so, in 1887, Jane Toppan—a classic psychopathic personality who longed to do harm—settled on the profession most congenial to her needs. She decided to become a nurse.

5

—⚬—

I solemnly pledge myself before God, and in the presence of this assembly: to pass my life in purity and to practice my profession faithfully. I will abstain from whatever is deleterious and mischievous, and will not take or knowingly administer any harmful drug.

—"THE FLORENCE NIGHTINGALE PLEDGE"

FOR MUCH OF THE NINETEENTH CENTURY, HOSPITAL nursing was typically handled by a bunch of remarkably unqualified women. In New York City, for example, the wards of Bellevue were staffed by former inmates of the Blackwell's Island workhouse—women, generally arrested for drunkenness or prostitution, who were paroled on the condition that they serve a stint as nurses. Needless to say, the quality of care they offered the patients left a lot to be desired, particularly since many of them were illiterate and unable to read the directions on medicine bottles—a circumstance that often produced disastrous results.

The situation was no less bleak in Boston. As early as 1850, a sanitary commission appointed by the Massachusetts State Legislature recommended "that institutions be formed to educate and qualify females to be nurses of the sick." It would be another twenty-three years, however, before the first nursing school was established in Boston. It was to one of these training facilities—the school attached to Cambridge

Hospital—that Jane Toppan applied for admission in 1887.

For the two years of their training, student nurses were subjected to a brutal regimen. They worked seven days a week, fifty weeks a year, with no Christmas, Easter, or Thanksgiving holidays. They slept in cramped, dimly lit, unheated cubicles, three women to a cubicle. Typically, they were roused from their cots at 5:30 A.M. by the clanging of a wake-up bell. After making their beds, dressing, and consuming a hurried breakfast (which they were required to fix for themselves), they repaired to a parlor for morning prayers. By 7:00 A.M., they were on the job. Between their shifts on the various wards and their professional instruction, they typically worked twelve- to fourteen-hour days, with about seventy-five minutes off for lunch and supper. Their meals tended to be so sparse and unpalatable that many of the women spent all their meager wages on extra food.

For her first month, the trainee was a probationer, consigned to the most menial drudge-work—scrubbing floors, emptying chamber pots, laundering soiled bedclothes, etc. By her second week on the job, she was also given charge of a handful of patients. Under the watchful gaze of the head nurse, the trainee learned how to give baths, dress bedsores, treat wounds, administer enemas, dispense medications. The head nurses—generally, stern, if not authoritarian, personalities—enforced discipline with a military rigor. The smallest infraction (grumbling about the quality of the food, for example) could get a trainee branded as a troublemaker. The rule book for one training school specified severe punishment for "any nurse who smokes, uses liquor in any form, gets her hair done at a beauty shop, or frequents dance halls."

If she successfully made it through her probationary period, the aspiring nurse was required to sign an agreement "to remain for two years in the Training School for Nurses as a pupil nurse and to obey the rules of the school and the hospital." In return, she was promised board, lodging, a white bib-apron and a cap made of lace-trimmed organdy, plus a monthly stipend of seven dollars, out of which she was expected to pay for her clothes, textbooks, and incidental expenses.

Typically, the trainee had charge of about fifty patients. Besides her medical duties—which involved everything from catheterizing patients to draining their suppurating wounds—she was responsible for keeping her ward in proper shape. Among her daily housekeeping tasks, she was expected to sweep and mop the floors, dust the furniture and windowsills, keep the furnace fed with coal, make sure the lamps were filled with kerosene. She was also required to prepare and serve the patients' meals, change their beds, launder their clothes, roll bandages, and keep her writing quills sharply whittled so that her records would be legible to the head nurse and attending physicians.

Once a week, generally between 8:00 and 9:00 in the evening, she was required to attend a lecture in medical theory presented by one of the hospital physicians. Subjects typically included: physiology, hygiene, dietetics, obstetrics, surgical emergencies, eye and ear diseases, pediatrics, and nervous disorders.

At the end of her second year, she was given a final examination by a board of physicians. If she passed, she received a handsome diploma, signed by both the examining doctors and the nursing-school board of

directors. The questions covered a wide range of top-
ics, from anatomy to sickroom care. Since administering medicine was such a major part of a nurse's duties,
particular attention was paid to the subject of "materia
medica." The questions included in the final examination of one school in the 1880s—the period in which
Jane Toppan received her training—reveal a great
deal, not only about the knowledge expected of
Victorian-era nurses, but about the kinds of medication commonly dispensed in those days:

What is the correct dose of sulfate of atropia?
Of sulfate of strychnia?

How much morphia would you give to a
child two years old? Four years old? Seven years
old?

What would you do for a patient who has
taken an overdose of opium or morphine?

What are poisons generally?

There is no doubt that, in many respects, Jane Toppan
had all the makings of a first-rate nurse. Having spent
twenty-two years of her life as a full-time house servant, she could easily handle the grueling drudge-work
required of her. She also had a winning bedside manner that charmed many of her patients. With her
increasingly roly-poly looks and bubbly personality, she
became known by a nickname that would stick with
her throughout the rest of her life: "Jolly Jane."

Not everyone, however, was quite so taken with her.
In fact, just as in high school, there were those who de-

tested Jane throughout her student-nursing years, and for the same reasons. Besides toadying up to her superiors—the head nurses and hospital physicians—she enjoyed spreading nasty gossip about people she disliked. She was exceptionally devious, with an uncanny flair for escaping the consequences of her own wrongdoing while implicating others as the culprits. In at least two instances, she spread slanderous rumors about fellow trainees that ultimately led to their dismissal. And she exulted in the trouble she caused. Even Jane's friends were somewhat taken aback by the unconcealed glee she displayed when the two disgraced (and wholly innocent) young women were expelled from the school.

In terms of sheer mendacity, the malicious lies she told about others were matched by the outlandish fabrications she invented about herself. As had been true since childhood, Jane was absolutely shameless about making up wildly boastful stories and insisting on their truth, even in the face of the most unassailable evidence to the contrary. On one occasion, for example, she let it be known that she was thinking of moving to Russia. According to her story, the Czar had heard of the wonderful strides being made by American nurses and—wanting only the best for himself and his family—had offered Jane an enormous salary to join his personal medical staff.

Lies weren't her only transgressions. Throughout her time at nursing school, she was suspected of stealing various items, from hospital supplies to small sums of money. Nothing could ever be proven against her, however. In all of her crimes, large and small, she was an expert at concealment. Despite the growing distrust and hostility she provoked among her peers, Jane's vibrant personality—the sunniness she could radiate when it suited her purposes—blinded most people to the dark realities of her nature. She continued to be a favorite among many of the patients, who brightened up visibly whenever "Jolly Jane" showed up on the ward.

In her own perverse way, Jane reciprocated their affection. She was particularly fond of certain patients, and felt so sorry to see them discharged that she would take steps to prolong their stay. Sometimes, she would falsify their records, inventing symptoms that they didn't really have or adding a few degrees of temperature to their fever charts. When that wasn't sufficient, she would administer small doses of medication that would make them feel worse—not seriously ill, just sick enough to remain in the hospital for an extra week or so.

And those were the patients she *liked*.

There were some that she actively despised. She was especially contemptuous of the elderly, and on more than one occasion was heard to remark that "there was no use in keeping old people alive." She said it with a smile, and her listeners assumed she was joking. But she wasn't. She was deadly serious.

Exactly how many patients died at Jane Toppan's hands during her time at nursing school is unclear. Even she couldn't say with any certainty, though, according to her estimate, she was responsible for at least a dozen murders during those years. In both their commission and concealment, her crimes were carried out with a methodical cunning. There was nothing haphazard about Jane's approach. On the contrary, she brought a terrifying rationality to the outrages she perpetrated. She set about studying the tools of her trade with a scholar's diligence, frequently asking her teachers questions about the properties of various poisons. She knew that her curiosity on the subject wouldn't arouse suspicion—not at a time when substances from arsenic to strychnine were routinely prescribed for a range of ailments.

She also pursued her researches in private. In later years, when investigators went through her belongings, they discovered a well-worn medical textbook from her student-nursing days. When they picked it up, the book fell open to a section that Jane had obviously pored over many times. It was the chapter on opium.

Throughout the nineteenth century, opium was a cheap, legal, over-the-counter drug—as easy to buy as aspirin is today. As a common ingredient in the countless patent medicines that flooded the marketplace in the 1800s, opium was used to relieve teething pains in infants, menstrual cramps in women, and diarrhea in dysentery patients. Insomniacs took it to promote sleep and consumptives to suppress coughing. Morphine, the principal derivative of opium, came into particularly wide use during the Civil War, when it was employed as a surgical anesthesia and painkiller. Some doctors also recommended it as a substitute for whiskey, believing that, of the two evils, morphine addiction was preferable to alcoholism, since (as a physician named J. R. Black wrote in 1889) morphine "calms in place of exciting the baser passions, and hence is less productive of acts of violence and crime."

Dr. Black, of course, had no knowledge of his deranged contemporary, Nurse Toppan, when he published those remarks. In her hands, morphine became everything he claimed it was not—productive of the most appalling acts "of violence and crime."

It is impossible to say exactly when Jane began conducting what she called her "scientific experiments." By the time she was caught, she had perpetrated so many of them that she could no longer remember all the details. She herself had become a kind of addict, profoundly dependent on the ecstasy—the intoxication—of murder. Poisoning, as she put it, had became "a habit of her life."

At first she appears to have relied exclusively on morphine, injecting it into her victims, then standing at the bedside to observe the effects. She liked to see their pupils contract—listen to their breathing grow loud and stertorous—watch as a clammy sweat covered their faces. With a large enough dose, they would sink into a coma almost immediately and die within a few hours. Sometimes, they simply stopped breathing. She found it far more satisfying, however, when—as occasionally happened—their deaths were accompanied by violent convulsions.

Her serious experimentation really began when she started combining the morphine with another drug: atropine. Derived from both the belladonna and datura plants, atropine has been employed throughout history—particularly in India—as a particularly deadly poison. In Victorian America it was used, like morphine, both as a painkiller and as a treatment for dozens of ailments: asthma, earache, night sweats, rheumatism, seasickness, tetanus, whooping cough, and many more.

Its symptoms, however, are very different from— and in some cases diametrically opposite to—those produced by morphine. The mouth and throat grow parched, and the pupils widely dilated. Victims lose control of their muscular coordination and reel around like drunks. They are possessed by a strange sense of giddiness that soon passes into a wild delirium. They may babble incoherently, burst into maniacal laughter, or emit constant, anguished groans. Perhaps the most grotesque symptom of all is their incessant picking at real or imaginary objects. They pluck at their clothing—pull at their fingers and toes—snatch at invisible objects in the air. Even when they lapse into their final stupor, they continue to mutter feverishly and make constant spasmodic motions, clutching at the bed-clothes or grasping at phantoms floating over their heads.

In experimenting on her victims, Jane began dispensing morphine and atropine in varying combinations. Often she would inject the morphine first, then—just before the patient lost consciousness—force him to drink a glass of water in which she had dissolved an atropia tablet. Or she might wait until the victim had lapsed into a coma, then roll him over and administer an enema laced with atropine, letting the poison flow directly into his bowels.

There was a twofold motivation to her method. First, it allowed her to mask her crimes. By varying the dosages and timing of the drugs, she produced a set of symptoms so perplexing that the doctors couldn't ascertain the true nature of the patient's condition, often ascribing it to diabetes or heart failure. Second, she did it for fun. She derived a keen, sadistic pleasure from playing with her victims—from doing terrible things to their bodies and watching the results—before deciding it was time for them to die.

Not that she killed every patient she poisoned. Sometimes, she waited until her victim was near death, then did everything in her power to save him. When she succeeded, she seems to have felt genuinely proud of herself, taking a deep sense of satisfaction in her professional skill. (In this respect, Jane Toppan was similar to other homicidal health care workers who have followed in her wake—Richard Angelo, for example, the Long Island "Angel of Death," who, in the 1980s, administered lethal injections to an indeterminate number of hospital patients so that he could rush to their aid and feel like a hero.)

The gratification she derived from being a savior, however—from rescuing one of her own victims from the brink of death—was nothing compared to the feelings she experienced when they succumbed. In describing that sensation, Jane tended to rely on Victorian locutions—"delirious enjoyment," "voluptuous delight," "greatest conceivable pleasure." In the end, however—and much to the horror of her contemporaries—she was extremely direct in her admission.

Killing, she would ultimately confess, gave her a sexual thrill.

6

The art of the poisoner is habit-forming; once the secret dose has been successful, the poisoner is urged on
by a desire to repeat his triumph.

—HENRY MORTON ROBINSON,
Science Catches the Criminal

AT THE SAME TIME THAT JANE TOPPAN WAS ATTENDING
nursing school, her great contemporary, Herman
Melville, was at work on his final masterpiece, *Billy
Budd*. Once a celebrated author, Melville had long
since dropped from public sight. In 1887—the year
Jane began her training at Cambridge Hospital—he
was residing in utter obscurity in lower Manhattan,
having retired from his job as a deputy inspector at
the New York City Customs House, where he had
worked for nineteen years. When he died in 1891, his
passing would go virtually unnoticed. In a perfunctory, three-sentence obituary, the *New York Times*
would describe him as a once-popular writer of "sea-
faring stories" and give his first name as "Henry."

In the few years between his retirement and death,
Melville's creative energies were devoted to the composition of *Billy Budd*. The work—which would not
be published until 1924, and even then in a seriously
flawed transcription—deals with one of Melville's obsessive themes: the eternal struggle between good and
evil, as embodied in its title character, the "handsome

sailor," Billy Budd, and his nemesis, John Claggart, the diabolical master-at-arms who sets out to destroy the innocent hero for no other reason than his hatred of Billy's beauty and goodness.

At one point in the novella, the author pauses to contemplate the source of Claggart's villainy. Living in a pre-Freudian age, Melville does not use the clinical language of modern-day psychology in accounting for the character's behavior, relying instead on such old-fashioned phrases as "natural depravity" and "the mania of an evil nature." But his description of the master-at-arm's malevolent personality makes it clear that Claggart is a classic instance of what we now call a criminal psychopath:

> Though the man's even temper and discreet bearing would seem to intimate a mind peculiarly subject to the law of reason, not the less in heart he would seem to riot in complete exemption from that law, having apparently little to do with reason further than to employ it as an ambidexter implement for effecting the irrational. That is to say: Toward the accomplishment of an aim which in wantonness of atrocity would seem to partake of the insane, he will direct a cool judgment sagacious and sound. These men are madmen, and of the most dangerous sort, for their lunacy is not continuous, but occasional, evoked by some special object.

Given his understanding of mankind's darker nature, it surely would have come as no great shock to Melville that, even as he composed this description, a being who matched it precisely—whose "even temper and discreet bearing" masked a heart that "rioted in" evil—was living in Boston. He might well have been amazed by one thing, however. Like most people, Melville apparently assumed that such extreme depravity was limited to members of the male sex—to "madmen." It would have undoubtedly surprised him to learn that the real-life counterpart of his fictitious maniac—a creature every bit as malign and diabolical as the fiendish Claggart—was a woman.

Despite the intense dislike she provoked in many of her acquaintances, Jane always had her champions. Cunning and manipulative, she was able to make a highly favorable impression on influential people. In 1888, that ability stood her in good stead when she decided to seek wider training at Massachusetts General Hospital, whose nursing school was one of the most respected in the nation.

The head nurse—an unreconstructed bigot who sniffed at Jane's "low origins"—initially opposed her admission. Jane's letters of recommendations, however—written by some of the most prominent physicians connected to Cambridge Hospital—were full of such glowing testimonials that the head nurse finally relented. Not only did Jane pass her probation without trouble; she struck her superiors as so proficient that, when the head nurse took a leave of absence the following year, Jane was named as her temporary replacement.

Like all sociopaths, however, Jane could not keep her worst impulses in check. It wasn't long before her behavior became a subject of whispered gossip among the other nurses, many of whom detested her. As in the past, she was widely perceived as a self-promoting liar, who routinely disparaged the efforts of her colleagues while taking all the credit for herself. There were constant rumors of falsified fever charts, tampered medical records, and petty thefts. And graver charges, too: of medications dispensed with such reckless disregard for proper dosages as to put the patient's health in jeopardy.

Even her most ardent detractors, however, never suspected the full appalling truth: that at night, when no one was about, Jane continued to conduct her secret "experiments" on unwitting patients.

As with her time in Cambridge Hospital, there is simply no way of telling how many people Jane killed during her stint at Massachusetts General. It appears that a fair number of patients died unexpectedly in her care. But in nineteenth-century America—when bleeding was still an accepted medical procedure and stomachaches were treated with strychnine—that was true for even the most respected physicians. Thanks to a striking piece of testimony, however, we do know something about the method she used. As it happened, one of Jane's intended victims managed to survive, and the story she would ultimately tell sheds chilling light not only on Nurse Toppan's MO but on the perverse erotic quality of her crimes: how tenderly she killed her victims, how lovingly she watched them die.

The woman's name was Mrs. Amelia Phinney. Thirty-six years old, she had been confined to the hospital with a uterine ulcer, which the doctors had subjected to the usual treatment, burning it with nitrate of silver, a powerful caustic agent. On the night following the procedure, Mrs. Phinney lay tossing on her cot, the pain in her lower body making it impossible for her to sleep. All at once, she became aware that someone was hovering over her bed. Opening her eyes, she saw the looming figure of Nurse Toppan, whose portly face—illuminated by the dull glow of the bedside oil lamp—wore a look of peculiar intensity.

When the nurse asked Mrs. Phinney how she was feeling, the poor woman gasped that she was suffering dreadfully, and implored Nurse Toppan to send for a physician.

"There is no need for that," Nurse Toppan said softly. "I have something to make you feel better. Here." Bending, she slid an arm beneath Mrs. Phinney's shoulders, raised her slightly from the pillow, and held a glass to her lips. "Drink this."

Mrs. Phinney swallowed the bitter-tasting medicine. Before long, a numbness began to spread through her body. Her mouth and throat felt uncomfortably dry, her eyelids heavily weighted. She felt herself subsiding into unconsciousness.

All at once, through her dimming perceptions, she became aware of something so peculiar that, for a long time afterward, she thought she must have dreamed it. She felt the bedclothes being pulled back—heard the creaking of the cot-frame—felt the mattress sag as another body slipped into bed beside her.

It was Nurse Toppan. Gently, she began stroking Mrs. Phinney's hair, kissing her all over her face, whispering softly in her ear that everything would soon be all right. At one point, she knelt on the bed and, bending low over the drugged woman, turned back her eyelids and peered intently at her pupils. Mrs. Phinney could feel the other woman's rapid, excited breathing on her face as Nurse Toppan examined her.

Moments later, Mrs. Phinney felt the glass being placed to her mouth once again, and heard Nurse

Toppan say in a husky voice: "Come, dear. Drink just a little more."

With all the strength she could muster, Mrs. Phinney tightened her lips and twisted her head to one side. Just then, something caused Nurse Toppan to rise hurriedly from the bed and flee, as though alarmed by the unexpected approach of another person.

The next morning, Mrs. Phinney was roused from a profound slumber by a young trainee named McCutcheon. Mrs. Phinney felt sick to her stomach, and so terribly groggy that it took several hours for her head to clear. Her recollections of the preceding night were so bizarre and bewildering that she hesitated to mention them to anyone. Surely, the whole dreadful experience *must* have been a bad dream.

It wasn't until years later—when jovial, fun-loving Jane was finally exposed for the monster she was—that Amelia Phinney realized just how close she'd been to death on that long-ago night when Nurse Toppan came to her bed.

While Jane's seriously criminal activities went undetected at Massachusetts General, the other infractions she committed—and the growing distrust she engendered in certain members of the staff—eventually got her into trouble.

Like other training facilities for nurses, the school at Massachusetts General followed the model established by Florence Nightingale, who had developed her methods during the Crimean War, when she was in charge of British army medical services in Turkey. Reflecting this military influence, early nursing schools demanded strict obedience from their students. Discipline was strictly enforced, and trainees who failed to display the requisite "ladylike" qualities—cheerfulness, piety, uncomplaining acceptance of their chores, and absolute submission to authority—were branded as incorrigible troublemakers and summarily dismissed.

In spite of the high regard in which she was held by various physicians—who swore by her competence and insisted on having her as a helper—Jane had managed to alienate a significant number of women on the nursing staff by the end of her first year at Massachusetts General. Increasingly, she was regarded as a "slippery" character, with a devious soul, a duplicitous tongue, and distinctly larcenous tendencies. She was suspected of stealing money from the hospital cash box, supplies from the storeroom, and a diamond ring from a wealthy patient. As usual, Jane made sure that nothing could be proven against her. She indignantly denied the accusations and did her best to shift the blame onto others.

Perhaps out of hubris, perhaps out of the compulsively self-destructive behavior that often undoes even the most cunning criminals, she finally made a misstep. In the summer of 1890, she committed a flagrant violation of the hospital rules, leaving the ward without permission. When her absence was brought to the attention of her nursing supervisors, they grasped at the opportunity to rid themselves of their increasingly troublesome subordinate. Though Jane had already passed her final examination and her diploma had been signed, she was discharged at once from the nursing school without receiving her license.

For a year, she worked as a private nurse in Cambridge and Lowell, garnering high recommendations from the doctors she assisted and the families she served. In the fall of 1890—seeking to obtain the license she'd failed to get at Massachusetts General—she returned to Cambridge Hospital. Before long, however, the old patterns reestablished themselves. On the one hand, her professional skill and personal charm made her a great favorite among the doctors and patients. At the same time, she was secretly and steadily engaged in a series of criminal activities, from larceny to homicide.

One of her intended victims was a nineteen-year-old trainee named Mattie Davis. Falling ill with a fever, the young woman took to bed and was tended by Nurse Toppan. After imbibing the medicine Jane gave her, Miss Davis, according to official accounts, "was seized with a sudden and violent collapse." Luckily for her, a doctor named Cleland happened to be passing by her room and, rushing to her aid, managed with great effort to save her.

Early the next morning, Jane reappeared in Miss Davis's room, with the evident intent of treating her to a second and more definitive dose of the medication. She was prevented from accomplishing her deadly purpose, however, by the presence of another nurse, who had been assigned to watch over Miss Davis by Dr. Cleland.

Though Cleland was deeply perplexed by Miss Davis's symptoms, he never suspected that she'd been poisoned. At least one other physician on the staff, however, began to have serious doubts about Jane after several of his convalescing patients died unexpectedly while under her care. To be sure, even he could not bring himself to believe that the affable, matronly nurse was a killer. He suspected, however, that she was dispensing opiates and other drugs with a dangerous disregard for the prescribed dosages—a charge that had been whispered about Jane throughout her career.

In the spring of 1891, he shared his doubts about Nurse Toppan's performance with the board of trustees, who wasted little time in dismissing her from the hospital.

She was now thirty-two years old. After four years of training, she had been discharged from Boston's two leading nursing schools without receiving her license. She had also left a long trail of corpses in her wake—perhaps two dozen in all—though no one, of course, was aware of that grim reality at the time.

Another person in Jane's position might have felt concerned about her prospects. But like other psychopaths, Jane possessed an unnatural sangfroid that allowed her to remain completely unfazed in situations that would engender intense anxiety in more normally constituted personalities. "I didn't care," she would breezily declare in later years when recalling her dismissal from Cambridge Hospital. She had already spent a year working for some of the most prominent families in Cambridge and knew that she "could make more money and have an easier time by hiring myself out."

And so, in the summer of 1891, Jane Toppan embarked on her career as a full-time private nurse.

7

In our society, the roles of women are still primarily
those of homemaker, of the preparer of meals, of the
rearer of children, of the nurse of the sick. . . . Abun-
dant temptations to commit crimes and opportunities
to carry them out in a secretive fashion follow from
these roles. Actually, woman's task of preparing food
for the members of the family has made her the poisoner par excellence, and her function in nursing the
sick has had a similar effect.

—OTTO POLLAK, *The Criminality of Women*

IT WAS TRUE—AS JANE BLITHELY DECLARED—THAT SHE
could do better financially by going out on her own.
Private-duty nurses did, in fact, receive good pay—but
only in comparison to the scandalous earnings of other
women in the late nineteenth century. According to a
survey conducted by the Department of Labor in 1888,
salaries for all female workers across the country aver-
aged from four to six dollars per week, hardly enough
to buy the bare necessities of life. By contrast, the average weekly pay for a highly trained private nurse was
twenty-five dollars.

Of course, like other freelancers, private nurses
tended to alternate between periods of intense, full-
time work and intervals of unemployment. And some
clients, even those who could afford it, failed to settle
up their accounts. Not infrequently, a nurse had to ac-

cept a fraction of her contracted wage, or even take barter goods in exchange for her services—food, clothing, household items.

As a result, even a successful nurse like Jane Toppan could count on a yearly salary of perhaps $600. To be sure, that was significantly more than her hospital salary. Still, it was hardly exorbitant—particularly given the grueling nature of the work.

True, not every nurse was terribly overburdened. The authors of a standard history of American nursing cite the case of "one trained nurse sent from New York to Europe, who found that her sole job was to make sure that the daughter of a millionaire never went out in damp weather without overshoes." In general, however, exceptionally heavy demands were made on full-time private nurses by the well-to-do families they served.

For the weeks or even months of her employment, the nurse was expected to keep virtually round-the-clock vigils at the patient's bedside. If the patient were seriously ill, she might, if she were lucky, snatch two or three hours of sleep each day on a couch beside the sickbed. If the patient suffered from insomnia, she was expected to stay up with him all night, tending to his comfort.

She was expected to anticipate the patient's every need, to obey the doctor's every direction, and to carry out the wishes of the family without question. While performing her duties, she was required to be a constant but unobtrusive presence, stepping softly when she moved about the sickroom, and refraining from making the slightest noise that might disturb the patient's repose. If she read a newspaper while the invalid slumbered, she took care not to rattle the pages;

if she passed the time knitting, she made sure the needles didn't click.

She was expected to maintain irreproachable personal habits, an unwaveringly cheerful disposition, and a docile manner, never displaying the slightest trace of discourtesy, fatigue, or irritation. If the patient were well enough to do without her care for a few hours, she was obliged to help around the house with the sewing, laundering, and other domestic chores. Circumstances permitting, she was allowed to take a brief daily walk. Otherwise, she had no time off, spending her days within the closed and fetid confines of the sickroom at the continuous beck and call of her employers.

It's no surprise that, after enduring such trying conditions for several weeks or longer, nurses themselves needed time to recuperate, often taking extended respites between jobs.

In spite of its demands, private-duty nursing suited Jane Toppan very well. At thirty-four, she possessed the physical stamina and practical experience necessary for the job. Her competent, take-charge manner inspired confidence in her employers, and her lively personality made her a household favorite. For a period of eight years, from 1892 until 1900, she was reputedly the most successful private nurse in Cambridge, highly recommended by respected physicians and eagerly sought-after by some of the city's best families.

To be sure, her reputation during those years wasn't entirely spotless. Some of her employers were taken aback by her tendency to spin elaborate lies about her life and accomplishments—though, for the most part, they dismissed her fondness for extravagant tale-telling as a function of what they euphemistically

called her "Celtic ancestry." She also had a habit of
borrowing small sums of cash from her employers and
neglecting to repay her debts. And on several occasions, she was suspected of committing small thefts.
At least one of her employers took the precaution of
making periodic counts of his silverware while Jane
was employed in his home.

Even he, however, never thought seriously about
dismissing her. Whatever her minor flaws—her chronic
fibbing, her cavalier attitude toward borrowing money—
she was an indispensable person to have around at times
of crisis, when a sick wife or suffering child required the
best care available, and the other members of the
household relied on the reassuring presence of a cheerful and capable nurse.

If Jane was able to beguile her employers with her
professional skill and personal charm, there were others who saw through her pleasant facade. To the
household servitors she worked among and the
friends she socialized with, she often showed a very
different face: jealous, bad-tempered, vindictive. While
she always took care to appear well-mannered to her
employers—using ladylike language and abstaining
from drink—she loved to guzzle beer on her off-time
and tell dirty stories whose vulgarity often shocked her
listeners. She delighted in gratuitous troublemaking—
in carrying tales, spreading rumors, turning people
against each other for no apparent reason.

Polite and respectful in public, she was often scur-
rilous in private, maligning her employers, her patients, and the physicians she worked with in the crud-
est terms. And her lies grew increasingly bizarre and
irresponsible. At one point, she caused a near-panic in
her neighborhood by fomenting the rumor that a se-

vere epidemic of typhoid had broken out in a nearby seminary.

For the most part, however, Jane was regarded as a gem and treated with affection, respect, and gratitude. And no one—not even those who caught glimpses of her uglier side—had any inkling of her darkest secrets: of the things that sometimes happened late at night, while the rest of the household slept and Nurse Toppan was alone with her patients.

8

These women take great delight in their secret hidden power. In watching the suffering and slow death of her victims, she receives the utmost stimulation. . . . She strives for the will to power which is characteristic of her sadistic nature and obtains this through the anguish and suffering of her victims.

—J. PAUL DE RIVER, *The Sexual Criminal*

GIVEN HOW GOOD IT MADE HER FEEL TO HOLD A DYING victim in her embrace, it is hardly surprising that Jane Toppan enjoyed her work as a private nurse. No other profession could have afforded her such choice opportunities to fulfill her twisted needs. The exact number of patients whose lives she ended during her nearly decade-long career remains a mystery, though estimates range as high as 100. Thanks to her own subsequent confessions, however, we do know the identities of some of her victims.

Two of them were her longtime landlords, an elderly couple named Israel and Lovey Dunham. When Jane wasn't engaged as a live-in nurse, she boarded for several years at the Dunham home at No. 19 Wendell Street, Cambridge.

In May 1895, Jane poisoned seventy-seven-year-old Israel Dunham because, as she later put it, he was getting "feeble and fussy." His death was attributed to heart failure brought on by a strangulated hernia.

For the next two years, Jane continued boarding with the grieving widow. By the fall of 1897, however, Mrs. Dunham, in Jane's estimation, had become too "old and cranky." When the old lady took ill that September, Jane nursed her to death with the usual combination of morphine and atropine dissolved in Hunyadi water, a popular, somewhat bitter-tasting mineral water imported from Budapest.

In killing the Dunhams, Jane was acting on a sentiment she had harbored at least as far back as her nursing school days, when she was repeatedly heard to remark that "there was no use in keeping old people alive." Another of her elderly victims was a wealthy seventy-year-old widow named Mary McNear.

On Christmas day, 1899, Mrs. McNear left her home in Watertown and traveled by carriage to visit her ailing daughter in Cambridge. On the way, she caught a chill. By the time she returned home that evening, she felt sure she was coming down with a cold.

The following afternoon, a Tuesday, she was visited by her married granddaughter, Mrs. Evelyn Shaw, who found her grandmother in the parlor. She was seated on the horsehair sofa, a woolen shawl around her shoulders, basking in the warmth from the black-marble fireplace. The old lady seemed her usual cheerful self, though she sneezed every now and then and sounded slightly hoarse to her granddaughter.

By Wednesday afternoon, Mrs. McNear had developed a cough. Taking to her bed, she sent for her longtime physician, Dr. Walter Wesselhoeft. Though he detected a bit of congestion in her lungs, Dr. Wesselhoeft seemed unconcerned, and when Mrs. McNear's relatives proposed hiring a trained nurse to care for the old lady, he dismissed the idea as unnecessary.

All she needed was bed rest, hot tea, and a little cod-liver oil for her cough. There was already a servant in the house who could easily minister to her needs.

Her family was insistent, however, and asked the doctor for a recommendation. Wesselhoeft told them to leave the matter to him. He would send over "one of his best nurses."

When Evelyn Shaw returned the following day— Thursday, December 28—she found her grandmother under the care of a buxom, pleasant-faced nurse who introduced herself as Miss Jane Toppan. Nurse Toppan had arrived early that morning and immediately taken charge. Her obvious professionalism and affable manner impressed Mrs. Shaw, who was relieved to see how well her grandmother was doing. Seated upright on the bed, her back propped up by feather pillows, the old lady was in high spirits, "laughing and chatting and making plans for some little New Year's celebration we were going to have," as her granddaughter would later recall.

After a pleasant visit that lasted an hour or so, Mrs. Shaw returned to Cambridge, feeling much reassured. She had only been home a short time, however, when her grandmother's coachman arrived in a state of extreme agitation. Something had happened to Mrs. McNear. She had passed out and could not be revived.

By the time Evelyn Shaw got back to her grandmother's house, Dr. Wesselhoeft was already there, having been summoned by Nurse Toppan. Taking Evelyn aside, he explained that her grandmother had "suffered a stroke of apoplexy." According to Nurse Toppan, the old lady had just taken a dose of her prescribed medication when "a quiver passed over her face, followed by a second" and she "fell back unconscious." Nurse Toppan had immediately gone downstairs to inform the servants that Mrs. McNear had passed out but that they "need not be alarmed, as she would do everything that was necessary."

The cook, however, Mrs. Grose, had thought it best to notify her family and had immediately dispatched the coachman to Cambridge.

Evelyn Shaw spent a long, sleepless night at her grandmother's bedside, holding the old lady's hand and praying for her recovery. Her prayers went unheeded. Early the next morning—Friday, December 29, 1899—Mary McNear died without ever having regained consciousness.

Shortly after the funeral, Mrs. McNear's relatives discovered that some of her best clothes were missing. Could Nurse Toppan have made off with the items? When they conveyed their suspicions to Dr. Wesselhoeft, however, he became deeply incensed. Jane Toppan, he declared, was "one of the finest women and best nurses he knew." He "would not listen to anything against her."

The family decided to let the matter drop. To be sure, as Mrs. Shaw later said, it pained them "to think that someone else might be wearing poor Grandma's clothes, and she laying in her grave." But in the end, some missing apparel was a trivial loss compared to the old lady's death. Besides, in view of Dr. Wesselhoeft's testimonial, it seemed unlikely that Nurse Toppan had stolen the garments.

That she had done something infinitely worse to their beloved grandmother was a thought that never even crossed their minds.

Considering how Jane felt about old people, it's hardly surprising that she did away with seventy-year-old Mary McNear. In another respect, however, Mrs. McNear was an unusual victim. Jane had never set eyes on the old lady until the day of the murder; they were complete strangers to each other. As a rule, Jane preferred to kill people she knew.

This preference is typical of women serial killers, and one of the traits that most distinguishes them from their male counterparts. In general, there is a promiscuous, impersonal quality to male serial murder, reflecting the stereotypical pattern of male sexuality. Whether straight or gay, a male psychopath will generally gratify his cravings on strangers—prostitutes, pickups, random victims snatched from the street. To be sure, he might look for someone with a specific physical trait that turns him on: blue eyes, brown skin, straight dark hair parted down the middle. But when the frenzy to kill comes over him, he will vent it on any available object that matches his fantasy.

By contrast, female serial killers prefer a certain level of intimacy with their victims. Their behavior is a grotesque travesty of the normal responses of women. Inflicting harm on anonymous strangers doesn't excite them; they achieve their deepest satisfaction in the context of personal relationships. They take pleasure in killing people they are closest to. Husbands and wives. Neighbors and friends. Their nearest blood kin.

Or their foster relations.

In the years since she'd left home, Jane had maintained superficially cordial relations with her foster sister, Elizabeth Brigham. On her occasional trips back to Lowell, Jane always stayed with Elizabeth and her husband, Oramel, who were more than happy to put her up in her old bedroom for a few days or a week. They were pleased that "Jennie" (as they fondly called her) had succeeded so well on her own. And they enjoyed her company. With her amusing personality, she always managed to brighten up the household. It felt like old times when Jennie came to stay.

Beneath her sociable exterior, however, Jane harbored virulent feelings against her foster sister. Like most psychopathic personalities, Jane Toppan bore a profound grudge against the world. Severely damaged in childhood, such individuals grow up full of envy and malice—and their bitterest hate is reserved for those who seem to have been granted everything in life that they themselves have been denied.

For Jane Toppan, her foster sister was the living embodiment of the world's inequities. Since childhood, Elizabeth had enjoyed all the advantages that Jane felt herself so unjustly deprived of: wealth, social status, parental devotion, and—later on—the blessings of love and marriage.

Not that Oramel Brigham was exactly a romantic figure. In 1899, he was a portly gentleman of advanced middle age with a double chin, bald dome, and bushy, gray, muttonchop whiskers. Still, as a deacon of the First Trinitarian Congregational Church and depot master for the Boston & Maine Railroad, he was a respected man in the community. And he was utterly devoted to his wife.

For several years, Jane had vacationed each summer on Cape Cod. In August 1899, she invited her foster sister to join her for a few days at her rented cottage in the seashore town of Cataumet. At her husband's urging, Elizabeth—who had been suffering from a mild but persistent case of melancholia—wrote back to Jane, eagerly accepting the invitation. A few days at the beach, she felt sure, would do her good.

She arrived late Friday, August 25. The following day, she and Jane—wearing white summer dresses and striped sailor caps—carried a picnic basket down to Scotch House Cove, where they spent several pleasant hours, chatting merrily, snacking on cold corned beef and taffy, and basking in the glories of the ocean, sky, and weather.

That night, Elizabeth—feeling slightly drained from her long afternoon in the sun—retired early to her upstairs bedroom. The following morning, she did not respond when called down to breakfast. Shortly afterward, Jane appeared at the house of her landlords. Her sister, she said, had taken sick. Having done all she could to make her comfortable, Jane thought it best to summon a physician.

Late that afternoon, back in Lowell, Oramel Brigham received a telegraph from Jane, informing him that Elizabeth was dangerously ill. Alarmed, he quickly made arrangements to take the first available train to Cape Cod. He arrived in Cataumet early the next morning, Monday, August 28, to find his wife in a coma. According to the physician who had responded to Jane's summons, Mrs. Brigham had suffered a stroke of apoplexy. Early the next morning, Tuesday, August 29, Elizabeth Brigham died with her tearful husband and dry-eyed foster sister at her bedside.

Shortly thereafter, Oramel began gathering up his dead wife's belongings for the journey back to Lowell. Glancing into her handbag, he was surprised to discover that it contained only five dollars. While discussing her vacation plans, he and Elizabeth had agreed that she should take no less than fifty dollars with her for expenses.

When Oramel asked Jane if she knew what had become of the missing money, she claimed ignorance. As far as she knew, Elizabeth had arrived with only the few dollars in her purse.

Taking Jane at her word, Oramel was about to return to his melancholy task when she placed a hand on his arm and told him that Elizabeth had made a final request. Just before slipping into her final coma, she had expressed the wish that Jane be given her gold watch and chain as a keepsake.

The information brought renewed tears to the deacon's eyes. How like his wife to make such a loving gesture! He turned the articles over to Jane without hesitation, then went back to arranging for his wife's final trip home to Lowell.

In subsequent years, Oramel never once saw Jane with the gold watch on her person. He assumed that she regarded it as too precious to carry, and kept it safeguarded with her other treasures.

He would not learn the truth until much later, when the police—searching through Jane Toppan's possessions—found a stash of pawnshop tickets in one of her bureau drawers.

Of all forms of homicide, poisoning is, by its very nature, the most secretive, accomplished by a killer who operates with the utmost stealth and perpetrated on a victim unaware that he or she is being murdered. Unless the killer confesses, it is impossible to tell precisely what took place during the commission of the deed.

Ultimately, Jane Toppan did confess to many, if not all, of her enormities, including the murder of her foster sister. From her brief but vivid account, we know what occurred in the rented summer cottage on the evening of August 26, 1899, after the two women returned from their pleasant afternoon at Scotch House Cove.

Jane admitted that she had harbored a bitter resentment against her foster sister for many years, and saw Elizabeth's visit to Cataumet as a "chance to have my revenge on her." Elizabeth, she claimed, "was really the first of my victims that I actually hated and poisoned with a vindictive purpose."

So inimical were her feelings toward Elizabeth that Jane didn't merely want to kill her; she wanted to see her suffer. "So I let her die slowly, with griping torture," she wrote. "I fixed mineral water so it would do that, and then added morphia to it."

Then, as she had done with so many other victims, Jane slipped into bed beside the dying woman, snuggled close beside her, and gave herself over to the voluptuous feelings that cruelty and death aroused in her:

"I held her in my arms and watched with delight as she gasped her life out."

9

This, above all, is what we must understand about extremely violent women, as we have always understood it about men. They were once needy girls, yes. Their lives were exploited, indeed. Patriarchal oppression incited them to desperate measures, perhaps. But none of that can be relevant to our social response. They are human first, and gendered second. They will destroy you in an instant, no slower than the men.

—PATRICIA PEARSON, *When She Was Bad*

FED UP WITH THE ENDLESS ACCOUNTS OF BLOODSHED and crime that constitute the daily news, many people long for the good old days, when a reader could pick up his morning paper without being assaulted by the latest evidence of human vice and depravity. A look at the front-page stories that ran in the *Lowell Sun* during the summer months of 1899, however, suggests that such a golden age never existed.

To be sure, some events that made the headlines bespeak a more quaint and innocent time. When a young couple from Nashua, New Hampshire—seventeen-year-old Mary Tessler and her eighteen-year-old beau, Alfred Salvall—eloped to Lowell to get married against their parents' wishes, the story was featured at the top of page one. The plight of six Lowell citizens who suffered food poisoning after eating badly preserved boiled lobster received equally prominent coverage, as did the four-month sentence imposed on Miss Angeline Fontaine for shoplifting fifteen yards of ribbon worth seventy-five cents a yard.

Running alongside this trivia, however, were stories about crimes every bit as shocking as the horrors that dominate today's headlines: matricide, lust-murder, juvenile sadism. In the short span of a few weeks, the front page of the *Lowell Sun* carried reports of a twenty-four-year-old prostitute named Dollie Hudson, found dead in her apartment with her throat slashed, the apparent victim of a sex-killer; a man named William Keating, who hanged himself in his jail cell with his suspenders after fatally shooting his wife and wounding two of her friends; a woman named Ella Shattuck, who shot her husband, Clarence, in the head and back, then placed his corpse in a wagon, hauled it across town, and laid it across the tracks of the Erie motor line; a pair of brothers, John and Joseph Seery, accused of beating their mother to death; and a thirteen-year-old named Arthur Slausen, who threw an eight-year-old playmate into a river, then returned to his fishing while the little boy drowned.

Readers of the *Lowell Sun* who sat down with their papers on the morning of Thursday, August 31, would have learned news of a tragic crime that had occurred many years in the past—the murder and disappearance of a local girl named Emily Newton, who had been killed by her lover in 1827 and whose skeletal remains had recently been turned up during the excavation of a vacant lot. They would also have learned the details of a very different, if no less tragic, event: the funeral of one of the town's most prominent citizens, Mrs. O. A. Brigham, who had died so

unexpectedly while enjoying a brief vacation on Cape
Cod.

The obsequies were held in the parlor of the
Brigham home, 182 Third Street. The furniture and
knickknacks had been moved aside and folding chairs
set up to accommodate the mourners. So many people showed up, however, that the latecomers were
forced to sit through the services in the dining room.

The Reverend George F. Kennegott, pastor of the
First Trinitarian Congregational Church, officiated. In
his eulogy, he described Mrs. Brigham as

> a devoted wife and mother, and a true and help-
> ful friend. The sorrowing sought her for sympa-
> thy, the needy for help. Always careful for the
> welfare of others, forgetful of self, her noble and
> generous nature readily responded to all. She
> was one with whom to form an acquaintance
> was a pleasure, and her noble life and her en-
> dearing manner won for her a high place in the
> estimation of all who were fortunate enough to
> come in contact with her. Her beautiful life will
> ever remain a loving memory. Because she has
> lived, the world is brighter and better.

Following the services, Mrs. Brigham's remains
were conveyed to the Lowell cemetery in a hearse
driven by undertaker Charles C. Hutchinson and
drawn by four plumed horses. Messrs. John C. Blood,
J. V. Keyes, Daniel A. Eaton, and Charles Frothing-
ham acted as pallbearers. As the casket was lowered
into its place in the family plot, Reverend Kennegott
led the assembled mourners in a final hymn of
farewell:

Now she's crossed the land of shadows,
    Crossed the river's brimming tide;
Wears a starry crown immortal.
    Stands among the glorified.

The funeral over, the dispersing crowd paused to pay their final condolences to the members of Mrs. Brigham's immediate family: her tearful husband, Oramel, and her foster sister, Jane, who had made the trip from Cataumet to see Elizabeth buried and to offer the grieving widower whatever comfort she could.

10

For poison, it must be pointed out, is the most intimate form of murder; one can be stabbed or shot by an enemy, but the bane-draught is usually poured by an intimate, posing as a friend.

—HENRY MORTON ROBINSON,
Science Catches the Criminal

THE ARRIVAL OF JANUARY 1, 1900, WAS GREETED WITH none of the hoopla or apocalyptic hysteria that surrounded New Year's Day a century later. On the contrary, little significance was attached to the event. The *New York Times* ran more than a dozen front-page stories that Monday morning, on everything from the fighting in the Philippines to the case of a New Jersey man who was "driven nearly insane" when a cricket crawled into his left ear. Nowhere, however, does the paper take any special note of the date. For most Americans, 1900 represented the last year of the nineteenth century, not the first year of the twentieth—an end, not a beginning.

Jane Toppan's case was somewhat different. For her, January 1900 did, in fact, bring the promise of something new, something she'd been waiting for—the opportunity to lead a different kind of life.

That opportunity presented itself when Mrs. Myra Connors—described in contemporary newspaper accounts as one of Jane's "intimate friends"—fell ill during the last week of January. A forty-year-old widow, Mrs. Connors had been employed for many years as the matron of the refectory of St. John's Theological School in Cambridge. Her only surviving photograph shows a prim, severe-looking woman in pince-nez eyeglasses, who might have served as the model for the mythic Mrs. Grundy. Exactly how the two women first met is unknown, though they had been friends for several years before Jane Toppan decided to kill her.

The day after Mrs. Connors was stricken, she called for her physician, Dr. Herbert H. McIntire, who diagnosed her condition as "localized peritonitis" and prescribed powdered opium and arrowroot poultices. A week later, on February 7, Jane Toppan showed up to help care for her old friend. Almost immediately, the patient—who had been "progressing favorably," according to Dr. McIntire's subsequent testimony—took a violent turn for the worse. On the morning of February 11, she died in great agony, suffering such terrible convulsions that her left arm was bent nearly double.

Though Dr. McIntire was baffled by the symptoms—which, as he would later state, resembled the effects of strychnine poisoning—he didn't seriously suspect foul play. He knew nothing, of course, about the long and growing list of patients who had succumbed to Nurse Toppan's ministrations. Nor was he aware that—along with her usual sadistic motivations—Jane Toppan had other reasons for wishing her old friend out of the way.

Though Jane had borne a particularly bitter grudge against Elizabeth Brigham, her foster sister was not the only person she envied. Another was Myra Connors. For some time, she had secretly coveted Myra's job at the Theological School.

Exactly why is unclear. By early 1900, her homicidal impulses were growing stronger by the day. It is possible that she was trying to stop herself from spiraling totally out of control by quitting the nursing profession. Like other people in the grip of irresistible drives, compulsive killers sometimes try to restrain their behavior by removing themselves from temptation.

On the other hand—given the nature of Myra Connors's position as dining hall matron—the opposite may also be the case. For a confirmed poisoner like Jane, the thought of overseeing the daily food intake of dozens of unwary theology students might have seemed like a dream come true: a classic case of setting the wolf to watch the sheep.

And then, of course, there were the perks of the position, which included a spacious apartment in Burnham Hall, complete with a private maid to do her housework and wait on her at mealtimes.

No sooner had Myra Connors been laid in the ground than Jane approached the dean of the Theological School, Dr. Hodges. She explained that, before getting sick, Myra had been making plans for a sabbatical and—intending to recommend Jane as a temporary replacement—had instructed her in all the duties of the matron.

With no one else to assume the position, Hodges offered it to Jane. With her usual cunning, she professed some reluctance, and asked for a little time to consider the offer. A few days later, she informed the dean that, despite her reservations about abandoning nursing, she had decided to accept the job. She felt she owed it to poor Myra. Privately, Jane exulted in the success of her scheme. Everything had worked out just as she'd planned. And killing her old friend with strychnine—a method Jane occasionally used when she sought some variety from her usual MO—had provided her with almost as much pleasure as the murder of her foster sister, six months earlier.

Her sense of contentment didn't last long, however. Questions about Jane's competence began to arise almost immediately. She was accused of poorly superintending the dining hall and suspected of various financial irregularities. When the school broke for summer vacation, she took a job at the mess hall at the newly established biology institute at Woods Hole. The following fall, she resumed her job as matron of the Theological School. By early November, however, so many complaints had been lodged against her that Dean Hodges could no longer ignore them. When several employees under her direct supervision accused her of failing to pay their salaries, she was finally asked to resign.

Her dismissal was a devastating blow. Like other psychopathic personalities, Jane Toppan was certainly capable of feeling pity—but only for herself. After being discharged by Dean Hodges, she returned to her apartment in Burnham Hall to pack her belongings.

Then, this middle-aged spinster who had murdered dozens of people without feeling anything besides sexual arousal, threw herself on her bed and blubbered like a baby.

PART THREE

BUZZARDS BAY

11

~m~

It has commonly been claimed that nowhere in the world would you find a State with a population more generally enlightened, orderly, and humane than in Massachusetts. Yet [it] is in Massachusetts that this monstrous deed has been committed. It is in Massachusetts, whose common schools have been the first and foremost in our country, that this act of barbarism and bloody superstition has appeared. Massachusetts has had deeds of black wickedness, deeds of atrocious cruelty and crime; but never, I think, in all its history . . . has it had a deed quite parallel to this in cold, deliberative, unnatural horror.

—FROM A SERMON PREACHED BY THE
REVEREND WILLIAM J. POTTER ON THE
POCASSET TRAGEDY, SUNDAY, MAY 11, 1879

THE SUMMER COTTAGE IN WHICH JANE TOPPAN KILLED her foster sister, Elizabeth, was located in Cataumet, a picturesque little village at the extreme western end of the Cape Cod peninsula on the shores of Buzzards Bay.

The cottage belonged to a man named Alden Davis, Cataumet's most prominent—and notoriously eccentric—citizen. The son of a stonecutter, Davis grew up in Sandown, New Hampshire, where he learned his father's craft. In early manhood, he moved to New Orleans and saw action during the Civil War

as a lieutenant in the Confederate Army. Not long
after Lee's surrender, he returned to New England,
settling in a suburb of Boston, where he continued to
ply his trade.

Though Davis did well enough at his stonecutting
business to support his family in comfort, he had larger
ambitions. Throughout much of the nineteenth century, Bostonians looking to summer on the Cape were
forced to endure the rigors of stagecoach travel—a
mode of transportation so slow and uncomfortable as
to discourage all but the most determined vacationer.
All that changed on July 18, 1872, when the first train
linking the city to Woods Hole made its maiden,
round-trip journey. Foreseeing the tourist boom that
the new railroad line was sure to create, Davis moved
his wife and children to the seaside hamlet of Cataumet.

Before long, he had become a leading figure in the
community. He bought up real estate and constructed
a hotel called the Jachin House—a rambling wood-
frame building with a wide wraparound porch where
(according to the recollections of one old-timer)
"guests could sit rocking on summer evenings, enjoying the cool breezes that swept in from nearby Buzzards Bay." To draw tourists to the area, he catered
large, festive clambakes on his property, and chartered
trains from the city to bring in the crowds.

Besides his activities as a land developer and hotelier,
Davis applied himself to a variety of enterprises. He
worked tirelessly to make sure that the little village got
its own post office and railroad station and took on the
duties of both postmaster and station agent. He also
ran a general store across from Depot Square and continued to practice his skills as a marble worker. Even
today, his handiwork can be seen in the little cemetery

in Cataumet, where—as one local historian notes—
"many of the stones were engraved by Mr. Davis."

Thanks in large part to his efforts, Cataumet became a popular watering place for vacationing city
dwellers by the late 1800s. In spite of all he accomplished, however, Davis was by no means a universally
admired figure. On the contrary. According to many
of their neighbors, the Davis family never really managed to fit in. They "held aloof from other residents
and kept by themselves," as one contemporary reported. Davis himself quickly gained a reputation as a
decidedly "peculiar" personality, prone to violent outbursts and erratic, even unbalanced, behavior.

That reputation was solidified as a result of his role
in the infamous Freeman affair—a case that stunned
late-nineteenth-century New England, which hadn't
witnessed a more appalling episode of religious fanaticism since the Salem witch persecutions of the 1690s.

In a town composed mostly of Methodists, the Davis
family held unorthodox beliefs. Davis's wife, Mary—or
"Mattie," as she was called—was a Christian Scientist.
Davis himself belonged to the Second Advent Church,
a millenialist sect that had been gathering adherents in
New England.

One of Davis's fellow Adventists was a man named
Charles Freeman, a local farmer who lived in the
neighboring town of Pocasset with his wife, Hattie,
and two young daughters—six-year-old Bessie Mil-
dred and four-year-old Edith, her father's favorite. A
man of "upright life and conduct" (as the newspapers
would later report), Freeman was much admired—
even revered—by his fellow believers for the fervency
of his convictions. He had frequently spoken of the
need to prove his faith through sacrifice, and declared

that "he had given his whole family to God." None of his associates doubted his sincerity—though they could hardly have guessed at the dreadful fixation that was growing stronger in him by the day.

During the latter half of April 1879, Freeman became obsessed by the notion that God required an ultimate test of his faith. He was perfectly willing to offer himself in sacrifice. After two weeks of prayer, however, he decided that God was demanding something even more extreme: the life of one of his children. He shared this revelation with his wife, who did all she could to dissuade him—but to no avail. On the evening of April 30, 1879, Freeman tucked his daughters into the bed they shared and kissed them good night. "They never seemed so dear to me as then," he would later testify. He then retired to his own bed and quickly fell asleep.

At about half-past two in the morning, he awoke with a start, shook his wife's arm, and told her that the time had come. "The Lord has appeared to me," he said. "I know who the victim must be—my pet, my idol, my baby Edith."

Weeping, her teeth chattering in horror, Hattie made one final plea. Her husband, however, would not be deterred. "The Lord has said it is necesary," he declared.

In the end, it was she who relented. "If it is the Lord's will, I am ready for it," she said at last. Her words seemed to lift a terrible burden from his heart.

Singing praises to the Lord, he rose from bed, rapidly dressed, then repaired to the shed, where he got a large sheath knife. He then returned to the house, lighted an oil lamp, and stepped inside his daughters' bedroom. Bessie, the older child, awoke at his entrance. Freeman instructed her to go into the other room and get into bed with her mother.

He then placed the lamp on a chair, pulled down the bedclothes covering Edith, and lowered himself to his knees. Silently, he prayed that Edith not awake, and that God might stay his hand at the last moment, as Abraham's had been stayed. Getting to his feet, he stood over the body of his four-year-old child and raised the knife high above his head.

At that instant, Edith opened her eyes and gazed up at her father. The look on her face did not stay Freeman's hand. Nor did divine intervention. He drove the blade deep into her side.

"Oh, Papa," she gasped. A moment later, she was dead.

Climbing into bed beside his child's corpse, Freeman took her into his arms as though lulling her to sleep and remained there until daybreak. For the first two hours—as he would later state—he suffered "a good deal of agony of mind." Eventually, however, a great feeling of peace, even exultation, came over him. He had been tested and found worthy. He had done God's will.

The following day, several dozen of Freeman's neighbors were summoned to his home, where—according to his message—they would be vouchsafed a great revelation. Among the invitees were the town constable, the selectmen, and the Methodist minister. In the end, about twenty-five people, nearly all of them Adventists, showed up at his home at the appointed time.

The group crowded into the parlor, where Freeman proceeded to deliver a rambling, hour-long harangue, interrupted by stretches of silence and bouts of weeping. He spoke of the imminent coming of Christ, as foretold in the twenty-fourth chapter of Matthew, and of the overwhelming conviction that had taken possession of his soul during the preceding fortnight. Then—with his sobbing wife beside him—he led them into the adjoining bedroom, where a little form lay draped beneath a stained sheet. Reaching down, he drew back the covering and revealed to his neighbors the glorious sacrifice that he had made at God's behest.

As his fellow church-members looked on in confusion, Freeman assured them that they need have no concern for the child. In three days, Edith would rise again. Her resurrection would be a sign that the Son of Man had come!

Shaken by the sight of the butchered child—but inspired by the rapturous intensity of Freeman's belief—the crowd soon dispersed to their homes.

In a town the size of Pocasset, it didn't take long for word of the atrocity to reach the ears of the constable. By the following day, Freeman was under arrest. Eventually, he would be declared insane and consigned to the asylum at Danvers.

Contrary to his expectations, his slaughtered child did not return to life. Three days after her murder—on the morning of her promised resurrection—the dead girl disappeared forever into the sod of Pocasset cemetery. A plaque on her coffin read: *Little Edie— lived only 57 months. She shall surely rise again—John vi. 39.*

The horrific crime provoked a burst of communal indignation. At least one of Freeman's neighbors, however, remained staunchly loyal to him. That man was Alden Davis, who chose the occasion of Edith's funeral to declare his allegiance to his fellow Adventist. Before the child's tiny casket had been lowered into the ground, Davis stood beside the newly dug grave and proclaimed her father's goodness to the assembled crowd of mourners. "There never lived a purer man than Charles Freeman," he declared.

His defense of the filicide so outraged the community that, for a while, Davis himself became a figure nearly as detested as Freeman. Stories about his own dangerous fanaticism began to circulate. According to gossip, Davis had declared that—since Edith had been buried before her resurrection could take place— it might be necessary to sacrifice another child, perhaps one of his own. Neighbors reported that his older daughter, Mary—or "Minnie," as everyone called her—had been seen wandering in tears through Cataumet, "afraid that her father was going to kill her."

Whether these rumors had any basis in fact is impossible to say, though it is certain that many of Davis's townsmen never doubted their truth. And his sympathetic support for the maniacal Freeman was never entirely forgotten. Indeed, even twenty years later, when the unspeakable happened, there were those in Cataumet who believed that it was the long-delayed fulfillment of a terrible curse that Alden Davis had brought down upon himself, his wife, and his children.

12

Never before that night had I *felt* the extent of my own powers—of my sagacity. I could scarcely contain my feelings of triumph. To think that there I was, opening the door, little by little, and he not even to dream of my secret deeds or thoughts.

—EDGAR ALLAN POE, "THE TELL-TALE HEART"

IN SPITE OF HIS INVOLVEMENT WITH THE "POCASSET Horror" (as the Freeman affair came to be known), Alden Davis retained the respect, if not the affection, of his townsmen. As the decades passed, he became a venerable figure in the community—a white-haired, white-bearded gentleman whose neighbors conferred upon him the ultimate New England honorific. "Captain Davis," they called him—though the mariner's life had never been among his many occupations.

Thanks partly to Davis's enterprising spirit, Cataumet and its environs had become a popular seaside resort. President Grover Cleveland himself had a home on Buzzards Bay, and Joseph Jefferson—the most famous American actor of his day, who delighted audiences for forty years with his comic portrayal of Rip Van Winkle—summered nearby.

By 1901, however, Davis himself had retired from the tourist business. In March of that year, he turned sixty-five. He and his wife had grown too old for innkeeping. Their daughters, Genevieve and Minnie, were grown women with families of their own. The Jachin House—with its wide veranda open to the ocean breezes—no longer took in guests. Now, it served solely as the family home. There were several small cottages on the property, however, that the Davises continued to rent out to summer visitors.

Their favorite was Nurse Jane Toppan.

She had first vacationed there in 1896. At the time, she was living with the family of Mr. L. W. Ferdinand of Cambridge, who had rented out the cottage closest to the main house. With her plausibly warm and affable personality, Jane had quickly ingratiated herself not only with the Davises but with their neighbors as well. People enjoyed her company—her easy laughter, her funny stories, her lively conversation. They also benefited from her medical expertise. Jane was always happy to offer advice when one of her new summer friends was afflicted with some minor malady—a sick headache, case of nasal catarrh, or bout of dyspepsia. Before long, she was a popular figure around town— everyone's favorite spinster aunt. Neighbors would leave their children in her care when they went off for the day. Years later, people still recalled the sight of "Jolly Jane" leading a troop of little ones, Pied Piper-like, down to the beach on Squiteague Bay for a mid-day picnic.

So fond were the Davises of their tenant—and so grateful for her help whenever one of the family took ill—that they let her have the cottage at a discount. Exactly how much they charged is unclear, though it was considerably less than the usual seasonal rent of $250. Even at that rate, however, Jane was unable to come up with the full amount when the summer ended. When she asked for an extension, the Davises were only too happy to oblige. Already, they seemed to have regarded her as a member of the family. It is a mark of their affection that they welcomed her back year after year without ever pressing her for the money. By the end of her fifth summer vacation at the cottage, Jane owed her landlords $500.

That was when Mattie Davis finally reached the limits of her generosity.

The younger of the two Davis daughters—thirty-one-year-old Genevieve—had married an upstanding young man from Lowell named Harry Gordon. The Davises were exceptionally fond of Harry. Their single complaint about him was that—having been promoted to an important position in the home office of the Equitable Life Insurance Company of Chicago—he had taken their daughter so far away from her family. Even so, Alden and Mattie saw Genevieve regularly. Every summer, she and her little girl would flee the confines of the city and return home to spend a few months by the bracing shores of Buzzards Bay.

In June of 1901, just prior to her departure from Chicago, Genevieve had written to her mother, explaining that—before proceeding to Cataumet—she intended to stop off and visit her in-laws in a suburb of Boston.

Even before receiving Genevieve's letter, Mattie had made up her mind to travel to Cambridge and collect Jane Toppan's long-overdue debt. She was dreading the trip, however. A diabetic, she had been feeling particularly weak for the past few days, partly as a result of the unusual heat. It would be a strain to make the journey there and back all alone.

When she learned that her daughter would be stopping in Boston, Mattie saw it as a golden opportunity. She would still have to travel to Cambridge by herself and confront Jane Toppan about the money. But once that unpleasantness was finished, she would be able to meet up with Genevieve and return to Cataumet in her daughter's company.

And so, on the evening of Monday, June 26, she announced her plan to Alden. Concerned about her health, he tried to dissuade her. Mattie was adamant, though. With Genevieve coming to Boston, there wouldn't be a better time to make the trip.

It was, she insisted, now or never.

The summer of 1901 was one of the most brutal on record, and in the Northeast—as elsewhere throughout the country—the heat took a heavy toll. In late June and early July, the papers in New York and Boston were full of front-page horror stories about the "hot wave" (as it was called back then). Each day brought grim new headlines: "Prostration from the Heat Ends in Death"—"One Woman Driven Insane"—"Hottest Day in Thirty Years"—"No Relief from the Fiery Sun." By the end of one six-day span, the number of heat-related fatalities in New York City and Boston had topped 400.

When Mattie awoke early on the morning of Tuesday, June 25, the temperature was already nearing seventy degrees. The day was going to be another scorcher. Maybe Alden had been right when he'd tried talking her out of the trip. Well, if she didn't hurry up, he'd get his wish after all. At sixty years old and in poor health, Mattie tended to move slowly. An hour after she awoke, she was still getting ready for the trip. The 6:45 to Cambridge was due to arrive any minute, and Mattie was in danger of missing the train.

When Alden saw the time, he volunteered to run over to the depot and have the conductor hold the train. Fortunately, he didn't have far to run, the Jachin House being located only 300 feet from the station. He got there just as the train was pulling in. It was a small train, consisting of a locomotive and two cars.

As Alden conversed with the conductor—Charles F. Hammond of Woods Hole—Mattie emerged from the house, made her way down the long flight of front steps, and bustled toward the station. All at once, at the foot of a hill leading up to the depot, she tripped over her feet and went sprawling. Seeing her fall, Alden hurried to her aid. Before he reached her, she had picked herself up with a moan and was limping toward the platform.

Dusty, dishevelled, and badly shaken, Mattie was assisted to the nearest boarding point, at the rear of the second car, by her husband and Conductor Hammond. Hammond then helped her through the baggage compartment and into a seat. After making sure that she was comfortably settled, he went off to collect tickets.

Several men were standing around the car, smoking. One of these was George Hall, representative of a Boston meat and provision house. Through a window, Hall had observed Mrs. Davis's accident and was surprised that her husband had allowed her to board the train. She had seemed in such a bad way when Conductor Hammond escorted her to her seat that Hall feared she might collapse before she reached it.

Turning to one of the men beside him, Hall remarked that he wouldn't be surprised if the fall turned out to be Mrs. Davis's "death blow."

As the train got under way, however, Mattie seemed to improve. A neighbor named Willard Hill, who had also witnessed the mishap through the window, took the seat across from her and asked how she was feeling. Mattie assured him that she was fine.

"Nothing hurt but my dignity," she said.

As the train moved along, they continued to chat. When Mattie explained the purpose of her journey, Mr. Hill seemed amazed to hear that "Jennie" Toppan—a woman he knew well and had always thought highly of—had been so negligent about paying her rent. Clearly she was taking advantage of her landlords' good nature. It was time to get tough with her, Hill advised. If he were in Mrs. Davis's shoes, he wouldn't leave Cambridge until Nurse Toppan had made good on her debts.

Since the death of her former landlords, Israel and Lovey Dunham—whom she had murdered in 1895 and 1897, respectively—Jane had been boarding at another house in Cambridge just down the street: Number 31 Wendell Street, owned by an ex-city councilman named Melvin Beedle and his wife, Eliza. Apparently on a whim, Jane had recently poisoned the Beedles, too—though only enough to give them a violent bout of gastrointestinal illness that their physician attributed to ptomaine.

She had also drugged their housekeeper, a young woman named Mary Sullivan whom Jane wanted out of the way. After persuading Mrs. Beedle that the servant was tippling in secret, Jane had slipped the young woman just enough morphia to send her into a stupor. She had then led Mrs. Beedle up to the housekeeper's room, where Mary lay sprawled on her bed, apparently drunk. Mrs. Beedle had not even waited for the young woman to regain her senses before firing her. She had immediately called for a carriage, loaded the half-dazed servant into the vehicle, and sent her on her way.

Since then, Jane Toppan had effectively taken charge of the household.

As soon as she disembarked from the train, Mattie Davis made her way to 31 Wendell Street, where she found Jane Toppan and the Beedles just sitting down to dinner. Evidently, Jane immediately guessed the reason for her friend's unexpected visit. When the Beedles invited Mattie to join them at the table, Jane quickly repaired to the kitchen, prepared a glass of her favorite concoction—Hunyadi mineral water doctored with morphia——and carried it back out to the dining room.

"You must be very thirsty after your trip," she said.

Her visitor took the proffered drink and sipped. By the end of the meal—much to Jane's satisfaction—Mattie Davis had entirely drained the poisoned glass.

When dinner was over, Jane suggested that they walk to the bank, so that she could withdraw the money she owed. Mattie—who wanted to deposit some cash she had brought along—readily agreed. When she rose from the table, however, she felt strangely woozy.

"Perhaps it was that fall," suggested Jane. Over dinner, Mattie had regaled her hosts with the story of her embarrassing accident. "Should we wait for a while?"

"No, no, I'm fine," Mattie insisted. Now that she was so close to achieving her goal, she wanted no further delays.

No sooner were they outside, however, than Mattie let out a fluttering groan and collapsed.

No one else was around on the sweltering street. Bending to the fallen woman, Jane managed to get Mattie onto her feet. Fortunately, they were still close to home. Even so, Jane found herself grunting with effort as she helped the limp old woman back to the house.

Inside, Jane and Melvin Beedle carried Mattie upstairs to the second floor. She was placed in a vacant bedroom. Assuming that she had fainted from the heat, Beedle hurried downstairs to fetch a glass of cold water. In the meantime, Jane stepped into her own room, got her hypodermic needle, and quickly returned to Mattie's side. Low, whimpering noises were coming from the old woman's throat.

"So I gave her another small dose of morphia," Jane would later state, recalling the moment. "And that quieted her."

That night, Jane sent a message to Alden Davis, informing him that his wife had taken sick. She also telegraphed Genevieve Gordon in Somerville, who had been growing increasingly anxious as the day progressed with no sign of her mother.

The following afternoon—Wednesday, June 26—Genevieve traveled to the Beedles' home in Cambridge. She found her mother lying unconscious in a darkened room hung with iced sheets, Nurse Toppan seated by the sickbed. Though Jane insisted that she could care for Mattie by herself, Genevieve persuaded the Beedles to send for a doctor at once.

It took a while to find one who hadn't fled the suffocating heat of the city. Only after putting in telephone calls to four different physicians did the Beedles succeed in reaching somebody.

That person turned out to be Dr. John T. G. Nichols—the very same Dr. Nichols who, fifteen years earlier, had been called to the bedside of Prince Arthur Freeman, one of the many victims of the "American Borgia," Sarah Jane Robinson. In that earlier case, Nichols had misdiagnosed his patient's condition as "disease of the stomach." His failure to recognize the symptoms of arsenic poisoning in Freeman had allowed Mrs. Robinson to continue her murderous career until several more of her family members were dead.

In the succeeding decade-and-a-half, Dr. Nichols had lived down the notoriety he had reaped from the Robinson affair and had established himself as a trusted and reliable general practitioner. Now—in the kind of bizarre twist of fate no novelist would dare to invent—he had been summoned to treat the victim of another female serial killer. It was as though life were offering him a chance to redeem himself for his earlier failure.

Unfortunately—both for him and for Mattie Davis—Dr. Nichols was about to be fooled again.

Arriving at the Beedles' home, Nichols found the patient attended by a buxom, briskly professional woman who introduced herself as Nurse Jane Toppan, an old friend of the Davis family. She informed Dr. Nichols that Mattie Davis was a diabetic, who—in defiance of Jane's warnings—had treated herself to a slice of Mrs. Beedles' white-frosted velvet cake at dinnertime and had collapsed shortly afterward, probably as the result of her overindulgence.

Examining the patient, Nichols found that her symptoms were consistent with a diabetic coma—a diagnosis seemingly confirmed when the sugar content of her urine was found to be abnormally high. Nurse Toppan had thoughtfully collected the urine sample before the arrival of Dr. Nichols—who, of course, had no reason to suspect that it might have been tampered with.

Jane took her time murdering Mattie Davis. For the next seven days—under the very noses of Dr. Nichols, Genevieve Gordon, and the Beedles—she played with her helpless victim, administering atropine and morphine in varying doses to produce a range of interesting effects. At times, she would inject Mattie with slightly smaller amounts of narcotic, allowing the old woman to emerge into partial consciousness and giving her loved ones a sudden glimmer of hope. On one occasion, she even raised Mattie to a state of full lucidity before plunging her back into a deep coma.

Why Jane carried out the murder in this way—prolonging it for a full week before putting Mattie Davis to sleep for good—is an interesting question. Partly, it was a matter of pure cunning, a calculated effort to make the old woman's death seem like the result of natural causes. But along with this motive, there was almost certainly an element of sadism involved—the delicious pleasure of inducing death at a slow, exquisitely measured pace in a helpless human being. And then, of course, there was the exhilarating sense of power. Power not only over the unresisting victim but over the rest of the Davis family, who could do nothing but wait and hope and pray while Jane secretly guided their loved one to her grave. And power, too, over Dr. Nichols, who—for all the professional status he enjoyed—was nothing more than Jane's unwitting pawn.

As the attending nurse, Jane was in sole charge of the

patient during the night, sitting up at Mattie's bedside while the rest of the household slept. The arrangement was ideal for her purposes, allowing her to do whatever she wished to the comatose woman. Sometime in the early-morning hours of Tuesday, July 2—one week after she first poisoned Mattie with the drugged glass of mineral water—Jane injected her with a final, fatal dose of morphine, then watched intently while the old woman stopped breathing. Whether—as she'd done so many times before—she climbed into the deathbed and trembled with pleasure as she felt the life drain from her victim is something Jane never revealed.

From her later confessions, however, we *do* know what was going through her mind at the time of Mattie Davis's burial. That somber event took place on the morning of Friday, July 5, 1901—one day after Mattie's mortal remains arrived home by train from Cambridge. Jane and Melvin Beedle had accompanied the coffin on its final journey, Genevieve Gordon having hurried back to Cataumet immediately after her mother's death to be with her grief-stricken father.

So many of Mattie's friends and neighbors showed up for the services that the parlor of the Jachin House couldn't accommodate them all. Afterward, at the grave site, Jane stood beside the sorrowing members of the Davis family—Alden, Genevieve, and the older daughter, Mrs. Minnie Gibbs, who lived in the neighboring village of Pocasset with her husband, Paul, a coastal schooner skipper away on a voyage.

Though the "hot wave" had broken, the day was uncomfortably warm. Gathered in the little cemetery, the mourners—the men in their black Sunday suits, the women in their long dresses and whalebone corsets—sweltered in the sun. As soon as the funeral was over, they began to disperse. Several relatives from Cambridge began to make their way to the railroad station. Jane watched as they headed for the depot and, smiling inwardly, thought: *You had better wait a little while and I will have another funeral for you. If you wait, it will save you going back and forth.*

Already, she was imagining the horrors to come; for, in her spiraling madness, Jane Toppan had decided to wipe out the remaining members of the Davis family, one by one.

13

~m~

Bloch, in his endeavor to explain the pyromaniac tendency, has recourse to the assumption of a sadistic impulse and of a sexually toned destructive tendency. He points out that red is a color which plays a tremendous role in our *vita sexualis*. The thought or sight of the dark red flames exerts a sexually exhilarating influence, similar to the sight of the reddened bodily parts during flagellation, or of the flowing blood in sadistic indulgences.

—WILHELM STEKEL, *Peculiarities of Behavior*

GIVEN THEIR LUST FOR DESTRUCTION—THE JOY THEY take in doing harm—it's no surprise that, among their other twisted pleasures, many serial killers love to set fires, a practice they often begin at an early age. Indeed, along with animal torture and abnormally prolonged bed-wetting, childhood pyromania is one of the classic warning signs of budding sociopathology. Some of the most notorious serial killers of modern times, like David "Son of Sam" Berkowitz, were juvenile arsonists. And their incendiary habits didn't always end at adolescence.

Ottis Toole, for example—Henry Lee Lucas's loathsome accomplice (whose alleged atrocities included the abduction and beheading of little Adam Walsh)—never lost his taste for torching buildings. And Carl Panzram—arguably the most unrepentant killer in the annals of American crime—took positive pride in the havoc he could wreak with a matchstick. Besides serial murder and forced sodomy, arson was Panzram's favorite pastime, and in his remarkable jailhouse memoirs, he provides a running tally not only of the people he slaughtered and raped, but of the property he incinerated during his lifelong vendetta against the world.

But it's more than sheer malice that underlies the incendiary crimes of serial killers. According to specialists in the psychology of perversion, there is always an erotic motive at the root of pyromania. "There is but one instinct which generates the impulse to incendiarism," writes Wilhelm Stekel in his classic work on aberrant behavior. "That is the sexual instinct, and arson clearly shows its connecting points with sex." True, there are often "secondary motives" behind a pyromaniac's acts—anger, frustration, revenge. But above all (as Stekel writes), "the incendiary is sexually excited by the flames; he likes to watch them burn." In short, serial murderers who enjoy starting fires do so for the same reason that they love to torture and kill.

It turns them on.

Exactly when Jane Toppan began setting fires for pleasure is unclear. Certainly—based on what we know about psychopathology in general and pyromania in particular—it seems unlikely that she didn't develop this perversion until middle age. It is entirely possible that, like other serial killers, she began committing arson as a child, though the documented facts about her early life in Lowell are too meager for us to say.

What we do know for certain is that, during that terrible summer of 1901, in the throes of her increasingly unbridled madness, Jane Toppan seemed bent not only on exterminating the entire Davis family but on obliterating their very home—reducing it to a smoldering heap of ashes.

Throughout his adult life, Alden Davis had always been known as an erratic, if not unstable, personality. Indeed, in the aftermath of the Freeman affair, he had suffered a nervous collapse and been confined to an asylum for a brief period. Now—fearful for the old man's well-being after the devastating loss of his wife—Genevieve Gordon decided to defer her trip home to Chicago and remain with her father for as long as necessary. She was joined by her older sister, Minnie Gibbs, whose husband was still away at sea. Within days of the funeral, Minnie had closed up her home in Pocasset and, with her two young boys, Charles and Jesse, moved back into the Jachin House.

When Jane informed the sisters of her intention to return to Cambridge, they urged her to stay for the summer as their houseguest. At first, she put on a show of reluctance but eventually agreed. Both Genevieve and Minnie were vastly relieved. Grief-wracked as they were, they felt incapable of managing on their own. Jane—with her great competence and energy—could help run the household and keep an eye on their father's fragile health. And her bubbly personality—what contemporary accounts consistently referred to as her "irrepressible, ever-present Irish love of fun"—would buoy up their spirits.

Having "Jolly Jane" around the house was sure to be a tonic—like drinking a tall, bracing glass of Hunyadi mineral water.

• • •

According to her later accounts, it was shortly after she settled into Jachin House that Jane set her first fire on the Davis premises.

It happened on a muggy night, less than a week after the funeral. Waiting until the family had retired to their beds, Jane stole into the parlor and ignited some old papers in a closet. As the flames sprang up and smoke began to billow, she retreated to her room and—as she described it—"danced with delight."

Fortunately for the intended victims, Alden Davis—who had been suffering from insomnia since his wife's death—smelled the smoke and rushed into the parlor in his nightclothes. Frantically, he shouted for help. To avoid suspicion, Jane came hurrying from her bedroom as though roused from a sound sleep and helped douse the fire. Beyond some charring of the parlor walls, there was little damage to the house—much to Jane's disappointment.

"I was hoping all along that the house would burn down," she later recounted. "But it didn't."

She tried again just a few days later. This time, after setting fire to a pantry, she strolled to the house of a neighbor—a Boston businessman summering in Cataumet—and, after knocking on his screen door, engaged him in a casual conversation. As the two stood on the porch, chatting about nothing in particular, the man noticed smoke pouring from a window of the Davis home. With Jane at his side, he immediately went for help. Once again, the fire was put out before substantial damage could be done.

A week or so later, Jane set yet another fire in the house. Again, it was caught and extinguished in time. Afterward, Jane took Alden Davis aside and told him that she'd spotted a stranger skulking about the property just before the outbreak of the blaze. Rumors quickly spread through the village that a "firebug" was on the loose—though why he'd targeted the Davis home no one could say.

To their neighbors, it must have seemed as if a dark cloud of misfortune had settled over the Davis home. First Mattie's death, now a string of mysterious fires. The truth, of course, was far worse than anyone could have guessed. The Davises weren't experiencing a run of terrible luck. They were being deliberately tormented by a monster they had invited into their home—a madwoman bent on their utter destruction.

14

Poor thing, she was grieving herself to death. . . . So life wasn't worth living for her anyway.

—FROM THE CONFESSION OF JANE TOPPAN

IT IS IMPOSSIBLE, OF COURSE, TO MEASURE THE DEPTH of another person's grief, and there is no doubt that Mattie Davis's death was a terrible blow to all her survivors. Of her two married daughters, however, Genevieve Gordon appears to have been hit particularly hard by her mother's passing.

Perhaps, as is sometimes the case, she had closer (or at least more complicated) emotional ties to her mother than her older sister did—though we know so little about the inner workings of the Davis family that it is impossible to say how any of them related to the others. Certainly, the circumstances surrounding Mattie's death would have been particularly unsettling for Genevieve. While her sister, Minnie Gibbs, lived within easy walking distance of their parents' home, Genevieve hadn't seen her mother for a year, and had traveled from Chicago specifically for a long-awaited visit. Then—on the very day of their expected reunion—she had received the shocking news of Mattie's collapse. She had spent the following week keeping a tense and increasingly desperate vigil at what turned out to be her mother's deathbed.

Adding to her despondency was her longing for her

husband, Harry, who had remained at home to attend to business. True, Minnie Gibb's husband was also away. But as the wife of a sea captain, Minnie was used to frequent and prolonged separations. Genevieve, who would be away from Chicago until summer's end, felt especially bereft of her husband's comforting presence. Though she did her best to put on a show of strength—particularly for the sake of her father (whose fragile emotional and mental state was a continuous source of worry to both his daughters)—it was clear even to the neighbors that Genevieve was suffering badly.

It was certainly clear to Jane Toppan, who was living in the same household with the sorrowing young woman. And that was why—by her own admission—Jane resolved to kill Genevieve Gordon next.

It was not the first time that Jane had concluded that someone was better off dead. During her nursing school days, she had made that decision about at least a dozen people, who—in her estimation—were too old, sickly, or just plain bothersome to live. Telling herself that she was doing them a favor by ending their miserable existences was, of course, simply a way of rationalizing her own sadism.

On the sick wards of Cambridge Hospital, slipping a bedridden patient a fatal combination of morphine and atropine posed little problem. Genevieve Gordon, however, was no invalid. She was a healthy thirty-one-year-old with no history of medical problems. Dispatching her without arousing suspicion posed a greater challenge.

Jane, however, was equal to the task.

Sometime in the last week of July, she took Genevieve's older sister, Minnie, aside and told her a worrisome bit of news. According to Jane, she had been strolling on the grounds earlier in the day, when she had spotted Genevieve inside the garden shed, closely inspecting a small container. Becoming aware that she was being watched, Genevieve quickly replaced the container on a shelf and hurried from the shed. Something about her demeanor had aroused Jane's suspicions. She had waited until Genevieve was back inside the house, then returned to the shed to see what had so absorbed the young woman's interest. At her first glimpse of the container, she had felt a jolt of alarm.

It was a round cardboard box of "Pfeiffer's Strictly Pure Paris Green," a popular insecticide compounded of arsenic and copper. The extreme toxicity of this substance was apparent from the green-and-black label, which—in addition to a skillfully rendered drawing of a potato bug—featured a boldly printed "Poison" warning, complete with skull and crossbones and instructions in case of accidental ingestion ("Give immediately any emetic, such as mustard and water, hydrated sesquioxide of iron in large tablespoonful doses, large doses of castor oil").

Given Genevieve's extreme despondency since her mother's death, her keen interest in this deadly substance was—so Jane told Minnie—a cause of real concern. Minnie couldn't believe that her sister was seriously contemplating suicide. Still, melancholia—what we now call depression—ran in the family, Alden Davis having been subjected to periodic bouts of the affliction, among his various other "eccentricities." The two women agreed to keep a close eye on Genevieve.

Just a few days later, on the evening of Friday, July 26, Genevieve Gordon became violently ill soon after finishing her dinner. She vomited until her throat was raw, then took to her bed. A few hours later, she was seized with another bout of nausea. When she emerged from the bathroom, she found Jane Toppan waiting for her with a glass of Hunyadi water. At Jane's urging, the pale and trembling woman managed to empty the glass, then sank into her bed with a groan. It was after midnight by then, and the other two inhabitants of the house—Minnie Gibbs and Alden Davis—were fast asleep.

Jane entered Genevieve's bedroom and locked the door behind her.

Just after daybreak the next morning, Minnie was roused by Jane Toppan, who grimly informed her that Genevieve had died during the night. The family physician, Dr. Leonard Latter, was immediately summoned to the house. On his official certificate, he ascribed the young woman's death to "heart disease," though the neighbors insisted she had perished of grief.

Jane stuck to her suicide story. Later that same day, she spoke to Captain Paul Gibbs, Minnie's seventy-year-old father-in-law, who had hurried over to the Jachin House as soon as he heard the bad news. Taking the old captain aside, Jane told him that Genevieve had died by injecting herself with Paris Green. According to Jane, she had found the empty syringe lying beside poor Genevieve's body, but—wishing to shield Minnie and Alden from the painful truth—she had thrown the needle down the hole of the outhouse.

At the grave site two days later, Jane wore a suitably mournful expression as Genevieve was interred beside her mother. Beneath her mask of solemnity, however, she exulted in the occasion.

"I went to the funeral and felt as jolly as could be," she would later confess. "And nobody suspected me in the least."

15

I made it lively for the undertakers and gravediggers that time—three graves in a little over five weeks in one lot in the cemetery.

—FROM THE CONFESSION OF JANE TOPPAN

TWICE IN THE SPAN OF A SINGLE SUMMER MONTH, Alden Davis had trudged to the Cataumet cemetery and watched in grief as two of his dear ones—first his wife of forty-odd years, then his beloved youngest child—disappeared forever into the ground. So perhaps, when Jane struck again, there was some validity to her usual rationalization. Perhaps putting the old man to death really was a mercy.

She did it less than two weeks after killing Genevieve Gordon. On the evening of Thursday, August 8, Alden Davis returned to the Jachin House after a day trip to Boston. The moment he entered his parlor, he practically staggered over to the horsehair sofa. The day had been another scorcher—nearly as brutal as the one on which his wife had made her own ill-fated journey just six weeks earlier. He was sweat-soaked, desperately thirsty, and tired to the point of prostration.

Thankfully, Nurse Toppan was there to offer relief. She fussed over him for a few minutes, then bustled off to the kitchen and returned with a tumbler of Hunyadi water.

Then she stood by and watched with satisfaction

as the parched old man gulped down every last drop.

The next morning, Alden Davis failed to show up for breakfast. Harry Gordon—Genevieve's widower, who had traveled from Chicago to attend the funeral—sent his young daughter upstairs to check on the old man. A few moments later, the little girl came hurrying back downstairs, looking frightened and confused.

There was something wrong with Grandpa. He wouldn't wake up.

Instantly, the three adults at the table—Harry, Minnie Gibbs, and Jane—leapt to their feet and dashed upstairs. One glimpse of the gray-skinned figure on the mattress was all they needed to know that they were looking at a corpse.

Dr. Latter was summoned once again. After confirming the obvious, he consulted with Jane, who theorized that Alden's heart had given out. The combined travails of the past month—the devastating losses, the alarming string of fires, the stress of his ill-advised trip to Boston—had taken their inevitable toll.

According to Jane, Alden had also been under strain from another source, having become embroiled in a nasty quarrel with the undertaker over the presumably exorbitant charges for Genevieve's coffin, which, he felt, should have been given to him at its wholesale price. Jane also raised the possibility that the grief-wracked old man might have taken his own life.

In the end, Dr. Latter came to his own conclusion, diagnosing the cause of death as "cerebral hemorrhage."

At the funeral, the neighbors seemed unsurprised to find themselves standing at the Davis family plot for the third time in less than two months. For years,

Alden had been notorious for his periodic break-downs. Even a far more stable personality would have found it hard to bear up under the crushing burden of woe that the Good Lord had seen fit to place on the old captain's shoulders.

It is often true of serial murderers that their blood lust becomes more urgent and irresistible the longer they continue to kill—as if (to quote Hamlet) "increase of appetite had grown by what it fed on." Each new atrocity only makes them hungrier for more. The intervals between their killings—the so-called "cooling-off periods"—grow shorter and shorter. Eventually, they may lose control altogether and give way to a frenzy of sadism. To cite just one notorious example, Jeffrey Dahmer's first two murders were separated by a nine-year span; his last two victims were slaughtered only four days apart.

That Jane Toppan was out of control in that terrible summer of 1901 is beyond question. Her murders were occurring with increasing frequency: a month between Mattie and Genevieve; two weeks between Genevieve and Alden. Only Minnie was left—and Jane would kill her just four days after Alden's funeral.

But it wasn't just the frenzied speed with which she wiped out the entire Davis clan that revealed her deepening mania. There was something else. For while murdering Minnie, Jane perpetrated an act of singular perversity.

Among the members of the Davis clan who assembled in Cataumet for Alden's funeral was Minnie's cousin, Beulah Jacobs, a vivacious, thirty-nine-year-old widow who lived with her parents in Somerville. Beulah had always been close to Minnie and—at the

latter's urging—agreed to stay on as a guest at the
Jachin House to help cheer her cousin up.

On the morning of Monday, August 12, Beulah
proposed that the entire household—she, Minnie,
and Jane, along with Harry Gordon and his daughter—take a jaunt to Woods Hole. It was a splendid
morning, and the carriage ride would do everyone
good.

Before leaving, Jane took Minnie aside and urged
her to drink a glass of cocoa wine "to brace her up for
the drive." Minnie—reeling from the string of tragedies
that had decimated her family—agreed. The drink,
however, only made her feel worse. She chided herself
for listening to Jane. Alcohol in any form never agreed
with her, and she hardly ever indulged.

She had no way of knowing, of course, that the
cocoa wine had been doctored with a tablet of morphia.

By the time they got home in the early afternoon,
Minnie was feeling so poorly that she sank onto the
parlor sofa with a groan, unable to drag herself upstairs. Jane immediately bustled away and returned
with a glass of Hunyadi water. Minnie didn't want to
drink it, but Jane was insistent. The bitterness of the
mineral water disguised the two tablets of poison—
one of morphia, one of atropia—that Jane had dissolved in it.

Several hours later, unable to rouse Minnie from
her stupor, Jane covered her with a blanket and retired upstairs. In the middle of the night, however,
Jane slipped back down to the parlor and injected
Minnie with more poison. By now, Minnie was in a
deep coma. Apart from some twitching on the left
side of her mouth and an occasional contraction of
her left leg, she lay profoundly inert.

Under similar circumstances in the past, Jane liked to climb into bed with her moribund victims and savor the feel of their bodies as they slipped into death. This time, however, she did something even more grotesque.

It wasn't until much later that she revealed what went on that night to another human being—specifically, to a court-appointed alienist named Henry Rust Steadman, who examined her after her arrest. What Jane told Dr. Steadman was that—instead of taking the comatose woman into her arms—she went back upstairs and gently woke up Minnie's ten-year-old son, Jesse.

Then she brought the little boy into her own bed, and held him close while his mother lay dying downstairs.

Beulah Jacobs arose before dawn the next morning—Tuesday, August 13—and hurried downstairs to check on Minnie. At her first glimpse of her cousin, she was seized with alarm. Minnie still lay fully clothed on the sofa, her face ashen, her breathing so shallow as to be barely perceptible.

Beulah immediately roused Harry Gordon, who managed to carry the shockingly limp woman upstairs to her bedroom. Then he ran to the little general store near the depot and used the telephone to summon Dr. Latter, who arrived shortly after 5:00 A.M.

Consulting with Nurse Toppan, Latter learned about the previous day's outing. Minnie, Jane opined, was "all tired out." Though the trip was meant to boost her spirits, it had clearly been too much for the debilitated woman.

Latter prescribed absolute quiet and regular sips of cocoa wine as a stimulant. Then he took his leave, promising to come back after breakfast.

In his absence, Jane remained at the patient's bedside, lavishing her usual depraved attention on the helpless woman. In her stuporous condition, Minnie couldn't be made to drink any more drugged cocoa wine; the concoction simply dribbled from her lips. So Jane prepared a poison enema by dissolving a morphia tablet in a mixture of whiskey and water and administered it rectally. As the narcotic coursed through Minnie's bowels, Jane stood at her side, gently stroking the strands of hair away from her forehead and making soft, comforting sounds. Minnie Gibbs had always been Jane's favorite member of the Davis family. Indeed—as she later confessed—she always thought of Minnie as her "best friend."

When Dr. Latter returned shortly after 9:00 A.M., he was dismayed to find that Minnie's condition was even graver than before. He spent the next several hours vainly attempting to rouse her back to consciousness. By early afternoon, the situation had grown so critical that he summoned a colleague, Dr. Frank Parker Hudnut of Boston, who was vacationing nearby in North Falmouth.

Dr. Hudnut arrived around 2 P.M. By then, Captain Paul Gibbs—Minnie's seventy-year-old father-in-law—had gotten word of the crisis and hurried to her bedside.

Hudnut, like Dr. Latter, was thoroughly perplexed by Minnie's symptoms. Her skin was dry and deathly pale, her fingers discolored. Lifting her eyelids, he saw that the pupils were dilated and totally unresponsive. When he tried her limbs, he was unable to elicit the slightest reflex. Her pulse was racing at such an accelerated speed that he couldn't take an accurate count, while her heartbeat was so faint that he had trouble detecting it.

He tried different medications, administering a fiftieth of a grain of nitroglycerin, followed by the same dose of digitalin. When neither drug produced a discernible effect, he injected her with a twentieth grain of sulfate of strychnine.

Nothing worked.

At approximately 4:10 P.M on Tuesday, August 13, thirty-nine-year-old Minnie Gibbs died without ever regaining consciousness. Dr. Latter certified the cause of death as "exhaustion."

Remarkably, even the death of Minnie Gibbs—the fourth and final member of the Davis family to perish suddenly and unexpectedly within a month-and-a-half—failed to arouse the suspicions of the community at large. On page two of its August 19, 1901 issue, for example, Barnstable's weekly newspaper, *The Patriot* ran the following story:

ENTIRE FAMILY WIPED OUT

Four Members of a Cape Family
Die in Period of Six Weeks

The death of Mrs. Irving F. Gibbs, which occurred at her home in Cataumet last Tuesday,
takes away the last member of a family of
four in six weeks. Mrs. Gibbs was the daughter of Mr. and Mrs. Alden P. Davis, well-
known throughout this section as proprietors
of the "Jachin," the first summer hotel to be
built on Buzzards Bay shore.

Mrs. Davis died July 4th after illness resulting from a fall. The younger daughter, Mrs. Harry Gordon of Chicago, who was with her mother, died very suddenly July 31st. Mr. Davis succumbed to paralysis Friday morning, 9th last. The death of Mrs. Gibbs from exhaustion removes the entire family.

Mr. Davis built his hotel in 1873, and thus began the development of Cataumet as a watering place. Through his efforts a railroad station was built, and in 1884 a post office established, he holding the positions of station agent and postmaster. He also carried on the marble business, and for a number of years was proprietor of a general store.

Perhaps the most striking thing about this article is what's missing from it—i.e., the slightest hint that foul play might have been involved in the swift and utter destruction of one of the area's most prominent families. To the residents of Cataumet, the tragedy appeared to be a singular act of God's inscrutable will, what their Puritan forebears would have called a "remarkable providence": a phenomenon to be noted and perhaps marveled at, but only as a particularly dramatic demonstration of the Lord's awesome power to smite mortal man whensoever He chose.

Not everyone, however, took such a biblical view of the matter. Old Captain Gibbs had paid a visit to his daughter-in-law on the day before her final carriage ride. Though suffering badly from the loss of her loved ones—as who wouldn't be?—she had appeared to be in good physical health. Forty-eight hours later, she had died under the watchful care of Jennie Toppan—the same kind, loving nurse who had ministered so faithfully to the three preceding members of the doomed family. The old captain wasn't a man who acted rashly, and he was reluctant at first to share his thoughts with anyone.

But alarming suspicions had begun to stir within his breast.

16

In general, treachery, though at first sufficiently cautious, yet in the end betrays itself.

—LIVY, *History, Prologue*

IN THE DAYS IMMEDIATELY FOLLOWING HIS DAUGHTER-in-law's death, Captain Paul struggled with his doubts. It seemed inconceivable that Jennie Toppan—a woman well liked and trusted by everyone who knew her (including the old seaman himself)—was really a monster capable of wiping out an entire family of her closest friends. At the same time, it was inescapably true that all four of the Davises had died with shocking suddenness while under Nurse Toppan's care.

And there were other disquieting circumstances, too. On the afternoon of Minnie's funeral, Captain Paul had talked to Harry Gordon, who claimed that, on the morning of her death, Minnie had briefly regained consciousness. Harry, who was in the room at the time, was startled to see that—when Jane approached the bed to check the patient's condition—Minnie seemed to cringe, as though in fear of the nurse.

Captain Paul himself had witnessed something odd. During his first visit to Minnie's sickbed, he had come upon Jane in the act of administering an injection to the enfeebled young woman. There was something so furtive in her manner that the old captain asked what she was doing. Jane had calmly replied that she was just following Dr. Latter's orders. Captain Paul had thought no more of the matter. But now, the picture of Jennie Toppan, hunched over Minnie's bedside, sliding a needle into poor Minnie's arm, kept haunting him.

Still, he couldn't yet bring himself to share his worst thoughts. Surely, he must be imagining things! Jolly Jane Toppan a fiend? It seemed too unbelievable. And so he decided to say nothing about his suspicions—not even to his newly bereft son, Irving.

Minnie had already been buried when her husband's schooner, the *Golden Ball*, docked at Norfolk, Virginia. There, the young skipper found a telegraph waiting from his father, conveying the tragic news. He hurried back to Cape Cod at once.

Evidence suggests that Jane—who bore a deadly malice toward female acquaintances with happy homes and families—had killed Minnie Gibbs at least partly in the deluded hope of supplanting the thirty-one-year-old woman in her husband's affections. It is certainly the case that, soon after the younger Captain Gibbs arrived back in Cataumet, Jane offered to move into his household and help care for his two now-motherless children. Irving Gibbs declined the offer—though not, evidently, out of any suspicion of Jane's motives. That he still regarded her as nothing other than a devoted friend and attentive nurse is demonstrated by a bitterly ironic fact.

Shortly after his homecoming, he presented Jane with a ten-dollar gold piece as a token of appreciation for the care she had given to his wife during her sad final hours.

Jane—disappointed in her deluded dreams of taking Minnie's place—turned her sights in another direction. In the third week of August, she packed her belongings, bid good-bye to her surviving acquaintances in Cataumet, and journeyed back to her childhood town of Lowell.

Her destination was the home of another widower whose wife had died at her hands: Oramel A. Brigham, husband of Jane's late foster sister, Elizabeth, whom she had poisoned in Cataumet exactly two summers before.

As it happened, the elder Captain Gibbs wasn't the only person whose suspicions had been aroused by the swift destruction of the Davis family.

The day before his death, Alden Davis had taken the morning train to Boston to lodge a complaint against the coffin makers who had overcharged him—so he felt—for Genevieve's casket. When he returned late in the day, a fellow passenger—a Brookline physician named Ira Cushing, who was vacationing in Cataumet for the summer—had observed Davis as the latter left the train. Knowing that Alden had recently suffered two terrible losses, Cushing was interested to see that the old man appeared to be in solid health. And so he was shocked to learn, the very next day, that Davis had suddenly taken sick and died. When Minnie Gibbs perished just a few days after her father, Cushing decided to take action.

It seemed to him that Captain Paul Gibbs—a venerable old-timer with close ties to the Davis clan—was the right man to get an investigation started. Cushing, however, barely knew Captain Paul and hesitated to approach him directly on so sensitive a matter. As it happened, the two men had a mutual acquaintance—another old salt named Ed Robinson. Cushing immediately sought out and spoke with Robinson, confiding his belief that the Davises had been poisoned, probably with arsenic. Robinson wasted no time in conveying the information to Captain Paul.

With his own suspicions now validated, Captain Gibbs was finally ready to do something about them. He wasn't quite sure how to proceed, however. Fortunately, he was acquainted with a man who had no trouble taking quick and decisive action in a crisis.

The man's name was Leonard Wood.

Apart from a handful of professional historians, few people today have heard of Leonard Wood. In his own time, however, he was a figure to be reckoned with. The son of a country doctor, he graduated from Harvard Medical School in 1884 and joined the U.S. army the following year as an assistant surgeon. His service in the Southwest—where he took part in the Indian campaign of 1886 that led to the capture of the Apache chief, Geronimo—earned him a Congressional Medal of Honor. (According to the citation, Wood "voluntarily carried dispatches through a region infested with hostile Indians, making a journey of 70 miles in one night and walking 30 miles the next day. Also for several weeks, while in close pursuit of Geronimo's band and constantly expecting an encounter, [he] commanded a detachment of Infantry, which was then without an officer, and to the command of which he was assigned upon his own request.") By 1891, the thirty-one-year-old Wood had been promoted to captain.

Seven years later, at the outbreak of the Spanish-

American War, he and his friend Teddy Roosevelt (who called him "the best fellow I ever knew") formed the 1st U.S. Volunteer Calvary—the legendary "Rough Riders." Though most Americans think of Roosevelt as the leader of the unit, Wood was actually the officer in charge. "T.R." was his second-in-command. Wood's meritorious conduct at the battles of Las Guasimas and San Juan Hill brought him promotion to brigadier general. From 1899 to 1902, he served as military governor of Cuba, earning praise as an effective administrator who helped modernize the island's educational, judicial, police, and sanitation systems.

At the time of the Davis murders, Wood—then serving his second year as military governor of Cuba—had returned for a summer visit to his boyhood home of Pocasset, where he had grown up in a square white-washed house known locally as the Josiah Godfrey place, or simply "the old house on the bay," an ancient dwelling with vines snaking through the shingles and a stairway so narrow that, according to local legend, a particularly obese visitor had once become wedged inside it while climbing to the second floor. Wood had come home to refresh his spirits—never imagining, of course, that he would end up playing a role in one of the most notorious multiple murder cases in the annals of U.S. crime.

Captain Paul Gibbs had been good friends with the Wood family for many years, and had implicit faith in Leonard's judgment. And so, in the last week of August, he visited the general at home and confessed his suspicions.

As Captain Paul had hoped, Wood knew just what to do. By the following day, he had contacted a former teacher of his at Harvard Medical School, a man who shared his last name (though the two were unrelated): Dr. Edward S. Wood. A distinguished professor of medical chemistry and renowned toxicologist, Dr. Wood had unique qualifications in such matters. Fifteen years earlier, he had been instrumental in bringing about the arrest of Sarah Jane Robinson—the "American Borgia"—after determining that her son, William, had been poisoned with a massive dose of arsenic.

With the involvement of both Leonard Wood and his eminent namesake, the investigation into the calamitous end of the Davis family finally got under way. Within days, the district attorney of Barnstable County, Lemuel Holmes, had assigned a state detective to the case, a man named Josephus Whitney.

Holmes took another critical step, too. Operating under the assumption that, of all four Davis deaths, the most unaccountable were those of the two previously healthy young women—Genevieve Gordon and her sister, Minnie Gibbs—the DA ordered that their bodies be exhumed from Cataumet cemetery and autopsied for signs of foul play.

17

Everything seemed favorable for my marrying Mr. Brigham. I had put the three women to death who had stood in my way.

—FROM THE CONFESSION OF JANE TOPPAN

ON HER WAY BACK TO LOWELL, JANE STOPPED OFF AT Cambridge to pay a brief visit to Harry Gordon's seventy-one-year-old father, Henry Sr. Inevitably, they spoke of little else besides the terrible events at Cataumet. When Jane asked him how he accounted for the shocking sequence of death, the senior Mr. Gordon gave a sad, philosophical shrug. The most likely explanation, he opined, was that "as the family was an old one, it was dying out."

It quickly became clear to Jane that the possibility of murder had never crossed the old man's mind. As far as he believed, the deaths were all due to natural causes. Certainly, he hadn't heard or read anything to make him think otherwise.

After a few hours in the old man's company, Jane took her leave and boarded a train to Lowell—satisfied (as one of her alienists would later report) "that her guilt had escaped discovery, and that it would be safe for her to go on killing."

Since murdering her foster sister, Elizabeth Brigham, exactly two summers before, Jane had continued to harbor connubial fantasies about Elizabeth's stodgy, sixty-year-old widower, Oramel. She had, in fact, taken active steps to eliminate any potential competition for his affections. The previous January, during a holiday visit to her old family home, she had poisoned Oramel's longtime housekeeper, a middle-aged widow named Florence Calkins, because (as Jane later put it) "I was jealous of her . . . I knew she wanted to become Mr. Brigham's wife."

When Jane arrived in Lowell on Saturday, August 24, therefore, she expected to have Oramel all to herself. Much to her dismay, she found another female in the house—Oramel's older sister, Edna F. Bannister.

A seventy-seven-year-old widow who lived with her married daughter in Turnbridge, Vermont, Mrs. Bannister had been hoping to visit the great Pan-American Exposition in Buffalo since it opened in May. Because of her recurrent heart trouble, however, she hadn't felt strong enough to undertake the journey until mid-August. It had been nearly a year since Edna had last seen her younger brother, so she decided to combine her trip to the exposition with a family visit. During the last week of August, she bid farewell to her daughter, Mrs. Annie Ordway, and took the train down to Lowell, arriving at the Brigham house at 182 Third Street just a few days before Jane showed up.

Early in the afternoon of Monday, August 26— shortly after Oramel, his sister, and Jane finished lunch—Mrs. Bannister began to complain of dizziness. She immediately went to lie down in her room. By late afternoon, she was feeling much better. Jane, however, insisted that she continue to rest, and brought her a tumbler of mineral water.

Sometime during the night, while Jane kept watch over the patient, Mrs. Bannister slipped into a coma. Early the next morning, Dr. William Bass—the same physician who had attended Oramel's late housekeeper, Florence Calkins—was summoned to the Brigham home. His efforts to revive Edna Bannister were in vain. She died that morning, Tuesday, August 27, 1901, at approximately ten o'clock. Dr. Bass attributed her death—as he had Florence Calkins's—to heart disease.

That Jane felt compelled to murder Mrs. Bannister so soon after destroying the Davis family says a great deal about her rapidly deteriorating mental condition. Obviously, Oramel's sister was not a romantic rival. Nor—since Edna planned to leave Lowell within days—did she represent an impediment to Jane's (bizarre) matrimonial schemes. Despite her usual rationalizations ("Mrs. Bannister was a poor old woman," she later wrote, "and was better off out of the way anyhow"), Jane kept killing because she couldn't control herself.

It is also likely that, by this point, she had lost all rational sense of the risks involved in her behavior. After all, she had not only gotten away with dozens of murders throughout the years, but had just committed one of the most shocking crimes in New England history—the annihilation of an entire family under the very noses of their relatives and friends—without (to all appearances) arousing suspicion. It must have seemed to her that she was invulnerable—too cunning for the law. Certainly, such grandiose delusions are not uncommon among serial killers, who often compensate for their profound feelings of worthlessness with a belief in their own supposed omnipotence.

If so, her sense of confidence must have been badly shaken when she saw the front page on the *Boston Globe* on Saturday, August 31. "INQUIRY IS UNDER WAY," blared the headline. "INVESTIGATION OF DEATHS OF CATAUMET FAMILY. A. P. DAVIS, WIFE, AND DAUGHTERS DIED SUDDENLY."

According to the story, the bodies of Genevieve Gordon and Minnie Gibbs had been disinterred from their graves in Cataumet cemetery early the previous day. State detective Josephus Whitney had superintended the exhumation. The corpses were then carried to a nearby barn, where they were dissected by Dr. Robert H. Faunce, the medical examiner of Sandwich. Also present were Professor Edward Wood of Harvard; the Davises' physician, Dr. Leonard Latter; and the Reverend Mr. Dicking of the Methodist Church of Cataumet.

Several internal organs, including the stomach, were removed from each cadaver, and these were given over to Professor Wood, who had transported them back to his laboratory in Cambridge. The results of his analysis were not expected to be known for some time.

To be sure, Jane might have taken comfort from certain statements in the article. Though she was identified by name as the nurse who had been "the attendant of each of the patients," there was no suggestion that she had given them anything other than the best care "that medical skill and professional training could provide." The article also stressed that, according to initial indications, the autopsies had turned up "nothing to warrant any suspicions as to the deaths having resulted from other than natural causes."

Still, it must have come as a blow to Jane—who

had felt so reassured after her recent talk with Henry Gordon Sr.—to learn that the Cataumet tragedy was under official investigation. And that, as the nurse in whose care the whole Davis family had perished, she herself was now an object of attention by the public, the police, and the press.

As it happened, the developments in Cataumet—which seemed so newsworthy on August 31—were about to vanish entirely from the papers, and Jane would enjoy a temporary respite from her budding notoriety. Within days of the exhumations, the country would be rocked by a killing so momentous that it would make every other crime—even a possible case of multiple murder in New England—seem trivial to the point of utter insignificance.

18

I don't believe that Christians in this country had any idea of prevailing on God through prayer to work a miracle, even to save our President's life. Their prayer was that God might give guidance to the surgeons, medical skill to the physicians, and care to the nursing.

—Rev. Dr. Withrow, "Did the Death of the President Prove Prayer Useless?"

Even now, a hundred years later, the city is still haunted by the tragedy. In September 1901, Buffalo, New York, was in its prime—a proud and wealthy metropolis with booming industries, splendid mansions, and a seemingly limitless future. In the century that followed, it suffered a stunning collapse, sliding from the eighth largest city in the nation to the fifty-ninth, and becoming a gray and dreary symbol of urban blight and Rust Belt decay. Various factors, of course, contributed to its deterioration. But to many of its inhabitants, the decline and fall of Buffalo could be traced to one shattering event—a single terrible moment that cast a permanent pall over their once-shining city and marked the beginning of the end.

It happened at the very place that was intended to ratify Buffalo's status as one of the nation's leading cities—the great Pan-American Exposition of 1901. First planned in the heady days following the country's triumph in its war against Spain, the exposition was designed to be the most spectacular event of its kind in nearly a decade. Like its celebrated predecessor—the Chicago World's Fair of 1893—the Buffalo exposition was a blend of high-mindedness and low pleasure, part cultural showplace, part carnival midway: a 350-acre tribute to American progress in the realms of science, industry, and the arts, balanced with a healthy dose of crude, Barnumesque fun.

Compared to the Chicago fair—dubbed the "White City" in tribute to its marblelike, neoclassical look—the Buffalo exposition was a baroque fantasyland of riotous color and garish design. The "Rainbow City" some called it. In keeping with its overarching theme—a celebration of our country's hemispheric bond with its Latin-American neighbors—the prevailing architectural style was something called "Spanish Renaissance." Red roof tiles were ubiquitous. But many of the pavilions featured a wildly eclectic mix of elements, from Islamic minarets to Corinthian columns, Italian loggias to medieval turrets.

Sculptures were everywhere—adorning the fountains, lining the esplanades, flanking the entrances of the buildings. Some were historical, others allegorical, many purely ornamental. Within the space of six months, a small army of sculptors, working under the supervision of Vienna-trained artist Karl Bitters, churned out more than 500 plaster statues, from demurely draped classical nudes symbolizing the Four Seasons of the Year, to overall-clad laborers representing the Spirit of American Manufacturing.

And then there were the lights: more than two million of them festooning every building in the fair. At the very center of the grounds loomed the great Tower of Electricity, 400 feet high and covered with nearly half-a-million eight-watt bulbs. At night, when the switches were thrown, the exposition was transformed into a glittering "fairy city" that left many observers breathless with wonder.

The level of innovation—industrial, scientific, technological—symbolized by this glorious spectacle was celebrated elsewhere throughout the fair: in the Machinery Building, the Hall of Manufactures, the Railway Exhibit, the Geodetic Survey Display. For countless fairgoers, however, the real highlight was not an edifying tour of the Hall of Ethnology or a glimpse of a hydraulic turbine in action but rather a trip to the Midway. Here, visitors could indulge in hours of Coney Island-style amusement and sideshow titillation. They could ride a camel, enjoy a simulated trip to the moon, or take a hair-raising spin on the Thompson Aerio-Cycle (a gigantic, Erector-set seesaw that suspended its passengers nearly 300 feet aboveground). They could descend into Dreamland, watch a graphic re-creation of the Johnstown Flood, or see premature babies kept alive in the amazing Infant Incubator. And all for the general admission fee of fifty cents.

The festivities on opening day—May 1, 1901—drew a crowd of 20,000. More than five times that number showed up for Dedication Day several weeks later. By the time the exposition ended on Saturday, November 2, it had drawn a total of 8,120,048 people. How many more dreamed of attending is, of course, impossible to say—though we know of at least one person who longed to see the fair but never made it: Oramel Brigham's sister, Edna Bannister, whose journey to the grand Pan-American Exposition was violently aborted when she stopped off to visit her brother in Lowell, Massachusetts and had the misfortune of being present at his home when Nurse Toppan showed up.

Needless to say, however, it wasn't the poisoning of an obscure Vermont widow that gave the Buffalo fair its permanent association with tragedy. It was another, infinitely more earthshaking crime that delivered a deathblow not only to the illustrious victim, but to the Exposition itself—and even, some say, to the city of Buffalo.

President William McKinley held an exalted opinion of world fairs. To him, they were not merely gala events but "the record of the world's advancement"— "the timekeepers of progress." He had enjoyed himself mightily at Chicago's Columbian Exposition in 1893 and Atlanta's Cotton States Exposition two years later. Now—like so many of his countrymen—he was eager to visit the great Pan-American Exposition.

Originally, he intended to travel to Buffalo in early June. But the sudden illness of his beloved wife, Ida—a chronic invalid who suffered from a range of ailments, including petit mal epilepsy—necessitated a postponement of the trip. The couple passed the summer of 1901 at their modest home in Canton, Ohio, where Ida enjoyed a steady recuperation, while her husband indulged himself in the simple relaxations of the placid Midwestern town—picnics, drives in the family roundabout, excursions to nearby farms and county fairs, evening hymnsings, and an occasional game of euchre. As the summer progressed and Ida continued to improve, his plans to visit Buffalo were renewed. By late August, newspapers around the country were announcing that President's Day at the Pan-American Exposition had been officially rescheduled for Thursday, September 5.

Not everyone was thrilled with the plan. George Cortelyou—McKinley's fiercely devoted personal secretary—was especially concerned about the proposed public reception, slated for the afternoon of September 6 and certain to draw enormous crowds hoping to shake the President's hand. Fearful for McKinley's safety, Cortelyou urged him to reconsider. But McKinley pooh-poohed his worries. "I have no enemies," he serenely declared. "Why should I fear?"

At fifty-eight years old and six months into his second term, McKinley was, in fact, a widely beloved leader—the country's most popular President since Lincoln. Even so, Cortelyou's anxiety was far from unfounded. At a time when Pennsylvania coal miners made less than $400 a year while millionaire industrialists dined from solid gold plates and smoked cigars wrapped in hundred-dollar bills, the country was seething with labor unrest. Only a short time earlier, a Secret Service operative named Moretti had managed to infiltrate an Anarchist cell in New Jersey and uncovered an international plot to kill members of the ruling elite—two of whom, Empress Elizabeth of Austria and King Humbert of Italy, had already been assassinated by the summer of 1901.

Desperate to dissuade McKinley from holding the planned public reception, Cortelyou tried a final tack. At best, he argued, the President would be able to shake hands with only a few of the thousands who would undoubtedly show up to greet him. The rest would go away deeply disappointed.

Once again, however, McKinley brushed aside the objection. "Well," he said, "they'll know I tried, anyhow."

In the end, Cortelyou was forced to bow to his

chief's wishes. Before the special train departed for Buffalo, however, he made sure to fire off a telegram to local officials, warning them that no security precaution was to be spared during the President's planned two-day trip to their city.

The President's three-car Special arrived in Buffalo at precisely 5:00 P.M. on Tuesday, September 3. No sooner had it pulled into the Terrace Railroad Station overlooking Lake Erie than Cortelyou's worst fears about Anarchist violence appeared to be confirmed. As the locomotive clanked to a halt, the station was rocked by a thunderous explosion. Smoke billowed—the train shook as if torpedoed—passengers were hurled to the floor—glass flew through the cars as windows were blown out by the force of the blast.

Among the crowd of spectators who had turned out to welcome the President confusion reigned. An outraged cry went up: "Anarchists! Anarchists! They've wrecked the train!" Spotting a short, swarthy man standing near the tracks, the inflamed crowd advanced on him, convinced he was the culprit. Only the timely intervention of a well-dressed bystander, who had observed the incident from a nearby carriage, saved the fellow from injury—or worse. Leaping from his vehicle, the man interposed himself between the mob and their scapegoat and, raising his hands, shouted: "There's nothing wrong, gentlemen! This man had nothing to do with the blast! It was caused by the cannons! Dynamite would have blown off the wheels of the car!"

The name of this Samaritan has gone unrecorded by history, but he was, in fact, correct. The incident was the result not of Anarchistic terrorism, but of official incompetence—specifically, of the carelessness of a

Coast Guard captain named Leonard Wisser, in charge of providing the President with a twenty-one-gun salute. In his zeal to make this greeting as spectacular as possible, Wisser had laid his artillery dangerously close to the tracks, and it was the detonation of one of the cannons that had rocked the cars carrying McKinley and his retinue.

Eventually, calm was restored. The First Lady—whose nerves were easily unstrung—required the immediate attention of her traveling physician. Otherwise, no serious damage was done, and the incident was quickly forgotten.

Only in hindsight did it assume a sinister aspect—an omen of the disaster to come.

McKinley was slated to spend two days in Buffalo. Wednesday, September 5—President's Day at the Exposition—went exactly as planned. At noon, McKinley delivered an eloquent speech to an enthusiastic crowd of more than 50,000 listeners, crammed into the Esplanade under a sweltering sun. Afterward, he spent a full afternoon seeing the grounds, touring the buildings and exhibits, attending receptions, and greeting assorted dignitaries and well-wishers. In the evening—after a brief rest at the mansion of his host—he and Ida returned to the Exposition to enjoy a concert by John Philip Sousa and watch a dazzling display of fireworks, whose highlights included a line of twenty-two pyrotechnic battleships, a fiery representation of Niagara Falls, and a blazing portrait of McKinley himself, accompanied by the legend: "Welcome President McKinley, Chief of Our Nation and Our Empire."

Thursday was scheduled to be McKinley's "restful day." It began with a morning of sightseeing. Accom-

Jane as a young woman, circa 1880.

Jane shortly before her arrest, circa 1900.

Oramel Brigham.

Elizabeth Brigham,
Jane's foster sister.

The Jachin House, where the Davis family lived.

CAPT. PAUL GIBBS

Captain Paul Gibbs.

Mrs. Conners' death was other than a natural one," he said, "and I never heard until very recently about the disappearance of her money. It is quite true that Dr. McIntire refused to say anything in her favor when I sent to him to inquire about Miss Toppan, but neither did he say anything against her, and Dr. Wesselhoeft and others spoke of her in the very highest terms.

"When Miss Toppan came to me and told me that Mrs. Conners had been preparing for a vacation, and had instructed her regarding all of the matron's duties, she made no direct ap-

tance with Miss Toppan, he said:
"We first formed the acquaintance of

JAMES STUART MURPHY,
Counsel for Jane Toppan.

Miss Toppan in Cambridge, Mass. She became acquainted with my sister, who lives with me. I knew Miss Toppan merely as a trained nurse of much ability. It was several years ago that she commenced to make visits to Amherst. She hardly ever stayed longer than a day or two.

"I always entertained a high regard for her, and it is hard for me to sus-

MRS. CONNORS.
Matron of the Refectory of the St. John's Theological School in Cambridge, who died suddenly on Feb. 11, 1901, while she was being visited by Jane Toppan

(above) Newspaper clipping, showing Myra Conners, one of Jane's victims, and James Stuart Murphy, Jane's friend and counsel.

(right) Jane at her hearing, November 8, 1901.

MISS JANE TOPPAN.

Jane leaves the Barnstable courthouse on the arm of James Stuart Murphy following her arraignment.

Spectators swarm to the Barnstable courthouse on the morning of Jane's trial, June 23, 1902.

Attorney General Herbert Parker.

JANE TOPPAN HEARS THE JURY'S VERDICT.

JANE TOPPAN BECAME GREATLY INTERESTED IN DR. STEDMAN'S TESTIMONY

DR. JELLY   V.DR. STEDMAN

SKETCHES AT TRIAL OF JANE TOPPAN FOR MURDER AT BARNSTABLE.

Jane reacts to the verdict.

panied by Ida and a party of distinguished guests, he traveled on a special train of parlor cars to Niagara Falls, where he walked along the gorge, hiked halfway across the suspension bridge, toured the powerhouse ("the marvel of the Electrical Age," as he proclaimed it), and enjoyed a hearty lunch in the ballroom of the International Hotel. After capping off the meal with a cigar on the veranda, he reboarded the train with his wife and entourage and returned to Buffalo for his final appearance at the Exposition—the public reception that George Cortelyou had tried so hard to talk him out of.

The Temple of Music—whose pseudo-Byzantine design and garish color scheme had drawn the sneers of critics, even while delighting countless fairgoers—had been chosen as the site of the reception. From the moment the fairgrounds opened that morning, thousands of spectators had swarmed to the building, many standing on line for hours beneath a blazing sun. Finally, at precisely 4:00 P.M., the door was thrown open and the crowd began to make an orderly, single-file procession down the aisle toward the dais, where McKinley waited to shake their hands.

In accordance with Cortelyou's instructions, extra precautions had been taken to ensure the President's safety. In addition to the three Secret Service men who routinely watched over him, a squad of Exposition policemen had been stationed at the entrance and a contingent of Buffalo detectives posted in the aisle. Ten enlisted artillerymen and a corporal, all in full-dress uniform, had also been called in, with orders to prevent any suspicious-looking persons from approaching McKinley. Altogether, more than eighty guards were there to keep an eye on the crowd.

In spite of these heightened security measures, however, one cardinal rule for protecting the President was flagrantly disregarded. No visitor was supposed to get close to the Chief Executive unless both hands were plainly visible and completely empty. In those pre-air-conditioned days, however, the crammed reception hall was sweltering—at least ninety degrees. Sweat poured from every brow, and so many handkerchiefs were in evidence that the guards simply paid no attention to them.

At least, that was the only explanation ever given for what happened next. At 4:07 P.M.—just a few minutes after the reception began—a short, slender, mild-looking young man reached the front of the line. Like so many other other people, he was clutching a big white handkerchief. Or so it appeared. In reality, the hankie was wrapped around his right hand, concealing a short-barreled .32-caliber revolver. As McKinley reached out to greet him, the young man—a self-professed Anarchist named Leon Czolgosz—lurched forward and fired twice into the President's body.

A moment of stunned silence followed the shots. Then pandemonium erupted. While the President staggered back a few steps, Czolgosz was knocked to the floor by a bystander, then pounced on by the soldiers and guards, who began to beat him with rifle butts and billy clubs. "Go easy on him boys," gasped McKinley, now seated in a chair, his face drained of color, a spreading red stain on his shirt-front.

While Czolgosz was hauled to his feet and dragged to an inner office, the Temple was cleared. A few minutes later, an ambulance clanged up to the entrance and the desperately wounded President was carried out on a litter, loaded into the vehicle, and driven to the Exposition hospital.

Anyone looking into the history of the Toppan affair is bound to be struck by the shockingly primitive state of American medicine a century ago—a time when a dose of formaldehyde was the officially recommended treatment for the common cold, when drugstore shelves were stocked with "reinvigorating tonics" consisting largely of alcohol and opium, and when an entire middle-class family could be annihilated in the span of a few weeks under the very nose of their unsuspecting family physician. No one, no matter how eminent or powerful, was immune from the rampant medical incompetence of the age—as the case of the unfortunate William McKinley was about to prove.

Housed in a small, gray building a quarter-mile from the Temple of Music, the Exposition hospital was little more than an emergency first-aid station. Exactly eighteen minutes after the shooting, McKinley—fully conscious, though in severe shock—was carried into the rudimentary operating room and lain on the table.

As the nurses began to undress him, one of the bullets—which had glanced off his breastbone, causing only a scratch—fell from his underclothing. Even at a glance, however, it was clear that the other wound was far more serious, perhaps even fatal. It had torn through McKinley's abdomen, approximately five inches below his left nipple.

The first and most urgent order of business was to round up the best physicians available. Dr. Roswell Park—the Exposition's eminent medical director and a man with long experience in the treatment of gunshot wounds—was the obvious choice to take charge. But Park was in Niagara Falls, operating on a lymphoma patient. Arrangements were quickly made to rush him back to Buffalo at the earliest possible moment. In the meantime, the President's life was put into the hands of another prominent Buffalo physician, Dr. Matthew Mann.

A short, gray-bearded fifty-six-year-old, Mann had a worldwide reputation. He had trained in the United States and Europe, served on the staff of the Yale Medical School, and authored a standard textbook. His specialty, however, wasn't abdominal surgery. It was gynecology. Nevertheless, he was deemed the most qualified surgeon available at that moment of extreme crisis.

Though the city of Buffalo had recently opened a new General Hospital with a well-equipped operating amphitheater, Mann, in consultation with the other doctors who had gathered at the scene, chose to operate without delay—the first of several highly questionable decisions he would later be accused of making. At 5:20 P.M., the life-and-death operation on the Chief Executive of the United States began under the least favorable conditions imaginable. Mann, who had arrived without his surgical case, had to work with borrowed instruments. No one wore a cap or a gauze mask. Though the fairgrounds blazed each evening with the brilliance of millions of incandescent bulbs, there were no electric lights in the operating room. As the daylight waned, the doctors were reduced to using a mirror to reflect the rays of the setting sun onto the incision in McKinley's abdominal wall.

Exploring the President's wound, Mann discovered that the bullet had gone straight through the stomach, puncturing both the front and rear walls. He couldn't find the bullet itself, though. An X-ray machine was on display at the fair, but Mann declined to use it. He also chose not to drain the wound. The two holes in the stomach were sutured, the abdominal cavity was flushed with saline solution, and McKinley was stitched back up with the missing bullet still inside him. At 7:30 P.M.—two hours after the operation began—the groaning, corpse-pale President was taken from the hospital and transported back to the mansion of his Buffalo host.

If the operation revealed the deplorable state of American medicine in 1901, its aftermath was equally grim. Over the course of the next week, the public was reassured by a steady stream of rosy communiqués from Buffalo. On Friday, September 6, the doctors reported that McKinley was "rallying satisfactorily and resting comfortably." On Saturday, a bulletin described his condition as "quite encouraging." On Sunday, one of his physicians, Dr. Herman Mynter, described the President as "first rate." The official word on Monday was that his "condition [was] becoming more and more satisfactory." By Tuesday, newspapers throughout the country were proclaiming that the President was "on the high road to recovery."

Not everyone was quite so optimistic, however. Concerned about the bullet that remained lost somewhere inside McKinley, his ever-faithful secretary, George Cortelyou, urged the doctors to search for it. At Cortelyou's request, Thomas Edison himself shipped his most sophisticated X-ray machine to Buffalo, along with a trained operator. But the doctors refused to reexamine the wound.

Their official prognoses grew more cheerful by the

day. On Wednesday, September 11, Dr. Charles McBurney, a prominent New York surgeon, paid lavish tribute to his colleague, Matthew Mann, telling reporters that "the judgment of Dr. Mann in operating as he did within an hour of the shooting in all probability saved the life of the President."

But the President's life had not been saved. Once again, Cortelyou—who had tried so hard to keep McKinley from attending the reception in the first place—saw his worst fears come true. At 5:00 P.M. on Friday the 13th, his venerated leader suffered a heart attack.

Nine hours later—his stomach, pancreas, and one kidney poisoned by the gangrene that had spread along the path of the unfound bullet—William McKinley was dead.

19

_m_

They say that I do not like men, that I am a sour old maid and man hater. But it isn't so. I like them and I like to nurse them.

—FROM THE CONFESSION OF JANE TOPPAN

IN COMPARISON TO OUR OWN TIME—WHEN YEARS OF legal maneuvering typically elapse between the commission of a capital crime and the ultimate punishment of its perpetrator—justice moved swiftly in the old days. On Tuesday, October 29, 1901—less than two months after he murdered the President of the United States—Leon Czolgosz was put to death at the state prison in Auburn, New York. Immediately after his electrocution, the top of his skull was sawed off and his brain examined for signs of mental impairment. His corpse was then stuck in a black-stained pine box, doused with sulfuric acid (to obliterate its identity), and buried in an unmarked grave in the prison cemetery.

The utter ignominy of the assassin's death and disposal was reflected in the meager news coverage accorded the event. The announcement of his death barely rated a headline in most papers (the _New York Times_ relegated the story to page five)—as though the end of so contemptible a creature deserved nothing more than a passing notice. This was particularly true in New England, where Czolgosz's execution was overshadowed by an event that happened on the very same day: the arrest of Nurse Jane Toppan in the case of the Davis family deaths.

Though the McKinley assassination and the nation's subsequent mourning had diverted the public's attention from Jane, she had, in fact, been under constant surveillance since early September.

No sooner had the bodies of Minnie Gibbs and Genevieve Gordon been exhumed than a state police detective named John S. Patterson was assigned to keep a close eye on Jane. He was on the train when she left Cataumet during the last week of August, trailed her during her brief stopover at Cambridge when she paid a brief visit to Harry Gordon Sr., and followed her on to Lowell. There—under an assumed identity—he took a room in the home of a family named Stevens, not far from the Brigham house. For the next few weeks, wherever Jane went out in public—to the post office or the druggist or simply for a stroll—Patterson was close behind. Before long, he was thoroughly acquainted with her daily routines.

Of course, he had no way of knowing what was taking place in private, behind the walls of Oramel Brigham's residence at Number 182 Third Street. There, Jane's behavior was growing more alarming by the day. As her mind became increasingly unmoored from reality and she slipped deeper into madness, she began to resemble the kind of lovelorn, frighteningly fixated personality familiar to modern-day audiences from movies like *Fatal Attraction*.

At first, she sought to impress Brigham with her competence and devotion, taking over the running of his household and trying to prove herself indispensable to his daily life and happiness. When Brigham made it clear, however, that he had no intention of keeping her on in any permanent capacity—as either housekeeper or wife—Jane tried a different tack to "win his love" (as she later put it).

She poisoned his tea with morphia.

The dose was just large enough to make the sixty-year-old deacon sick. For the next several days, Jane remained constantly at his bedside, nursing him back to health. Surely, he would realize how much he needed her!

But this ploy, too, failed to produce the desired result. Seething with a sense of betrayal and rejection, Jane then resorted to blackmail. She threatened to destroy Oramel's reputation by spreading word among his neighbors that he was "the father of her unborn babe."

At that point, Brigham reached the end of his tether and ordered Jane out of his house. That same afternoon—Saturday, September 29—she took an overdose of morphine. When Brigham found her unconscious, he immediately summoned his physician, Dr. W. H. Lathrop, who administered an emetic that induced profuse vomiting. Before long, Jane had emerged from her stupor.

A private nurse named Ann Tyler was summoned to remain at her bedside. The following morning, Jane seemed to be in such good spirits that Nurse Tylor decided to leave her alone and go downstairs for some breakfast. When she returned a short while later, she was stunned to discover that Jane had evidently taken another dose of poison. Her complexion was badly discolored and her face muscles so tightly clenched that Nurse Taylor could not force an emetic through her teeth. Just then, Dr. Lathrop happened to arrive for his morning visit, and immediately injected apomorphine in both of Jane's arms. Within moments, she had emptied the contents of her stomach into a chamber pot.

Seated at her bedside, the doctor asked Jane why she had poisoned herself.

"I'm tired of life," she answered. "I know that people are talking about me. I just want to die."

In spite of her statement, there is reason to doubt that Jane was serious about killing herself. After all, she had successfully murdered nearly three dozen people with morphine, so it's hard to believe that she wouldn't have known what constituted a fatal dose. More likely, she was just trying to win Brigham's sympathy and keep him from throwing her out.

If so, the tactic didn't work. No sooner was Jane back on her feet than Brigham finally managed to expel her permanently from his home.

Jane spent the next several days recuperating in Lowell General Hospital under the care of Dr. F. W. Chadbourne. Even there, she was being watched. Feigning illness, Detective Patterson had himself admitted to the hospital. From his bed in an adjoining ward, he was able to keep constant tabs on the suspect.

After being discharged, Jane—still shadowed by Patterson—traveled to Amherst, New Hampshire, to stay with her old friend Sarah Nichols, a middle-aged spinster who lived with her brother, George, in a handsome yellow farmhouse about a mile outside the village. The trip did wonders for her spirits. "I had a fine time out there," she would later write, describing her visit to Amherst. "I don't think I ever enjoyed myself as much as I did that fall. There was a jolly lot of people there, and I had the kind of time I like to have."

The good times, however, weren't destined to last. On Tuesday, October 29, Detective Josephus Whitney arrived in Amherst, accompanied by two other officers, Inspector Thomas Flood and Deputy Marshall Wheeler. Seeking out Patterson, who was lodged at a boardinghouse a short distance from the Nichols residence, they informed him that the autopsy on Minnie Gibbs had turned up lethal traces of poison in the dead woman's viscera.

The four officers immediately proceeded to the Nichols house, where—brandishing a warrant—Whitney informed Jane that she was under arrest for the murder of Minnie Gibbs. Jane took the news with perfect composure. When Whitney ordered her to pack her belongings, she complied without a word of protest. Only one thing bothered her, she would later confess. "I was annoyed because the detective insisted on remaining in my room while I was getting ready, and I did not think it was very gentlemanly."

If Jane seemed unperturbed by her arrest, it came as a terrible shock to her hosts. They had no idea, of course, just how lucky they were.

Jane later revealed that—had Detective Whitney not shown up when he did—"I might have killed George Nichols and his sister, too." She never gave a reason. Apparently, after her pleasant four-week vacation at their home, she was feeling like her old self again, and drugging her longtime friends to death was just something she wanted to do. For the hell of it.

PART FOUR

MURDERESS

20

I have no statement to make. I do not even want to get my name in the newspapers.

—JANE TOPPAN, OCTOBER 31, 1901

FROM THE MOMENT SHE WAS TAKEN INTO CUSTODY, Jane Toppan was big news. On Thursday, October 31, her arrest made the front page of the *New York Times* (though a story about tainted pastry from a neighborhood bakery in Manhattan—"Scores Poisoned by Eating Crullers!"—was given even greater prominence). Unsurprisingly, the case was a particular sensation in New England, where it would dominate the headlines for weeks.

Within twenty-four hours of her arrest, newspapers throughout Massachusetts were already predicting that Nurse Toppan would prove to be one of the most extraordinary killers in the annals of American crime. According to the *Boston Herald*, the story was shaping up to be "the most famous poisoning case Massachusetts has ever had"; while the *Boston Journal* declared that it "promises to be one of the most remarkable cases the State has ever known." The *Boston Post* went even further, predicting that Nurse Toppan would turn out to be "one of the most remarkable of murderesses, a Lucretia Borgia without parallel in modern times."

Though Jane had only been charged with a single

murder at this point—that of Minnie Gibbs—she was clearly the prime suspect not only in the deaths of the other members of the Davis family but in a number of other cases as well. In its page one story of October 31, the *Post* referred to Oramel Brigham's "serious illness" while Jane was staying at his home in September; the "sudden and suspicious death" of his sister, Edna Bannister; and the "sudden and mysterious illness" of "Mr. M. C. Beedle of Cambridge while Miss Toppan was living with his family last winter."

No one yet guessed that these cases represented only a fraction of Jane's crimes. Another six months would pass before the full extent of her enormities became known to a stunned and disbelieving world.

In the meantime, Jane steadfastly maintained her innocence, insisting that she had nothing to do with the tragedy that befell the Davis family. "Those people all died of natural causes," she told her escort—a detective named Simon F. Letteney—on her way back to Cape Cod. "Excepting old man Davis. He was crazy, and I think he poisoned himself."

Her mood was relaxed and upbeat. Letteney reported that she had "chatted pleasantly" throughout the trip and even "laughed and joked about the stories of her arrest and alleged crimes which she read in newspapers on the train."

When the train arrived in Barnstable on Wednesday afternoon, a flock of newspapermen were waiting on the platform to catch a glimpse of the country's latest criminal celebrity. Jane seemed unperturbed by the attention. "She appeared cheerful and full of animation and good spirits" as she was led to the little red-brick jailhouse, one paper reported.

The situation was very different the following day—Thursday, October 31—when Jane was arraigned in the Bristol district court before Judge Swift. By then, her cheery mood had evaporated and the gravity of her situation had finally sunk in. According to her jailer—a balding mustachioed fellow named Judah Cash—she had passed a sleepless night. In the morning, she appeared to be "on the verge of collapse." A sizable crowd had assembled outside the courthouse for the occasion. As Jane approached the colonnaded building on the supporting arm of Detective Letteney, her steps seemed to falter. The *Boston Globe* offered a vivid, if slightly overwrought, description of scene:

> Miss Toppan was very pale, and beneath her jet black hair, but slightly streaked with gray, her sunken cheeks seemed very white, and there was the darkness beneath the eyes that showed that the night had not been a restful one in the county jail. She wore a black tailor[ed] skirt and jacket and a white shirtwaist with a band of black about her throat. Upon her head her hastily combed hair was concealed by a black hat trimmed with black muslin. She carried her gloves and veil, but even these light objects were a burden as she dropped them while ascending the two steps to the courthouse.

Entering the little courtroom with tottering steps, she seated herself on the wooden bench that served as the prisoner's dock of the district court. She had no legal representation, her attorney, James Stuart Murphy, having not yet arrived from Lowell. When her name was called, she arose unsteadily, clinging to the wooden railing in front of her as the clerk read the complaint.

"What do you say to this complaint?" he asked when he was finished.

"Not guilty" she answered in a shaky voice, then sank back onto the bench.

The case was continued to November 8 at the request of the state, and Jane was remanded without bail. The entire proceedings took less than three minutes. When it was over, Jane arose, stepped halfway through the doorway, then quickly clutched the frame, as if she required support. After pausing for a moment, she made her way unsteadily along the narrow hallway, keeping one hand on the wall to brace herself until she reached the exit. As she descended the courthouse steps, she nervously dropped her gloves and veil again. Detective Letteney gallantly stooped to retrieve them, then escorted her back to her cell on the second floor of the woman's wing of the jail, where she stripped off her jacket and hat and collapsed on her cot.

In a message transmitted through Letteney, reporters let Jane know that their papers "would be very glad to publish anything she cared to say in her defense." Jane, however, demurred. "Thank them very much," she had Letteney tell the newsmen, "but I think I shall keep my own counsel until I have an opportunity to talk with my attorney."

She repeated her claims of innocence, insisting that she knew "nothing about the deaths of the members of the Davis family, excepting that I supposed they all died from natural causes." Significantly (and characteristically), the only person she felt bad for was herself. "I am very sorry that I am obliged to endure this wide publicity," she said in her statement, "and the only wish I could offer would be that my name does not appear in the papers anymore."

However devout Jane's wish for obscurity may have been, she would never be anonymous again. A hundred years ago, no less than today, the press was only too happy to cater to the public's perennial craving for sensationalism. The major difference between then and now was technological. In the era before CNN and CourtTV (or, for that matter, radio bulletins and newsreels), people had to settle for print. In the weeks following her arrest, the Boston papers—the *Globe, Post, Herald, Traveler, Daily Advertiser, Morning Journal,* and *Evening Transcript*—devoted lavish attention to the Toppan case, describing each new development in minute detail and accompanying their stories with crude photographic portraits of the accused multi-murderess and engraved illustrations of the unfolding events.

Every vague rumor, wild speculation, and trivial detail of Jane's life was dished out for the titillation of the public. In an article headlined "Feared by Her Playmates," the *Boston Globe*—citing an unnamed and clearly not very reliable source—claimed that "in her childhood days, Miss Toppan's little playmates came to have a certain fear of her, and the result was that she had no intimates as a girl." The same article reported—as though it were unassailable proof of her aberrant nature—that as Jane grew older, "one of her peculiarities was to refrain from partaking of any breakfast save a cup of coffee." Equally inconsequential was a story headlined "Miss Toppan's Clothing," which broke the less-than-earthshaking fact that most of her personal effects had been left behind in Amherst, where they were being "closely guarded by the Nichols family."

Everyone even remotely connected to Jane was sought out by reporters. There was L. W. Ferdinand, for example, the gentleman who had briefly employed her in the summer of 1896, when she had accompanied his family to Cataumet and first fallen in love with the resort. Interviewed at his home in Cambridge, Ferdinand was asked if he "could throw any light upon the Davis case and the personality of Miss Toppan." "No I can't," was his reply. His complete lack of useful information did not prevent the *Globe* from devoting an entire story to Ferdinand under the headline, "He Rented the Cottage."

Ferdinand wasn't the only tangential figure to find his name in the papers. Another was a Chelmsford woman named Lottie Parkhurst, a telegraph operator at the Middlesex Street station. Describing herself as "an intimate friend of Miss Toppan for many years," Miss Parkhurst avowed that her confidence in Jane's good character was such "that I would as readily have suspected my own sister of wrongdoing." She did note, however, that "several years" earlier, her friend had been "jilted by a young man to whom she was engaged"—a "severe disappointment" that (so Miss Parkhurst implied) might well have started Jane on the road to multiple murder.

Other informants preferred to maintain their anonymity. A resident of Lowell—identified in the *Globe* as "one of the oldest women in the First Trinitarian Congregational Church"—described the peculiar changes she had recently noticed in Jane. "I have known Jennie Toppan since she was girl," this grandam declared. "What has come over her I do not know . . . I saw her at the harvest supper in the First Trinitarian Congregational Church vestry. She passed me without speaking, but I thought she was very pale. Her conduct that night surprised me, as she was always very jolly."

Another person who had recently had a surprising encounter with Jane was a gentleman named Drewett, who had run into her early on the morning of October 1, right after she'd been turned out of the Brigham house. According to Drewett, Jane—who was making her way on foot across the little bridge spanning the Merrimack River—told him that Brigham had thrown her out because of a letter she had sent to the wife of the Reverend Mr. Kennegott. Apparently in response to some unspecified snub, Jane had composed an abusive note in which she "used very plain language [and] told Mrs. Kennegott just what she thought of her." When Brigham—a deacon in Reverend Kennegott's church—got wind of what Jane had done, he had commanded her to pack up and leave.

At least that was Jane's version of events leading to her expulsion. Drewett himself had no further light to shed on the matter other than to say that "Miss Toppan's story had sounded very strange to me."

The press was especially interested, of course, in people closely connected to the case, beginning with Oramel Brigham himself. After a lifetime of obscurity, the elderly deacon and baggage master—rumored to have been the object of Nurse Toppan's desire—suddenly found himself in newspapers all across the state, his name in the headlines, his image plastered on page one. The widely reprinted portrait showed a stuffy-looking gentleman with a high, balding dome, full white muttonchops, and a look of bland benevolence.

The relentlessly proper, high-minded personality reflected in this picture was conveyed in his remarks concerning Jane. Despite her alleged crimes against him—poisoning his food, attempting to blackmail him into marriage—Brigham refused to speak ill of her, insisting that he felt "only the greatest charity toward Miss Toppan."

According to Brigham, there was only one reasonable explanation for Jane's recent behavior. "There is no doubt in my mind," he told reporters, "that she was addicted to the morphine habit. This is a habit that a great many professional nurses unconsciously get into. It is certainly a very sad occurrence. In justice to her, however, I think it is best not to tell all I know concerning her actions before the trial is held."

The assertion that Jane was addicted to morphine was, if not actively rejected, at least called into question by another important figure in the case: Dr. William H. Lathrop, Brigham's family physician, who had been summoned to treat Jane after her suicide attempts. Like Brigham, Dr. Lathrop was the soul of discretion in his public comments, though he clearly disagreed with the deacon on several key points.

Whereas Brigham expressed "little doubt that Miss Toppan is insane," Lathrop believed that attributing her crimes to "mental imbalance" was "a charitable view . . . of her case." Certainly, he insisted, "she showed no sign of aberration" when he was treating her. He declared, moreover, that he had "no personal knowledge of her [alleged] morphine habit."

What seemed to interest Lathrop most about the case were its forensic implications. Indeed, in an extended interview with a reporter for the *Globe*, Lathrop used the occasion to ride his favorite hobbyhorse—his opposition to the practice of cremation.

Lathrop was of the firm (and not entirely unjustified) opinion that "there are many more cases of willful poisoning than either the public or the medical profession have any idea of, and there have been some instances where bodies have been cremated under circumstances that, to my mind, were exceedingly suspicious." Such cases, he continued,

> do not, as a rule, occur among the poorer or more ignorant classes, but among the more intelligent, and the deed is likely to be done by persons who not only have some knowledge of the action of poisons but have intelligence enough to cleverly conceal their work.
>
> Arsenic is a favorite agency with such persons, partly because it is about the easiest poison to obtain, and partly because it is practically tasteless. In the case of a body which has been buried in the usual manner, traces of arsenical poisoning may be detected a long time after interment, but in the process of cremation, the arsenic is absolutely dissipated.

There was only one way, according to Lathrop, to stem the epidemic of arsenic murder: by making cremations illegal and performing compulsory autopsies on every fresh corpse. "This is a very important point that should be looked into both by our lawmakers and physicians," Lathrop declared.

He concluded his interview by taking issue with Oramel Brigham on one final point. Contrary to the latter's conviction that he had been poisoned the previous summer, Lathrop stuck to his own belief that "Mr. Brigham's illness was cholera morbus." There was absolutely "nothing in his case to indicate arsenical poisoning," he insisted.

Lathrop's defense of his original opinion was, he claimed, a matter of simple justice. "It is not fair to the woman to state absolutely that Mr. Brigham's own illness was due to the fact that he had been poisoned by his nurse." Still—though Jane was certainly entitled to the presumption of innocence—Lathrop's main concern appeared to be his own good name. To have misdiagnosed a case of arsenic poisoning was embarrassing (at best) for any physician, but particularly for one who presented himself as something of an expert on the crime.

One man who was unable to defend his somewhat tarnished professional reputation was Lathrop's medical colleague Dr. Leonard Latter—the Cataumet physician who had attended Alden Davis and his daughters without ever having his suspicions aroused. There was a good reason for his silence. Just ten days before Jane Toppan's arrest, Dr. Latter had died—of natural causes, unlike his three eradicated patients.

For investigators working on the Toppan case, his passing was a blow. For Jane, however, it was extremely convenient. Though publicly professing sorrow over his death, nothing could have suited her more. Without Latter around to contradict her, she could claim that he held the key to her exoneration.

On November 2, she did just that, issuing a statement through her attorney, James S. Murphy: "I know nothing about the poisoning either of Mrs. Gibbs or any members of the Davis family," she declared, repeating her claims of innocence. "I suppose they all died of natural causes. I am willing to tell all about these cases. I have nothing to conceal. I am sorry that Dr. Latter is dead. Were he alive, I would not have the slightest difficulty in clearing my skirts."

21

When we have told all we know to support the charge we have made against Jane Toppan, the Robinson poisoning case, the most famous that has ever been heard in a Massachusetts court, will sink into insignificance.

—STATE DETECTIVE JOSEPHUS WHITNEY

THOUGH JANE HAD HER SUPPORTERS—SOCIAL ACQUAIN-tances from Cambridge and Cataumet with fond recollections of her "jolly" personality, a few former patients who had recovered under her care—her guilt was never questioned by the press. On the contrary, each day's papers carried new and more damning accusations. By Friday, November 1, the list of her suspected victims had climbed to seven: the four members of the Davis family, plus three women connected to Oramel Brigham—his wife, Elizabeth; his sister, Mrs. Edna Bannister; and his housekeeper, Florence Calkins. As the apparent death toll mounted, it seemed clear that—as the *Boston Post* proclaimed—Nurse Toppan was nothing less than "a new Lucretia Borgia."

Fifteen years earlier, of course, the public had been riveted by another female serial poisoner who had also been branded a latter-day Borgia—Sarah Jane Robinson, whose victims included her husband, sister, brother-in-law, nephew, and as many as five of her own children. Languishing in a solitary cell in the East

Cambridge jail—where she'd been confined since her death sentence was commuted—Mrs. Robinson had largely been forgotten by the outside world. Now, with interest in the Toppan case running so high, an enterprising reporter for the *Boston Record* sought an interview with the former "poison fiend" in the hope of learning her thoughts about New England's newest celebrity killer.

Managing to gain admission to her cell during an inspection by the prison commissioners, the reporter found the forty-five-year-old multi-murderess in serene spirits—getting on "very nicely," as she herself declared. Apart from her jailhouse pallor and faded hair, she seemed healthy and content. Indeed, she had put on a good deal of flesh, a fact stressed again and again by the reporter, who appeared to be somewhat obsessed by her weight gain (or, as he euphemistically put it, "her tendency to *embonpoint*"). It seemed to strike him as a bitter irony that she should grow so fat in jail—this monstrous mother whose own children had died convulsing in digestive torment from the lethal meals she fed them.

From listening to her speak, of course, no one would have guessed at her pathology. She was perfectly composed as she conversed with the reporter. "Not a shadow of the seven relatives she sent to death with arsenic ever seems to float across her mind," he noted. "Never a sign of remorse, never a mention of their former existence to show that she ever thinks of her crimes." In the "calm blue depths of her eyes," the young man could detect no indication of madness. A stranger meeting her on the street, he asserted, "would see in her the typical church worker."

Her tiny cell was sparsely furnished with a bureau,

table, washstand, and bedstead. The walls were decorated with engraved portraits of her murdered children, clipped from newspapers, along with various small artworks brought by her son, Charles—the "last of his branch, the only one to survive her terrible death-dealing poison." The dutiful young man still visited his mother regularly, conversing with her through the mail-slot-sized opening in the steel door of her cell. Occasionally, Mrs. Robinson received visits from other callers, too—"religious people" who, in their "false zeal," believed that she had been "found unjustly guilty."

Her cell contained a window overlooking the prison yard. Flowers bloomed directly below the window, and vines clung to the wall. "But Mrs. Robinson sees them not," wrote the reporter. "The glazed glass shuts out the scene," allowing daylight into the room but affording her no glimpse of the outside world. Once a day, for the space of an hour, when the other prisoners were inside, she was allowed to take a stroll around the yard, an attendant guarding her every step.

Though she confessed that she was not especially fond of prison life, Mrs. Robinson never complained. However grim her existence, she had "never tried to escape, never thought of suicide. She calls herself a philosopher and grows fat."

The supervisor of the jail, Sheriff Fairbairn, considered her a model inmate. "Never was there a more tractable, calm, contented prisoner," he declared. "She gives no trouble and never did." When the commissioners asked if there was anything she needed, she replied that she had "everything she wanted." She enjoyed her occasional chats with the chaplain. She was permitted to borrow one book a week from the prison library. Invariably she chose religious works, her favorites being *The Lives of the Saints* and *Foxe's Book of Martyrs.* She regarded herself as a deeply devout person—"just as she did fifteen years ago," the reporter dryly noted, "when she was poisoning her own family."

As for the object of his visit—learning her thoughts on America's latest homegrown "Borgia"—the reporter came away disappointed. Shut away from the world, Mrs. Robinson had never heard of Nurse Jane Toppan—another homicidal nurturer whose own eating habits would eventually become a matter of keen public interest.

22

Prof. Wood has evidence which will prove beyond a doubt that the arsenic found in the bodies, and which caused death, was not in the preservatives injected by the undertaker. These women were murdered by the administration of arsenic which they took with their food or drink.

—District Attorney Lemuel Holmes

It was commonly believed that—like Sarah Jane Robinson and Lydia Sherman before her—Nurse Toppan had dispatched her victims with arsenic. Dr. William Lathrop, for example, was clearly operating under this assumption when he argued that, since Oramel Brigham had displayed no symptoms of "arsenical poisoning" the previous summer, his illness could not have been caused by Nurse Toppan. Neither Lathrop nor any other authority saw fit to question the findings of Professor Edward Wood of the Harvard Medical School, whose chemical analysis had turned up significant amounts of arsenic in the viscera of Genevieve Gordon and Minnie Gibbs—"enough to have depopulated the summer colony at Cataumet," according to the *Boston Globe*. Wood, after all, was the country's leading forensic expert. He had been involved in hundreds of criminal cases. His testimony had been instrumental in the conviction of Mrs. Robinson. And he had been a star witness at the most sensational murder case of the day, that of the Falls River parricide, Lizzie Borden.

It was only natural, therefore, that, in building its case against the suspect, the government began by attempting to tie Jane to the ostensible murder weapon—"to find evidence connecting Nurse Toppan to the purchase or acquisition of arsenic," as the *Boston Globe* put it. No sooner had Jane been taken into custody than detectives began visiting pharmacies in Falmouth where, according to unverified reports, she had bought her arsenic. They were hoping, the *Globe* wrote, "to locate any druggist who remembers having sold the deadly compound to Miss Toppan."

Nothing came of their efforts. Within days of Jane's arrest, papers were reporting that "there is at least one missing link in the government's chain of evidence against Miss Toppan. The government has failed to ascertain that Miss Toppan purchased at any place or any time any arsenic, the poison of which Prof. Wood says he found in the stomachs of Mrs. Gordon and Mrs. Gibbs."

There was a very good reason for this failure. Jane had never made such a purchase in Falmouth or elsewhere. In the long course of her murderous career she had never resorted to arsenic. Professor Wood, it turned out, had come to the right conclusion for the wrong reason. Jane's Cataumet victims had, in fact, been murdered—but not with arsenic.

How, then, did this substance end up in such lethal quantities in the intestines of the two sisters? The answer was provided by a gentleman named W. C. Davis. Davis (who was unrelated to the Cataumet clan murdered by Jane) was the owner of a large furniture store on Main Street in Falmouth. He was also the local undertaker, who had prepared the bodies of Minnie Gibbs and Genevieve Gordon for burial. Interviewed at his funeral parlor on Friday, November 1, Davis revealed that arsenic was a main ingredient in his embalming fluid.

Davis's revelation was a godsend for the defense. Jane's attorney, James Stuart Murphy, was now free to argue that Genevieve Gordon and Minnie Gibbs had died of natural causes, just as his client claimed, and that their organs had become infused with arsenic during the embalming process.

The press took immediate note of the state's vulnerability on this point. "It is understood here that the embalming fluid that the undertaker used in the preservation of the bodies of Mrs. Gordon and Mrs. Gibbs contained large quantities of arsenic," one newspaper reported on Saturday, November 2. "If the undertaker filled the cavities of the bodies of the members of the Davis family with fluid that contained arsenic, it is asked how can the government prove that there were traces of that poison in the body of Mrs. Gibbs before her death and that it was arsenical poisoning that caused her demise?"

In spite of this serious flaw in their case, authorities doggedly stuck to their belief that Nurse Toppan had murdered her victims with arsenic. Interviewed in Boston on Sunday, November 3, District Attorney Lemuel Holmes stated unequivocally that the "arsenic found in the intestines of the Davis sisters had been administered by way of the mouth" and "could not have been any residue of the embalming fluid."

By the following day, however, authorities were offering a revised theory. An unnamed official, quoted in the *Boston Herald*, acknowledged that the arsenic may indeed have come from W. C. Davis's embalming fluid. He pointed out, however, that Nurse Toppan was known to be in the "habit of assisting the undertaker in preparation of bodies for burial." "What would have been easier for her," he proposed, "than obtaining the arsenical solution used for embalming purposes and subsequently giving it to her patients in the Hunyadi water many of them seem to have been given?"

With the continuing failure of the police to find a druggist who had ever sold arsenic to Jane, this theory quickly gained ground, since it identified a possible source of the poison she had presumably used on her victims—a link between the suspect and the ostensible murder weapon. Without such a link, the prosecution would be forced to build its case on the notion of "exclusive opportunity"—i.e., the theory that Jane *had* to be the killer since no one else had been alone with the victims. The state wasn't eager to resort to this argument, which had been made, to no avail, at the Lizzie Borden trial.

In their blind faith in Dr. Wood, it seems never to have occurred to District Attorney Holmes or any other official that the professor was wrong and that Jane's victims hadn't been poisoned with arsenic at all. There was, however, one man who arrived at precisely that conclusion. Not only did he harbor serious doubts about Wood's findings; he had an alternate theory about Jane's MO that would prove to be startlingly correct. This unlikely individual wasn't a physician or a chemistry professor or an officer of the law. He was none other than Captain Paul Gibbs—the "bluff old veteran of the sea" (as the newspapers never tired of describing him) whose suspicions of Nurse

Toppan had helped lead to her arrest in the first place.

In their search for any scrap of information regarding Jane, reporters lost no time in tracking down Captain Gibbs. The first to interview him was a writer for the *Boston Journal*, who found the old man seated on a wheelbarrow at the sandy edge of the Drinnell estate in Cataumet, contemplating the waters of Buzzards Bay. No sooner had the reporter introduced himself than Gibbs—who hadn't seen a paper in several days—eagerly asked for the latest news about Professor Wood's analysis. The young man's reply—that massive amounts of arsenic had been found in the viscera of both Genevieve Gordon and Captain Gibbs's daughter-in-law, Minnie—left the old sailor deeply troubled.

Bowing his head, he stood silently for several moments, so deeply lost in thought that he seemed to forget about the reporter. When the latter finally asked what was wrong, Captain Gibbs shook his head and replied: "I'm surprised to hear that arsenic was detected in the bodies. I suspected that they had been poisoned, but I didn't think Jennie Toppan would use anything as easily detected as arsenic."

Even more striking than this response—which revealed a shrewder understanding of Jane's criminal cunning than the police or prosecuting attorneys seemed to possess—was the old man's next statement. When the reporter asked what sort of poison he believed Nurse Toppan had used, Captain Gibbs said that he "thought it might be found that Mrs. Gibbs and Mrs. Gordon had been killed by morphia and atropia." He then went on to explain "that atropia expanded the pupils of the eyes, whereas morphia contracted them, so that if a person had been killed by these poisons, the pupils of the eyes would practically be in their normal state, and to detect the traces of poison would naturally be very difficult."

Exactly how the long-retired fishing-boat captain knew so much about morphine and atropine was never explained. Evidently, Captain Gibbs was one of those practical, hard-headed Yankees who took a keen interest in the way things work, and who—in the course of his seventy years—had picked up information on a wide range of subjects, including the physiological effects of the opiates so freely dispensed by the physicians of his day. In any event, his speculations would turn out to be remarkably precise, putting the authoritative pronouncements of the experts to shame.

Gibbs went on to describe some of the things that had stirred his suspicions of Nurse Toppan. "She tried to make us believe that Mrs. Gordon committed suicide by taking Paris Green by injection," the old man told the reporter. "She said she threw the syringe into the lavatory." State Detective Whitney, however, had dug around in the outhouse muck and managed to locate the syringe, which had been sent to Professor Wood's laboratory for chemical analysis. No trace of the lethal insecticide had been found.

There were also the odd circumstances surrounding the shockingly abrupt death of his daughter-in-law, Minnie. According to Gibbs, the young woman was "as well as could be on the Monday before her death. We were all at Falmouth, and when we came back that evening she was lively and in the best of spirits."

The very next morning, however, Gibbs "was called to the Davis house, being told that Minnie was very sick. We knew she was not a rugged woman, but still it was strange that she could be taken so quick and in such a peculiar manner. She lay on her bed with her eyes partly open, barely breathing. I took hold of her hand and she could not speak. The next morning she was dead. Jennie Toppan had been caring for her all the time." Later that same day, Genevieve's widower, Harry, took the old captain aside and told him that, during the last hours of her illness, Minnie had seemed "afraid of Jennie Toppan, shrinking away from her whenever she came into the room."

On the subject of Jane's motives, Gibbs was firmly convinced that Nurse Toppan had perpetrated her outrages for the most mundane of reasons: money. According to the old man, Jane—who owed several hundred dollars to the Davis family—had asked Minnie to sign a paper relieving her of the debt. "This my daughter-in-law refused to do," said the old man grimly. "And so she died."

Gibbs also claimed that Alden Davis had received $500 as repayment of a loan shortly before his death. In fact, he was still carrying it around in his pocket when he took ill. The money had subsequently vanished without a trace. The old sailor insisted that Jennie Toppan—who had prepared Alden's body for burial—was "the only person who had the opportunity to take it."

Captain Gibbs's accusations—which he shared with other reporters—became immediate front-page news. "MOTIVE WAS TO GET CASH!" trumpeted the *Herald*. "DID JANE TOPPAN KILL FOR MONEY?" read the headline of the *Daily Mail*. The *Globe*—which had learned of Jane's amorous designs on Oramel Brigham (including her efforts to blackmail him by claiming that he had gotten her pregnant) ran a variation of the theme in its Saturday headline:

"MARRIAGE AND MONEY—MISS TOPPAN EVI-
DENTLY DESIRED BOTH."

Deacon Brigham himself—who had previously attributed Jane's actions to morphine addiction—now
seemed inclined to believe that she had been driven by
mercenary motives, as Captain Gibbs claimed. Jane, it
turned out, owed Brigham $800. Dr. Lathrop's opin-
ions notwithstanding, the deacon remained convinced
that he had been poisoned by Nurse Toppan the previous summer. Was it possible that she had tried to do
away with him in order to avoid repaying the debt?

Other witnesses soon came forward with tales of
Jane's "peculations," reinforcing the growing perception of her as a woman possessed by an "omnipresent
and insatiable greed for the almighty dollar" (in the
words of the *Boston Daily Advertiser*). A family friend
of Brigham's revealed that, after the sudden passing of
Mrs. Edna Bannister—Oramel's older sister, who had
died at the deacon's home while on her way to the
Buffalo Exposition—"a pocketbook belonging to her
and containing about $75 was found to be missing."
That Jane had a long history of such petty thefts
quickly became apparent. An unnamed physician who
had known her during her nursing days at Cambridge
Hospital, for example, declared that he had always
considered her "sly and deceitful and too much interested in matters that did not concern her," including
the "financial affairs" of her patients. According to
this doctor, money was always disappearing from the
sickrooms of her patients—a fact corroborated by another physician named Swan, who affirmed that there
had been constant complaints of stolen money during
Jane's stint at the hospital, not only from patients but
from other nurses as well.

Acquaintances from her vacation days in Cataumet testified that Jane's ill-gotten gains had been used to indulge her taste for high living. "All the money she ever possessed was quickly disposed of," the *Herald* reported. "It is said that she did not hesitate to spend $10 or $12 for a day's enjoyment in a carriage. Whatever she puchased was of the best. If she bought flowers, they were invariably the most choice of the season. If she purchased a box of confectionery, it was always of the finest."

As a result of her free-spending habits, her long years of "peculation" hadn't made her rich. "Whatever sums the woman may have obtained in this way," the *Herald* went on, "it is the opinion of her friends that she has comparatively little money now, probably not enough to allow her to retain the best legal counsel for her defense."

The belief that Jane was a creature compelled mostly by greed was by no means universal, however. In the view of many people, the enormity of her crimes was simply too great to be explained by her fondness for ten-dollar carriage rides and expensive candy. Every day brought new and higher estimates of her alleged victims. On Friday, the death toll stood at seven. By Saturday, three more names had been added to the "long record of mortality following Nurse Toppan's ministrations" (as the *Boston Traveler* put it): Israel and Lovey Dunham, the elderly couple she had boarded with for several years; and her old friend Myra Connors, whose position as dining hall matron at St. John's Theological School in Cambridge Jane had so desperately coveted. One day later—under the headline "DEATH LIST IS GROWING!"—the *Herald* reported that Nurse Toppan was now a suspect in no fewer than twelve cases, including that of William H. Ingraham of Watertown and another man whose identity the District Attorney refused to divulge.

That such wholesale slaughter had been committed for the sake of a few hundred dollars struck many people as flatly unbelievable. Nothing but insanity could account for evildoing on such an appalling scale.

And in fact—according to a woman named Jeannette E. Snow, who claimed to be her cousin—there was a long history of mental illness in Jane's background. Interviewed by a reporter for the *Herald*, Mrs. Snow revealed, for the first time, the basic facts of Jane's family history: her birth as Nora Kelly in Boston's North End; the early death of her "sweet-tempered" mother; her mistreatment at the hands of her father, whose extreme "peculiarities" of behavior earned him the nickname "Kelley the Crack"; and her subsequent adoption by Mrs. Abner Toppan of Lowell.

"It would not surprise me to know that Jane Toppan is insane," Mrs. Snow told the reporter. "And if she is, she inherited it from her father."

Indeed, according to Mrs. Snow, Jane had an older sister named Nellie who had gone "violently insane" in her twenties and been committed to a mental asylum for life. "When Nellie was a girl, she was one of the sweetest and prettiest little things I ever saw," Mrs. Snow told her interviewer in a sorrowful voice. "But even then there was something peculiar about her. She had a strange love for little colored children, and every time she saw one on the street, she picked it up and kissed it. When the real insanity began to show in her, she had experienced a great change, and her condition soon became so serious that she could not be looked after at home. I went to see her once when she was in the mental asylum, and I never felt so badly in my life as I did then. I gave her some fruit, and while she muttered some senseless expressions, she lifted her clothing and began to push the fruit down her stockings. Poor Nellie! She did not know me, and it was terrible to watch her idiotic actions.

"If Jane Toppan committed the crimes of which she is accused," Mrs. Snow insisted again, wiping tears from her eyes, "she has inherited insanity from the source which was responsible for her sister's condition."

Other longtime acquaintances of Jane's—including those who had kind words to say about her "jollity and bonhommie"—attested to her history of "erratic" behavior, going back to her childhood. Like Mrs. Snow, they could only conclude that—should the facts serve to show that Jane really *was* guilty—she must have been in the grip of inherited insanity: possessed, in the words of the *Boston Post,* by "a murderous mania." As that paper reported, "the theory of money troubles" was "far outweighed by the mass of evidence tending to show that Miss Toppan is classed by many people as a dangerous lunatic."

The debate over the true motive behind Nurse Toppan's atrocities—money or mania—would continue to rage for many months. It would not be fully resolved until she herself provided the answer, in a confession that would startle the experts and send shock waves throughout New England and beyond.

23

Don't blame me, blame my nature.

—JANE TOPPAN

JANE TOPPAN WASN'T THE ONLY KILLER NURSE WHO made the headlines in November 1901. In Illinois, two nurses at an insane asylum outside Chicago were accused of murdering a pair of female patients by deliberately starving them to death. The victims—Kate Neddo and Kate Kurowski—were given nothing to eat for nearly a month, beyond an occasional crust of bread and a few sips of weak tea. The motive for this outrage—according to the man who brought formal charges against the nurses, Secretary Follet Withbull of the Civil Service Reform Association—"was that the patients were especially obnoxious."

Crimes involving evil women appeared with striking frequency in the news. Under the headline "TAUNTED BY WIFE," the *Boston Globe* reported the case of a newlywed named Virginia Leslie who goaded her husband into slitting his own throat during an argument at a popular Manhattan restaurant. Another young wife, Elizabeth Habash of Boston—who, in her own words, was feeling "sulky" after a quarrel with her husband—permanently disfigured him by hurling a teacup full of carbolic acid in his face. And then there was the story headlined "VICTIM OF A WOMAN'S HATE," about Seamon L.

Witherell of Vermont, who had spent years in state prison on a phony rape charge, trumped up by a spurned lover.

Immigrants were also much in the headlines. Raids on gambling dens in Boston's Greek community ("GREEKS GRABBED!") and savage killings committed by Italians ("MURDERED ITALIAN FOUND IN BARREL!") were among the stories that conveyed a widespread anxiety about the social effects of unfettered immigration.

That anxiety was particularly acute in Jane Toppan's adopted hometown of Lowell, a manufacturing city that had experienced both a large influx of foreign-born workers and a sharp rise in crime in recent years. Two front-page stories appearing in the *Lowell Daily Mail* during the week of Jane's arrest reflected the growing concerns about the breakdown of law and order in the "spindle city" (so called because of its large number of textile mills). The first—headlined "LOWELL THE DANGEROUS"—recounted the ironic case of a New Yorker named Harry English who had come to Lowell from the sin-infested streets of Manhattan, only to be robbed and beaten in a Merrimack Street barroom.

The second described the Sunday sermon of Rev. George F. Kennegott of the First Trinitarian Congregational Church, who spoke on the subject of "crime in Lowell." The reverend stressed that—in spite of the mounting hysteria over the city's alarming moral decline—"Lowell is not a Sodom. It has not many dens of vice or sinks of iniquity. Our police department is efficient. Our city government is honest."

After offering this reassuring view, however, he immediately went on to contradict it by admitting that Lowell's "unenviable reputation" as a place of rampant criminality was not wholly unearned. "Sin in its most horrible form has visited us," he thundered. "Murder, embezzlement, and abnormal lust have raged. The same old causes—love of money, love of pleasure—are the influences that play havoc with the brain of man."

The solution proposed by Reverend Kennegott was of the sort that might be expected from a man of the cloth: self-restraint combined with religious piety. "If men would only try to live within their incomes—if men strong in passion and desire would only satisfy their desires in a normal way—if men were strong religiously—the problem would be solved. Pray to God that we may be kept clean. When temptation lures you to false pleasures, pray to God. And when you see someone taking his or her first step along the path of vice, save them with God's help at any cost."

Though he never mentioned her by name, it is hard to believe that Reverend Kennegott didn't have Nurse Toppan in mind when he delivered his sermon. Not only was the accused muti-murderess a lifelong resident of Lowell, she was a regular at Kennegott's own church, where her brother-in-law, Oramel, served as deacon.

Indeed, it was Reverend Kennegott who had delivered such an eloquent eulogy for Oramel's wife, Elizabeth, following the latter's shockingly sudden death in August 1899, while she was visiting her foster sister, Jane Toppan, in Cataumet.

Even as Reverend Kennegott was delivering his homily, religious services were taking place in the Barnstable jail, where his notorious congregant was spending her first Sunday.

The ceremony was held in the ground floor corridor, Reverend Mr. Spence of the Unitarian Church officiating. Jane, however, was not allowed to attend. Already her infamy was such that everyone wanted a glimpse of her. Her jailer, Sheriff Cash, felt that her presence would prove too disruptive, detracting attention from the minister and exposing Jane to the stares of the other prisoners.

From her cell in the southeast corner of the upper floor, Jane was completely isolated from the proceedings. She couldn't hear the prayers of the pastor or the singing of the worshipers. If she felt bad about missing the services, however, she showed no sign of it. She passed a pleasant morning, enjoying the ample breakfast prepared by Sheriff Cash's wife, who acted as the jailhouse matron.

In fact, to all outward appearances, Jane had made an easy adjustment to life behind bars. Though confined to her cell for all but one hour of the day (when she was permitted to walk up and down the corridor), she never complained about the conditions. Always an avid reader, she spent hours immersed in the women's magazines and popular novels supplied by Mrs. Cash. Her barred window afforded her a view of the railroad station, and she enjoyed watching the trains pass up and down the Cape and the people bustling to and from the depot. At mealtimes, Mrs. Cash would arrive with a tray and remain to chat while Jane tucked into the solid home-cooked fare (supplemented, as the papers reported, "with occasional dainties").

Prison life actually seemed to agree with her. With each new day, her spirits grew increasingly buoyant. Apart from her attorney and longtime friend James S. Murphy of Lowell, no outside visitors were allowed to see her. But she was not completely cut off from communication with the world. Old acquaintances wrote to her in jail. Many were former patients, offering moral support. (Jane, after all, had been a nurse for more than a decade, and—in addition to the nearly three dozen victims she had murdered for pleasure—there were scores of people she had ministered to with professional care.)

She was particularly cheered by the letters from her wealthy Cambridge clients, who—as the *Globe* wrote—"avowed their faith in her innocence and promised that they would help her secure the ablest counsel in Massachusetts." Jane diligently answered every piece of correspondence, sometimes writing until sundown.

She also spent hours poring over the papers. To be sure, there was much in the news that must have dismayed her, including virtually daily additions to the burgeoning list of murder allegations. Suspicions had now been raised about Mrs. Mary McNear, the elderly Watertown woman Jane had nursed to death in late December 1899. And more revelations about her pyromaniac tendencies were coming to light. In addition to the string of fires that had broken out on the Davis property during her summer visits, there was a report of a blaze that had mysteriously erupted the previous spring at 68 Brattle Street, Cambridge. As the *Boston Post* pointedly noted, "Miss Toppan was at the time employed in the house as a nurse, and on the evening when the fire occurred she was the sole occupant of the house."

There seemed little doubt—as the same paper observed—that Jane Toppan had been leading "a strange life, a double life, as it were":

Up to last August, Miss Toppan was thought by everyone with whom she came in contact to be a perfect example of a true, honest, conscientious Christian woman.

Today, because of the accusations hurled at her, a mass of evidence accumulates which shows her to be at least, if the stories be true, a woman entirely destitute of morals. Her episode with Deacon Brigham and her blackmailing threats were a great shock to her adherents. New reports from Cambridge add to the list. Charges are made that Miss Toppan was suspected by her patients who missed valuable articles and sums of money. Charges are also made of untruthfulness and deceit.

This is the reason people are now so willing to believe that the State has not erred in her arrest.

In spite of finding herself exposed to the world as a blackmailer, liar, and thief, however, Jane was apparently quite encouraged by the news—particularly by the ongoing failure of the police to find any conclusive way to link her to the death of Minnie Gibbs. The headline of the November 5 edition of the *Boston Post* neatly summed up the situation: "STATE HUNTS LONG BUT FINDS LITTLE." According to the story, the police were "doing their utmost to add to the array of evidence against Miss Toppan. So far, however, nothing has been obtained save a record of other mysterious deaths under her nursing, but it is doubtful this could be used as evidence in the Gibbs case. Evidence of the untruthfulness of Miss Toppan in small things, and of her great desire for money, has also been uncovered. But nothing really tending to clinch the case against her for the alleged murder of Mrs. Gibbs has come to light."

Indeed, the State's case seemed to grow shakier by the day. On Wednesday, November 6, W. C. Davis—the Falmouth undertaker who had prepared Minnie Gibbs's body for burial—told an interviewer that his embalming fluid "had been injected partially through the nostrils and down into the throat of the deceased." "Arsenic and alcohol make up the general basis of such fluids," Davis explained. "Naturally the arsenic would assert itself within a few hours and show upon all the organs of the body with which it came in contact. It would be an easy matter for the fluid to percolate in the mouth and leave evidence of arsenic." This revelation was a serious blow to District Attorney Holmes, who had been confidently declaring that—since traces of arsenic were found in her mouth and throat—Mrs. Gibbs must have been poisoned.

On the same day, Mrs. Beulah Jacobs—the Davis relation who had been staying at the Jachin House when Minnie Gibbs died—admitted to a reporter for the *Boston Traveler* that she "did not see Mrs. Gibbs take any liquid" after returning from their carriage ride to Falmouth. "Soon after entering the house," Mrs. Jacobs explained, "Minnie complained of a peculiar numb feeling in one side. I assisted her to a couch, where she sank down and soon became unconscious, even before Jennie Toppan entered the room."

As the *Traveler* pointed out, this information was "of inestimable benefit to the case of the defendant," since it raised serious doubts about the state's contention that Jane alone had the chance to kill the victim. Not only was someone else present when Minnie was stricken but—by Mrs. Jacobs's own admission—

Jane was in another part of the house when the young woman collapsed. "HENCE IT MUST BE ASKED," the paper declared, printing the question in caps to emphasize its importance, "WHAT EXCLUSIVE OPPORTUNITY WAS AFFORDED JANE TOPPAN TO POISON THE WOMAN?"

In light of this new information—which, as the *Traveler* declared, "proves most favorable to the nurse"—it is hardly surprising that Jane's lawyer and childhood friend, James S. Murphy, seemed to be brimming with optimism when he spoke to reporters on Thursday afternoon, November 7. Murphy had arrived in Barnstable that morning in preparation for the following day's hearing.

"The State, as usual, has made a great deal over the case, and dragged in outside matters which have nothing to do with the Gibbs case," Murphy declared. When a reporter asked what he meant by "outside matters," Murphy explained that he was referring to the "record of supposedly mysterious deaths under Nurse Toppan's care." These deaths, Murphy declared, were "simply a train of coincidences." It was true that "many of her patients had died one after another." He insisted, however, that "every nurse and doctor of standing has had a similar experience."

Speaking as a lifelong friend of the accused, Murphy avowed that he had "never known her to do anything which in any way reflected on her character. Her arrest was a great shock to all her friends. We will have no difficulty in proving her absolute innocence."

So confident was Murphy that the charges wouldn't stick that he didn't hesitate to offer an opinion on his client's mental condition. The debate over Jane's sanity had continued to rage, with different experts offering contradictory diagnoses. Dr. E. F. Chadbourne, for example—the physician who had treated her at Lowell General Hospital following her suicide attempts—told reporters that, while he had "found her to be suffering from nervousness," he "never detected the slightest evidence of insanity." Dr. Lathrop, on the other hand, was "inclined to the affirmative view"—i.e., that Jane was, indeed, "mentally unbalanced."

Murphy shared Chadbourne's opinion, proclaiming that he was "convinced of her mental strength. I do not believe that Miss Toppan is insane. I am not an expert, but that is my opinion."

For a defense lawyer to make such a statement was a sign of either professional incompetence or extraordinary faith in his client's innocence. After telling the world that he firmly believed she was sane, it would be very hard for him to turn around and mount an insanity defense—a stratagem that many observers believed would be Jane's only chance of escaping the gallows.

As for Jane herself, she appeared to share her attorney's serene confidence in the outcome of the case. Confined to her cell, awaiting trial, she displayed—according to a story in the *Boston Post*—not the slightest anxiety about the future:

> "You bear up well," someone said to her today.
>
> "Well, what must be, must be," replied Miss Toppan, using one of her favorite expressions.
>
> And that expression explains her whole composure and seeming indifference. For Miss Toppan is a fatalist. A Lowell friend once reproached her for telling a falsehood.

"Don't blame me, blame my nature!" exclaimed Miss Toppan. "I can't change what was meant to be, can I?"

It is this belief which enables her to smile in her prison cell, unconcerned at the dreadful shadow hanging threateningly over her. "What is to be must be."

Jane Toppan worries not for the future.

24

The preliminary hearing will be postponed to as late a date as possible, the government not being anxious to try the case until spring. The officers at work on the case say that it will likely take three or four months until they can complete their work. That the county will be put to great expense in carrying on the trial is admitted by the officers. It has been a long time since there has been a case of this magnitude in this county, and already many residents are expressing regrets that it did not happen elsewhere.

—*Boston Globe*, NOVEMBER 5, 1901

SHORTLY BEFORE 9:00 A.M. ON FRIDAY, NOVEMBER 8, Jane Toppan emerged from the jailhouse for the first time in a week. Accompanied by State Detective Letteney, her counsel, James S. Murphy, and jailer Judah Cash, she walked the short distance to the Barnstable courthouse, her gaze fixed on the ground, as though to avoid eye contact with the crowd that had turned out to gawk at her.

She was garbed in the same clothing she had worn on the day of her arrest: a dress of black cheviot, a black hat adorned with a red imitation flower, and a white lace bow tied loosely about her neck. The outfit was oddly accessorized with a high, white, standing nurse's collar—a peculiarity that caused a certain amount of comment among the spectators and received inordinate attention in the tidbit-hungry press.

The little courtroom was packed with curiosity seekers as Jane took her seat beside her lawyer. News accounts of her behavior during the proceedings differed dramatically. "MISS TOPPAN NERVOUS" the *Globe* proclaimed the following day; while the headline of the *Herald* read: "MISS TOPPAN UNCONCERNED." To one observer, she seemed "as calm as if she were simply one of the spectators, and did not seem particularly interested in what was going on." According to another, however, she "plainly evidenced the great mental strain under which she was laboring. She clutched her gloves and turned nervously in her seat and seemed to be on the point of collapsing."

The proceedings lasted less than five minutes. As expected, Judge Smith K. Hopkins—substituting for Judge Fred C. Swift of Yarmouth, who was otherwise engaged—granted another postponement, continuing the case until November 15. The only moment of interest in the otherwise perfunctory affair was provided by lawyer Murphy, who wanted more time to prepare his case. According to Murphy, he had been promised a continuance until December 4 by District Attorney Holmes. Hopkins replied that he was operating under strict instructions from Judge Swift, who had mandated "that the case should not be postponed longer than one week." The two argued back and forth for a few minutes, but Hopkins refused to be budged.

After ordering that the prisoner be held without bail until November 15, the judge ended the hearing. Once again, eyewitness accounts of Jane's reactions were wildly contradictory. "When she went from the courtroom," the *Herald* reported, "she went with a light, springy step and outside the door said something to her counsel and smiled." According to the *Globe*, however, "she could hardly keep her balance as she left the courthouse," and had to "grasp the arm of her counsel, who steadied her until she got to the jail."

All reports agreed, however, that by the time she was settled back in her cell, she had "quite recovered her composure." Later that morning, a statement was issued in her name. In it, Jane conceded that while the many sudden deaths of her friends, family members, and casual acquaintances might *seem* suspicious, there was a perfectly logical explanation for them, having to do with geography, climate, and diet.

"The fact that I am innocent will be established when the hearing is held next week," she proclaimed. "If there is any justice in Massachusetts, I shall be cleared. I cannot see how I can be convicted of a crime I never committed. I admit that the many deaths of which I am supposed to be the cause form strong circumstantial evidence, but they may have been due to many causes. All the deaths occurred in the summertime. The drinking water at Cataumet is bad. The land is low. The country is practically unwooded, and conditions favor diseases that can be transmitted through drinking water. I myself was sick at Cataumet.

"Moreover, Mrs. Brigham, Mrs. Bannister and Miss Calkins died in the intense heat of the summer, and Mr. Brigham's illness was also at this time of the year. All were of advanced age and ate freely of fruit that grew on the old place. Anyone who understands medicine or hygiene knows what this means.

"Each of the people who died I knew personally and was on friendly terms with. I would not kill a chicken."

Even as Jane was blaming her victims' deaths on everything from weather conditions to fruit, events were taking place a few miles away that would sorely test her much-noted composure.

At precisely 10:30 A.M., an inquest into the deaths of Minnie Gibbs and Genevieve Gordon got under way at Buzzards Bay, Judge Swift presiding. The proceedings were held under closely guarded conditions. No spectators or reporters were allowed to attend. Even the witnesses were kept waiting outside the courtroom until called in for questioning, one at a time.

Over the course of the following four hours, the prosecution heard testimony from more than half-a-dozen people, including Oramel Brigham, Dr. W. H. Lathrop, Captain Paul Gibbs, Beulah Jacobs, Professor Edward Wood, and medical examiner R. H. Faunce. At 2:35 P.M., the inquest was adjourned indefinitely. When District Attorney Holmes emerged from the courtroom, he was brimming with confidence, though he refused to divulge any information to the press.

Within hours of the adjournment, however, rumors were circulating that dramatic new evidence had emerged at the inquest—evidence that would seal the government's case against Jane. By the following morning—Saturday, November 9—the front pages were full of tantalizing hints of an imminent breakthrough. "SOMETHING IN TOPPAN CASE NOT YET MADE PUBLIC!" the *Herald* trumpeted. "A SENSATION PROMISED!" According to one unnamed official quoted by the paper, "The most important piece of testimony by which we hope to convict Miss Toppan has not yet been revealed to the world. When the proper time comes, it will be given out and will convince those who think we have a weak case against Miss Toppan."

The world didn't have to wait long. That very evening, the late edition of the *Boston Globe* ran a banner headline: "SECRET OUT! MORPHIA AND ATROPIA CAUSED MRS. GIBBS' DEATH! SUSPICIONS OF WOMAN'S FATHER-IN-LAW HAVE BEEN VERIFIED!"

Captain Paul Gibbs had been vindicated. After more than a week of insisting that Jane's victims had died of arsenic poisoning, the prosecution had finally acknowledged what the old sailor had been saying all along.

The change in the government's position resulted partly from a turnabout by Professor Wood, who had revised his initial opinion. Wood now agreed that the arsenic in Minnie Gibbs's body had indeed "come from the embalming fluid used by undertaker Davis and was in no wise responsible for her death." Further chemical analysis had turned up lethal traces of morphine and atropine in the victim's organs, leading him to conclude "that it was these drugs and not arsenic that killed Mrs. Gibbs."

Equally important to the government's case was the testimony of Mr. Benjamin Waters, proprietor of a pharmacy in the nearby town of Wareham. Waters told officials that, during the second week of July, Jane Toppan had telephoned his store from the Cataumet post office and "ordered a bottle of morphia tablets, the strongest kind." He had wrapped up the bottle in brown paper and shipped it to her on the next train. According to Waters, there was "enough poison in the morphia to send into eternal rest a score of persons."

Waters's story was substantiated by the Cataumet postmaster, Frank K. Irwin, who kept a record of every call placed from his establishment (which served not only as the town's post office and "telephone exchange" but also its general store). Irwin had not only noted Jane's call in his ledger but had overheard her place the order for the morphine.

Another crucial link in the State's chain of evidence was provided by a drugstore clerk named William Robinson, who recalled Jane's frequent purchases of Hunyadi mineral water. That Jane freely dispensed this beverage to her patients was confirmed by several witnesses, including Beulah Jacobs, who testified that Minnie Gibbs had been given a glassful to drink shortly before she sank into a coma and died.

Putting all these facts together, the government was now thoroughly (and correctly) convinced that it had figured out Nurse Toppan's murderous MO. Her victims, as the *Boston Post* reported, had all "died the same way—died after a poisoned glass of Hunyadi water was handed to them by Miss Toppan."

Indeed District Attorney Holmes felt so confident in the findings that, late Saturday afternoon, he announced that "the inquest will not be resumed, the government being perfectly satisfied that it has secured sufficient evidence against Miss Toppan to connect her with the death of Miss Gibbs."

Holmes had another announcement, too—even more unwelcome news for Jane and her lawyer.

He intended to order further exhumations. Sometime in the coming days, he declared, the corpses of the two elder members of the ill-fated Davis family, Alden and Mary, would be disinterred from their graves in the Cataumet cemetery and autopsied for traces of poison.

25

One may smile, and smile, and be a villain.

—SHAKESPEARE, *Hamlet*

PUBLICLY, AT LEAST, JANE'S LAWYER BRUSHED OFF THE revelations that had emerged from the inquest. "It makes me smile when I think of the stories that have been printed about the discoveries made in connection with this morphia purchase," Murphy told reporters. "I assure you that the defense is not the least bit worried about them."

Jane, too, appeared unfazed when she was next seen in public. Despite rumors that her incarceration was taking a terrible toll on her mental state— "MIND IS YIELDING!" cried the headline of the *Globe* on November 13—she seemed perfectly calm and cheerful when she emerged from the jailhouse on Friday morning, November 15, to attend her twice-postponed preliminary hearing.

Earlier that morning, shortly after eight, Murphy had arrived at her cell, bearing a large bunch of chrysanthemums and a basket of fruit for his client, who—according to reports—was "happy as a school-girl when he presented them to her."

After conferring for an hour, Jane and her counsel left the jail, accompanied by State Officer Letteney and Keeper Cash. Jane's face, according to reporters who had turned out for the event, was "wreathed in smiles." As the party made its way to the courthouse, Jane walked with such a brisk and sprightly step that she quickly outdistanced the others. Noticing how far behind they were, she came to a halt and jokingly remarked on their lagging pace.

Assembled in front of the big stone courthouse was a crowd of newspapermen, several of them wielding cameras. "Oh, look," Jane cried to Murphy. "They are trying to get a snapshot of me." Though one paper, the *Lowell Sun*, suggested that Jane was frightened of the photographers ("MISS TOPPAN STARTLED BY CAMERA FIENDS" read the headline), most observers agreed that she seemed somewhat amused to find herself the focus of such extraordinary interest.

Inside the courtroom, Jane took the same place she had occupied one week earlier. She was dressed in the identical outfit she had worn on that occasion—black dress, black hat, white tie, and incongruous collar. Hands folded on her lap, she sat calmly beside Murphy, observing the proceedings "with head erect and eyes bright" (in the words of one reporter).

Judge Fred Swift, who was already seated at the bench when the prisoner entered, promptly began the proceedings. "I will now hear what is to be said by the counsel for the prisoner as to the continuance of the case," he declared.

Rising, Murphy stated that he had arranged with the government to have the hearing continued yet again—this time until December 11—and asked the judge to grant his request. State Detective Letteney, representing the government, made no objection.

Judge Swift asked the prisoner to rise. Getting calmly to her feet, Jane looked him squarely in the face while he ordered that she be returned to jail and held there, without bail, until the agreed-upon date. With a rap of his gavel, Judge Swift then adjourned the court. The entire proceedings had lasted barely four minutes.

As Jane was escorted back across the lawn to the jailhouse, she appeared to be her old jolly self, "laughing merrily" (according to the *Globe*) as she chatted with her lawyer. Murphy remained in her cell until it was time for him to catch the 10:25 train back to Lowell. As he headed for the depot, reporters saw Jane watching him through the barred window of her cell—"casting longing glances after the one in whom she has confided all, and upon whom she relies to secure her freedom."

Accounts emanating from the jailhouse continued to stress Jane's serene acceptance of her situation. Though Keeper Cash had been ordered to keep a close eye on her because of her earlier suicide attempts, she showed no signs of depression. On the contrary, her famous "rollicking good-nature" was very much in evidence. When someone asked how she was bearing up behind bars, she reportedly replied: "Well, I am having a good rest in here, anyway."

Letters from supporters continued to arrive. A gentleman named Charles M. Dauchy—whose son had been stricken with typhoid fever during the Spanish-American War—expressed his everlasting gratitude for the "splendid care" Jane had lavished on his child. A woman named Gertrude L. Lafon, a onetime classmate at the Cambridge Hospital Training School for

Nurses, wrote to say how much she had always respected Jane.

Jane continued to find ways to beguile the time. With material furnished by the motherly Mrs. Cash, she had begun work on a new dress for herself. Seated in the morning sunshine streaming through her cell window, she contentedly plied her needle for hours at a time. She had also formed a warm attachment to Mrs. Cash's three-year-old granddaughter, Lucy, whose regular visits, according to the *Barnstable Patriot*, were "the brightest moments of Mrs. Toppan's prison life." Nearly every afternoon, the little girl would "toddle up to the cell door and, with her tiny fingers grasping the bars, stand for an hour at a time talking with the nurse."

Even the exhumations of Mr. and Mrs. Davis did not—to all outward appearances—cause her any particular consternation. The bodies were removed from their graves on the chilly, rain-swept morning of Thursday, November 21. Officials had intended to conduct the autopsies in a carriage shed adjoining the church across from the Cataumet cemetery. The little structure offered such poor protection from the weather, however, that the corpses were carried to the more sheltered precincts of the Major Allen house nearby.

Aside from several representatives of the press, those in attendance included Professor Wood, Undertaker Davis, and State Detectives Whitney and Letteney. The autopsy itself was carried out by Medical Examiner Faunce, with the assistance of Dr. C. E. Harris of Hyannis. Despite having lain in the ground for over three months, the bodies, according to witnesses, were "in a remarkable state of preservation."

The livers and stomachs were removed and given over to Professor Wood for transportation back to his lab at Harvard. Wood—who promised to "make all possible haste" with his analysis—estimated that his report would be ready in "less than two weeks," in plenty of time for Jane's rescheduled hearing.

Since Alden Davis's death had been officially attributed to cerebral hemorrhage, his skull was sawn open and his brain examined. Even at a glance, it was clear that the diagnosis on his death certificate was wrong. The brain showed no sign of ruptured blood vessels. "NOT DUE TO APOPLEXY," proclaimed the headline of the next day's *Herald*. "SOMETHING ELSE CAUSED ALDEN DAVIS' DEATH." That "something," of course, was now believed to be Nurse Toppan's lethal cocktail of poisoned mineral water. The discovery was a further boon to the state and a blow to the defense. Surely, the paper conjectured, news of this development would "cause Miss Toppan to lose the cheerfulness that has characterized her since she was last brought before the district court."

But the paper was wrong. According to Mrs. Cash—who was pumped by reporters each day for any scrap of information concerning the celebrity inmate—Jane's spirits remained as upbeat as ever.

If there was anything that worried her it was money. By all accounts, she was completely broke. Though she had earned a respectable income as a private nurse, she had nothing to show for her years of employment—no savings, no jewelry, no property. The financial support promised by her wealthy Cambridge friends had not materialized.

In the view of certain sympathizers, her circumstances made it impossible for her to mount a proper defense. Even her childhood friend James Murphy was representing her for free. A few days after her latest appearance in court, reports began to surface that the government itself might come to the aid of Nurse Toppan by assigning a number of state detectives to work on her behalf.

Since the government was, of course, intent on convicting her, this suggestion struck many people as highly peculiar. There was, however, a precedent for it. Eighteen years earlier, a sensational crime had occurred in the Boston area. A Watertown woman named Carleton had been brutally slain in the doorway of her own home, her skull crushed with a granite paving stone. Eventually, a man named Roger Amero was arrested for the crime. Unable to hire his own investigators, the penniless Amero appealed to then-governor Benjamin Butler, who agreed to put a pair of state detectives at the disposal of the defense. Pitted against members of their own force—who were doing their best to establish his guilt—the detectives managed to dig up enough evidence to win Amero's release.

With this episode in mind, one anonymous source close to the Toppan case argued that the same governmental assistance should be offered to Jane Toppan:

> Anyone who follows trials closely knows that it will take considerable time to reach the trial stage. The Grand Jury will not take up the case for months, and counsel will not be assigned until after the indictment. In the meantime, the State will be hard at work perfecting its case. The best

detective talent will be employed to this end.

If Miss Toppan is guilty of one-half the crimes which have been charged and implied against her, no punishment is too severe for her. In Massachusetts, however, a defendant is looked upon as innocent until proven guilty. Therefore, in the eyes of the law, Miss Toppan is an innocent woman. But she is deprived because of her incarceration, as well as because of her lack of means of seeking out evidence which might be of vital importance at her trial. The Commonwealth of Massachusetts can afford to be generous. At least it can afford to be fair. It has a large force of detectives whose business it is to investigate crimes and apprehend criminals. Two of the force are at work on perfecting the prosecution's case. Would it not be a magnanimous act if some of the other officers should be placed at Miss Toppan's disposal to look up evidence in her defense?

In truth, however, the government had no interest in assisting Miss Toppan. On the contrary. Even as this high-minded proposal was being bruited about in the press, District Attorney Holmes was planning a little surprise for Jane and her lawyer—a move that would catch them completely off-guard and place them at a distinct legal disadvantage.

The world learned the news before Jane did. In an extra that hit the streets late on Tuesday, December 3, the *Globe* announced a "decidedly sensational and unexpected move" on the part of the prosecution. Instead of waiting until April—when the Barnstable grand jury met for its regular session—District Attorney Holmes had taken the highly unusual step of summoning a special session. It was to be held in just a few days' time, on Friday morning, December 6.

This maneuver was clearly designed to "outflank" the defense (as the *Globe* put it). It was Holmes's way of avoiding the preliminary hearing, at which he would be required to reveal his evidence against the accused in district court. Both Jane and her lawyer had been counting on the hearing for precisely that reason—i.e., to get a preview of the prosecution's case. The hearing—already postponed twice—was scheduled for December 11. With the special grand jury convening on the 6th, however, there was no longer any need for the formality of a hearing at all.

The surprising step taken by Holmes thus deprived the defense of an important tactical advantage. Instead of tipping its hand in open court, the state would be able to lay out its findings in secret.

Jailer Cash had received word of this development early Tuesday morning, but had decided to withhold it from Jane, preferring that her lawyer break the bad news to her. Cash felt sure that this surprising turn would come as a serious blow to Jane, who seemed convinced that she would soon be out of jail. She had been planning to make a statement on her own behalf at the hearing, and was confident that the judge would release her on bail.

Just a few days earlier, while enjoying the Thanksgiving meal prepared by Mrs. Cash, Jane had jokingly remarked that "it was the first holiday she had ever spent in jail," but that she expected to be back home in Lowell in time to share Christmas dinner with her friends. Mrs. Cash's granddaughter, Lucy, was standing outside the cell at the time. Fingers gripping the bars, the child beamed with excitement as the kindly, round-faced woman she called "Jennie" promised to send her a special gift for Christmas.

Now, it seemed certain that "Jennie" and her new little friend were both in for a grave disappointment.

26

—◊—

The slow clanging of a harsh-toned bell at 9 o'clock announced to Miss Toppan that the superior court of the
county had assembled to hear her case. The bell was in
the tower of the little courthouse opposite the dreary-
looking jail, and the brisk, cold northeast wind which
blew down the bay sent the sounds of its funeral-like
tolling reverberating through the sand dunes.

—*Boston Herald,* DECEMBER 6, 1901

THE TWENTY-THREE MEMBERS OF THE GRAND JURY
came from towns all over the Cape—Brewster and
Bourne, Truro and Chatham, Orleans and Eastham,
Harwich and Mashpee, Wellfleet and Provincetown.
Some arrived in Barnstable County late Thursday afternoon, putting up overnight at a hotel in Hyannis.
Others waited until the last minute. When the bell
tolled in the tower of the Barnstable courthouse at
nine o'clock the next morning, three of the jurymen—William Chadwick and Daniel Phillips, both of
Falmouth, and Horace Percival of Sandwich—had yet
to arrive, though they made their appearance shortly
thereafter.

Chief Justice Albert Mason (who had traveled from
his home in Brookline) opened the court promptly
at 9:00. The venerable white-haired clerk, Smith K.
Hopkins, announced the start of the session, after
which Rev. Albert H. Spence of the Barnstable Uni-

tarian Church offered a prayer. The chief justice gave
the jurors no instructions, beyond advising them to
listen attentively "to such matters as the district attorney might lay before them."

The twenty-three jurymen then filed downstairs to
the same little courtroom in which Jane's previous appearances had taken place. The courtroom was cleared
of all spectators, and the doors closed. The witnesses
were sequestered in the judge's chambers. At precisely
9:15, District Attorney Holmes began his presentation
of the case.

The witnesses were brought into the courtroom
one at a time. Professor Wood entered first, carrying a
large suitcase. He emerged thirty minutes later and
was followed by Professor W. P Whitney of the Massachusetts General Hospital, who had assisted Medical
Examiner Faunce with the autopsies of the Davis family. Professor Wood was then called back inside the
courtroom for some follow-up questioning. By ten
o'clock, both Wood and Whitney had completed their
testimony. Ignoring the shouted questions of reporters gathered in the hallway, they proceeded directly to the train station to catch the 10:15 back to
Boston.

Beulah Jacobs was next. She remained inside for
more than two hours. She was followed by Officer
Letteney and General Josephus Whitney, both of the
state detective force. The latter had just completed his
testimony when the chief justice ordered a break for
lunch.

Oramel Brigham opened the afternoon session. He
was done at three o'clock, at which point Benjamin
Waters—the Wareham druggist who had sold morphine to Jane—was expected to testify.

He never got the chance.

Before he was summoned inside, the courtroom door flew open. District Attorney Holmes came striding out and went hurrying upstairs to the chief justice's private quarters. The two men remained closeted for nearly an hour.

In the meantime, the jurors began to drift from the courtroom and make their way to the treasurer's office to receive their per diem pay. Word quickly spread among the reporters. No further witnesses would be called; the grand jury had heard all the testimony it needed to.

Someone was sent to the jail to notify Keeper Cash. At 5:00 P.M., the jurymen—who had been milling about the corridors for forty-five minutes—were called back inside the courtroom. No sooner had they seated themselves than Jane Toppan—accompanied by her lawyer and flanked by a pair of deputy sheriffs— was escorted into the room.

Under the close scrutiny of the newspapermen (who were permitted to witness this portion of the proceedings), Jane strode briskly to her place and seated herself between the two deputies. The reporters studied her face for any signs of anxiety but saw none. Head high, she fixed her eyes on Chief Justice Mason and did not shift her gaze until the clerk, Smith K. Hopkins, turned to the jury foreman, Herman Cook, and said: "Mr. Foreman, have you anything to report to the Court?"

"We have, sir," said Cook. He then handed a batch of typewritten papers to Hopkins, who passed them to the judge without so much as glancing at them.

At that moment, District Attorney Holmes rose to his feet.

"May it please the Court," he said. "The grand jury has reported the indictments against the defendant, and I ask that she now be arraigned."

With a slight bow of the head, Chief Justice Mason handed the papers back to the clerk.

"Jane Toppan," intoned Hopkins.

Rising quickly, Jane placed her hands on the railing and stared intently at the wizened clerk.

Squinting down at the first indictment, the old man began to read. In the fading twilight, he had difficulty making out the words. Eventually, a kerosene lamp was brought in. Even so, the reading was a painful affair, Hopkins stammering and stumbling through the tortuous legalese of the indictment:

> The jurors for the Commonwealth of Massachusetts on their oath present: That Jane Toppan, late resident of Cambridge, in the County of Middlesex and Commonwealth aforesaid, on the twelfth day of August in the year of our Lord one thousand nine hundred and one, at Bourne, in the County of Barnstable aforesaid, in and upon one Mary D. Gibbs, did feloniously, wilfully and of her malice aforethought did make an assault, and to her, the said Mary D. Gibbs, did feloniously, wilfully and of her malice aforethought then and there give and administer, in some way and manner and by some means to the jurors aforesaid unknown, a certain large quantity, to wit: ten grains of a certain deadly poison called morphine, she, the said Jane Toppan, then and there well knowing the same to be a deadly poison, with the intent that the said Mary D. Gibbs should then and there take and swallow down the

same into her body; and that the said Mary D.
Gibbs the said morphine, so given and administered as aforesaid, did then and there take and
swallow into her body, the said Mary D. Gibbs
not then and there knowing the same to be a
deadly poison; by means whereof the said Mary
D. Gibbs became mortally sick and distempered
in her body, and the said Mary D. Gibbs of the
poison aforesaid, so by her taken and swallowed
down as aforesaid, and of the sickness and dis-
temper occasioned thereby, from the said twelfth
day of August in the year aforesaid until the thirteenth day of August in the year aforesaid at
Bourne aforesaid, in the County of Barnstable
aforesaid, did languish, and languishing did live;
on which thirteenth day of August in the year
aforesaid at Bourne aforesaid, in the County of
Barnstable aforesaid, the said Mary D. Gibbs of
the poison aforesaid, and of the sickness and dis-
temper occasioned thereby, died. And so the jurors aforesaid, on their oath aforesaid, do say that
the said Jane Toppan in manner and form aforesaid, the said Mary D. Gibbs, feloniously, wilfully
and of her malice aforethought did poison, kill
and murder, against the peace of the said Commonwealth and contrary to the form of the
statute in such case made and provided. . . .

As Hughes read, the reporters scribbled away, furiously transcribing the gist of the indictment in their
notebooks. Stripped of its jargon, the document
charged Jane with murdering the older Davis sister,
Mary "Minnie" Gibbs, by giving the unsuspecting
woman massive doses of morphine and atropine.

It took Hopkins almost fifteen minutes to make his way through the four-page indictment. By then, Jane (along with most of the other people in the room) was showing signs of strain.

There were still two more indictments to go. Before Hopkins could begin on the next one, Jane's lawyer sprang to his feet and, on behalf of his client, waived the reading of the other indictments.

"They are practically the same," he said, "and I do not see the necessity of reading them."

To the undoubted relief of everyone present, Chief Justice Mason readily agreed.

Turning to Jane, Hopkins then asked if she were guilty or not guilty of the charge according to the Gibbs indictment.

In a clear, calm voice—loud enough, according to one reporter, "to be heard almost in the corridor"— Jane replied: "Not guilty."

She was then informed that she had also been charged with the murders of Alden Davis and Genevieve Gordon.

Again Jane replied "Not guilty" when asked how she pleaded to each charge.

The proceedings lasted only a few minutes longer. Reseating herself, Jane listened calmly, hands folded in her lap, as Murphy asked the Court to "assign senior counsel" for his client, who, he explained, "was absolutely without financial resources."

"You say she has no money?" Chief Justice Mason asked.

"Yes, sir," said Murphy.

"Very well," said the judge. "The Court will take the matter under advisement."

A few seconds later, Mason dismissed the grand

jury and Jane Toppan was escorted back to her cell.

Immediately after the arraignment, the district attorney was besieged by reporters, clamoring for details. Holmes declined to comment on the proceedings. He did, however, offer a prediction that would prove to be extraordinarily inaccurate: "Now that we have Miss Toppan indicted," he declared, "there is much to be done to substantiate what we have charged, and I can safely say that when the case reaches the court, it will mean one of the longest trials Massachusetts has ever known."

The following morning, reporters grilled the jailer's wife, Mrs. Cash, about Nurse Toppan's state of mind. Surely, after the findings of the grand jury, Jane's famous composure had finally cracked? Surely she had passed a terrible night after being formally charged with so many counts of premeditated murder?

Mrs. Cash, however, quickly put these speculations to rest. After returning to her cell, Jane and her lawyer had held a lengthy consultation. Later, the portly nurse had polished off her dinner with her usual gusto. When Mrs. Cash came by to collect the dishes, Jane had seemed perfectly calm, even cheerful. The two women had chatted for a while.

Then Jane had retired early and—so far as Mrs. Cash could tell—had slept the sleep of the just.

PART FIVE

—⚏—

A POISONED MIND

27

How can I be insane? When I killed the people, I knew I was doing wrong.

—JANE TOPPAN

GIVEN THE PERENNIAL HUMAN FASCINATION WITH SENSA-tional crime, it's hardly surprising that the New England press played up the Toppan story for all it was worth. Then as now, serial murder sold papers, and the competition among Boston's various dailies was intense. The *Globe*, the *Post*, the *Herald*, the *Traveler*, the *Transcript*, the *Journal*, the *Daily Advertiser*, the *Morning Journal*, the *Evening Transcript*—all vied with each other for the attention (and the pennies) of the public. Every wild rumor and unsubstantiated charge became the basis of a blaring headline, and when dramatic new revelations were in short supply, reporters occasionally resorted to sheer fabrication (several supposedly exclusive jailhouse interviews with Jane, for example, turned out to be completely trumped-up).

With the handing-down of the indictments, however, the Toppan story disappeared for a time from the front pages. Only one significant bit of news found its way into the papers during the winter. In January, Chief Justice Mason granted James Murphy's request and named a new lawyer—Fred M. Bixby—to defend Jane. Justice of the Brockton police court and a summer resident of Hyannis, Bixby was known—in the words of the *Brockton Enterprise*—for his "good working knowledge of the law, good abilities as a public speaker, and a remarkable capacity for seeing a point quickly and turning it promptly to his own advantage. He has the gift of humor, he can wound with ridicule, and he can be impressively eloquent when occasion demands." He had served as junior counsel in a case that had received a good deal of local attention some years earlier—the trial of a man named Arthur Albee for the murder of a barber named Leaman. Thanks in large measure to Bixby's efforts, Albee had been acquitted.

Apart from Bixby's appointment, however, there were no new developments in the Toppan case for months following her arraignment. It was not until the spring of 1902 that her name reappeared in the news. On the last day of March, papers reported that Jane had undergone an intensive psychiatric examination by a panel of experts, who had determined that she was insane.

Contrary to the earlier statements of District Attorney Holmes—who had confidently predicted that her trial would be "one of the longest" ever conducted in Massachusetts—it now appeared likely that Jane Toppan might not be tried at all.

Dr. Henry Rust Stedman was one of Boston's most distinguished psychiatrists (or "alienists," as they were commonly referred to back then). A native of Boston, he received his bachelor's degree from Harvard in 1871, then entered its medical school, graduating four years later at the age of twenty-six after surgical and medical service at Massachusetts General and Boston City hospitals.

After a period of private practice, he embarked on the study of psychiatry. He spent five years as Assistant Superintendent of the Danvers State Hospital for the Insane before moving to Great Britain, where he served as clinical assistant in the Edinburgh Royal Asylum and the West Riding Asylum at Yorkshire, England.

By 1884, he was back home in Boston, where he established the Bournewood Hospital, a private facility for the treatment of nervous and mental diseases. For thirty-four years, he would serve as superintendent and resident physician at Bournewood (which remains in operation to this day). A frequent contributor to the literature of mental diseases, Stedman served as president of the American Neurological Association, the New England Society of Psychiatry, and the Boston Society of Psychiatry and Neurology. Often called upon for his medicolegal opinions, he had taken part in many highly publicized trials.

Sometime at the beginning of the new year, District Attorney Holmes and Jane's new senior counsel, Fred Bixby, approached Attorney General Parker with a proposal. To avoid the usual, befuddling courtroom situation—in which the opposing sides trotted out their respective expert witnesses to offer completely contradictory testimony—Bixby and Holmes wished to appoint an impartial commission of "insanity experts" to diagnose Jane's mental condition "with reference to her responsibility."

After considering the matter for several weeks, Parker agreed. Stedman was a natural choice for the commission. On March 20, 1902—along with two other prominent alienists, doctors George F. Jelly of Boston and Hosea M. Quinby, superintendent of the

Worcester Hospital for the Insane—he arrived at the Barnstable jail to conduct a series of interviews with the infamous killer nurse.

At first, Jane seemed suspicious of the doctors, treating them warily and giving terse, grudging answers to their questions. It wasn't long, however, before she loosened up and (as Stedman later explained in a paper he presented to the American Medico-Psychological Association) "talked freely, volubly, and intelligently." The calm, almost breezy, acceptance of her situation that reporters had noted since her arrest was very much in evidence. She appeared, as Stedman put it, "quite indifferent to her situation, and seemed to regard our visits as pleasant breaks in her monotonous life."

Several aspects of Jane's unwholesome personality quickly manifested themselves. There was, to begin with, the deep well of spite—even malignity—that lay just beneath the genial surface. "Her utter mendacity and disposition to speak slurringly of even her best friends and to make accusations against them, almost without exception—to praise one minute and blame the next—was very marked," Stedman noted.

Though not clinically delusional, she was certainly a pathological liar, making many of the same outrageous claims she had been asserting since childhood: that her father had resided in China, for example, and that her sister had broken the heart of an English lord. She also spoke emphatically "of her horror of the dead, which was so great that she sometimes fell senseless at the mere sight of a corpse"—this despite the irrefutable fact that, as Stedman noted, "she had often laid out dead bodies as a matter of course" in her capacity as private nurse.

About her guilt Jane also continued to prevaricate—though only for a while. At first, she stoutly denied that she had committed any of the crimes with which she was charged. Finally, however, the truth came spilling out.

Stedman and his colleagues had arrived in Barnstable knowing full well that Nurse Toppan was a criminal of an usually—even uniquely—pernicious stripe. They had, after all, been given full access to the evidence collected by the prosecution since the start of its investigation. And so they were unsurprised when Jane freely confessed to both pyromania and multiple murder. Even the number of homicides she initially admitted to—twelve—did not come as a shock, since government investigators had concluded by then that she was responsible for at least that number of deaths.

What Stedman and his colleagues weren't wholly prepared for was the manner in which she related her crimes, as well as certain details that she divulged for the first time. These factors, even more than the sheer number of her enormities, would ultimately determine their diagnosis.

Once Jane started to speak about her murders, she did so, in Stedman's words, with "utter calmness." She described the deaths of her victims in a perfectly matter-of-fact way, adding what the psychiatrist described as occasional "eulogistic remarks," i.e., fond reminiscences of the patients who had met such tragic deaths. She spoke of them as her friends, and "denied any hostility on either her side or theirs."

At the same time, she displayed "not the slightest sign of remorse" for her murders. On the contrary, "for much of the time during the interviews she manifested a lack of seriousness and often a levity which was in marked contrast to what was to be expected of one who had been brought to confess so many heinous crimes."

Even Jane seemed somewhat nonplused by her lack of normal human responses. "When I try to picture it," she told Stedman, "I say to myself, 'I have poisoned Minnie Gibbs, my dear friend. I have poisoned Mrs. Gordon. I have poisoned Mr. Davis and Mrs. Davis.' This does not convey anything to me, and when I try to sense the condition of the children and all the consequences, I cannot realize what an awful thing it is. Why don't I feel sorry and grieve over it? I cannot make sense of it at all."

When pressed for details of her crimes, Jane was only of limited help. She could not remember all the specifics because murder had become so routine. Poisoning, as she put it, "had become a habit of her life."

Those facts she did provide, however, were deeply unsettling. There was nothing rash or frenzied about her murders. She planned them carefully and carried them out in a perfectly "calm and clear-headed" way. After doctoring a glass of mineral water with poison and making sure that her victim drank every last drop of the lethal brew, "she always experienced great relief and went to bed and slept soundly." In the same bizarrely nonchalant tone, she revealed to the startled psychiatrists that she was in the habit of "laying in bed with the patient she had just poisoned." Even more grotesque was her admission that, after administering poison to Minnie Gibbs, she had "taken [the latter's ten-year-old son, Jesse] to bed with her." This claim seemed so incredible that investigators subsequently took pains to verify it by interviewing the boy, and in the paper he later presented to the American Medico-

Psychological Association, Stedman went out of his way to emphasize that this appallingly perverse incident was "*a fact.*"

Stedman and his colleagues, however, were even more shocked by the motive Jane finally gave for her crimes. When pressed as to "what prompted her acts," the plump middle-aged spinster let loose "with a shameless recital of a story of sexual excitement occurring in the presence of a dying person." She was driven to murder by "an irresistible sexual impulse." This need had grown increasingly powerful over the past year, and during the preceding summer she "had let herself go."

So "startling" was this admission (in Stedman's words) that he and his colleagues were reluctant to believe it. They had never heard of anything like it. There is something quaint in Stedman's insistence that—as he wrote in his paper—Jane's "representations as to the nature of this impulse and the conditions attending it were so at variance with any known form of sexual perversion that feigning was suspected by her interviewers." Clearly, these proper physicians from Puritan Boston were unfamiliar with Krafft-Ebing's *Psychopathia Sexualis*, whose pages are full of precisely such creatures as Jane Toppan—homicidal sadists who derive the greatest ecstasy from making other people die.

Beyond what Jane herself described as "the desire to experience sexual excitement by killing people," she had no explanation for her criminal behavior. "Something comes over me, I don't know what it is," she said. "I seem to have a sort of paralysis of thought and reason. I have an uncontrollable desire to give poison without regard to consequences. I have no objection against telling my feelings, but I don't know my own mind. I don't know why I do these things."

It did not take long for Stedman and his colleagues to reach a consensus on Jane's mental state. Their joint opinion was reported to the attorney general during the last week of March. Its main points, as summarized by Stedman, were as follows:

1. The prisoner, Jane Toppan, comes of a family in which intemperance and mental weakness and disorder are prominent disease features.
2. Her utter lack of moral sense has been evident from childhood in her incorrigible proclivity to falsehood, dishonesty, and mischief-making, general unreliability and probable theft. The good moral, mental, and religious training which she received in her youth resulted in no modification of her character, and were practically thrown away on her in that respect.
3. Her moral insensibility is further apparent in the absence of sense of fear before, during, or after the commission of her crime, and of remorse, sorrow, or genuine affection at any time. This defect is even more forcibly shown by the fact that her chief victims were her especial friends.
4. Her lack of any appreciation of her situation, her levity under such circumstances, and her inability to realize the enormity of her deeds are strong evidence of mental weakness.
5. That an irresistible propensity propelled her to crimes of arson and murder is shown by

the great frequency and variety of such acts
and her continuance in them, regardless of
consequences.

6. There is an absence of any apparent motive
   for her criminal acts in some cases, and inade-
   quacy of motive in many of the others. This
   is shown in the total lack of evidence of
   pecuniary gain or satisfaction in revenge as
   a rule, except minor thefts and transient
   enmity. These would be powerless with
   sane criminals as an incentive to habitual
   homicide.

7. The prisoner's disease-history and present
   mental state correspond with a well-recog-
   nized form of mental disease of a moral type
   due to congenital degeneration, in which
   there may be little or no intellectual disturbance that is apparent to the ordinary
   observer.

The mental features described in this summation—
the congenital duplicity; the complete lack of any
"moral sense"; the inability to feel either empathy or
remorse; the bizarre sangfroid under intensely stressful
conditions; the absence of any apparent "intellectual
disturbance"—are, of course, the classic hallmarks of
what we now call the psychopathic personality. In the
era of Jane Toppan, that phrase had not yet come into
use. Back then, the condition was technically known
as "moral insanity" (or "moral imbecility").

In his paper to the American Medico-Psychological
Association, Stedman devotes a considerable amount
of space to defining of that term, which he describes
in the following way:

These patients have good memory and understanding, ability to reason and contrive, much
cleverness and cunning, and a general appearance of rationality, coexistent with very deficient
control, absence of moral sense and human sentiments and feelings, perverted and brutal in-
stincts, and propensities for criminal acts of various kinds which may be perpetrated deliberately
and cleverly planned, yet committed with little
or no motive and regardless of the consequences
to themselves and others.

It would be hard to find a more concise description
of a criminal psychopath than this one. The real question, however, had to do with Jane's responsibility.
Stedman and his colleagues had no doubt that Nurse
Toppan was—as they stated in their report—a "moral
monster." But was she legally insane? Jane herself insisted that she could not possibly be insane because
she knew that she was "doing wrong" and had gone
to great lengths to avoid detection. And, indeed—
since sanity is generally defined as the ability to distin-
guish right from wrong—it is exceptionally difficult
for even the most egregious serial killers to plead insanity for precisely that reason. However horrific their
atrocities, the mere fact that they have taken pains to
conceal their crimes and evade capture proves that
they know that they have been engaged in wrongdoing.

Stedman and his colleagues recognized that Jane's
intellectual faculties were unaffected by her moral degeneracy—that, in perpetrating her crimes, she had
exercised "a cool judgment, sagacious and sound" (to
quote from Herman Melville's memorable description

of the psychopathic villain of *Billy Budd*). And so the conclusion they ultimately reached was somewhat surprising: "Therefore," they wrote, "we are of the opinion that the prisoner, Jane Toppan, was insane and irresponsible at the time of the homicide with which she is charged, and is so now; that her disease being constitutional, she will never recover; and that if ever at large again she would be a constant menace to the community."

Though the shocking details of the report were kept from the public, the gist of it became known in mid-April. As the *Barnstable Patriot* announced on the 14th, Nurse Toppan had been "officially adjudged insane by the three alienists secured by the State to investigate her mental condition."

The immediate and general belief was that there would be no trial. "It is expected that the Judge of the Superior Court will be asked by the District Attorney to dispose of Miss Toppan's case by committing her to an asylum," the *Patriot* reported. For the residents of Barnstable, this came as welcome news. For months, people had been grumbling about the fiscal burden of the case. The investigation had already cost taxpayers a considerable sum, and the local newspaper estimated that "if Miss Toppan is tried, the expense to Barnstable County will be in the vicinity of $15,000"—a substantial amount in 1902 dollars.

It was with a mixture of disappointment and relief that the citizens of Barnstable read the story that the *Patriot* ran on April 28. A trial would be held after all. After consulting with District Attorney Holmes and Fred Bixby, Attorney General Parker had "decided that Miss Toppan will be taken into court at Barnstable and evidence given about the crimes with which she is charged and about her moral and mental condition." Parker made this decision because he didn't want to establish a precedent. "If Miss Toppan were committed without the evidence being passed upon by a jury," he explained, "the same privilege might be demanded by some future defendant which the government might not feel like conceding."

The good news was that the proceedings were not expected to take long. Fred Bixby told a reporter for the *Brockton Enterprise*, "The trial of Miss Toppan will be very brief. My client will presumably be found not guilty by reason of insanity and will then be committed to an asylum, either the Worcester Insane Hospital or the Taunton Insane Asylum—and if she goes to either, it will be to pass the remainder of her life."

28

Her mania, as discovered by the medical commission, has no parallel in the history of extraordinary crimes and criminals in this country. To find an analogous case, one must go to the most degenerate localities of Europe and read the reports of scientists of most revolting passions that incited successions of murders that appeal only to psychologists.

—*Boston Globe,* JUNE 23, 1902

FOR WEEKS PRECEDING THE START OF NURSE TOPPAN'S trial, the people of Barnstable, it seemed, could talk of little else. Even the trial of the Pocasset fanatic Charles Freeman for the sacrificial murder of his four-year-old daughter hadn't generated as much excitement. Sightseers from up and down the Cape came to view the gray, Greek Revival courthouse, its four fluted columns half-concealed by shade trees. Even villagers who had passed by the building all their lives now paused to gaze at the place where the greatest murderess of the age would be brought before a jury during the last week of June 1902.

On the day before the trial, curiosity-seekers by the score poured into Barnstable. By Sunday evening, every vacant room within a mile of the courthouse had been rented out. The *Boston Post* reported that farmers were "sleeping in their kitchens and letting their own bedchambers." Even so, there were not

nearly enough rooms to accommodate the crush of
visitors. Dozens of people were forced to seek quarters in Hyannis, five miles away. Others chose to
forgo lodgings at all. One party of women—
determined to secure the best seats in the house—
arrived from Truro late Sunday afternoon and
camped out overnight on the courthouse lawn. To
cater to the crowd, a lunch counter was set up in the
corridor of the courthouse.

That the impending trial had provoked such intense fascination was only to be expected. Though
the details of the alienists' report had not been made
public, enough information had leaked out to the
public to make it clear that Jane Toppan was a monster whose crimes had no precedent—at least in this
country. To find parallels to her atrocities, the *Boston
Globe* suggested, one would have to turn to scientific
accounts of European serial killers—degenerate for-
eigners whose "revolting passions" incited them to
commit "successions of murders." In America, there
were no analogous cases at all—with one possible exception. "The nearest approach to it," the *Post* noted,
"is that of Jesse Pomeroy"—the notorious "Boston
Boy-Fiend," whose mutilation murders of young children, perpetrated in the early 1870s, had terrorized
the city.

Despite the *Post*'s insistence that such "revolting"
matters could "appeal only to psychologists," these
tantalizing hints about the appalling nature of Jane's
crimes were guaranteed to inflame the prurient interest of the God-fearing, law-abiding folk of New England. Those who flocked to Barnstable to have their
morbid curiosity fully gratified, however, were
doomed to disappointment. "So horrible is the plain,

unvarnished description of Miss Toppan's homicidal mania," declared the *Post*, "that it is doubtful if only the most general terms can be used to indicate its character to the jurors."

Nevertheless, the journey to Barnstable was clearly worth the trouble for many people. Even if the juicy details of Jane's atrocities were to be withheld from them, they would still get something deliciously titillating from the trip—a first-hand glimpse of one of the most depraved murderers the country had ever produced.

The village was astir early on June 23, a warm, sparkling Monday. The sun had barely risen when spectators began swarming into town. Within a few hours, the lawn that stretched between the jail and courthouse was packed. The jurors began arriving around 7:00 A.M., some by carriage, others on the morning train from Provincetown.

A second train—this one from Boston—steamed into the Barnstable depot at around 9:40 A.M. Most of the court officials were on board, along with nearly all the witnesses, including Harry Gordon, Professor Wood, Mrs. Beulah Jacobs, Oramel Brigham, State Detective Whitney, and the three alienists, Drs. Stedman, Jelly, and Quinby.

The iron doors of the courthouse swung open at precisely nine o'clock. Within minutes the gallery was filled to capacity—the floor being reserved for the fifty-five prospective jurymen and nearly thirty-five witnesses. Shortly before 10:00, the two judges who were to hear the case—Charles U. Bell and Henry K. Braley—entered. Following the roll call of the jurors, Rev. Mr. Spence of the Unitarian church offered a prayer. Attorney General Parker then asked that Assistant District Attorney General of Fall River be appointed to assist him. The request was promptly granted by the court.

Then, straining forward in their seats for a better view, the spectators fixed their eyes on the doorway to watch Jane Toppan make her entrance.

Prisoners were normally awakened at 6 A.M., but Jane was allowed to sleep late on the morning of the trial. The day was bound to be long and stressful, and the kind-hearted matron, Mrs. Cash, persuaded her husband to grant Jane an extra hour of rest.

When Mrs. Cash showed up with the breakfast tray, Jane seemed her usual composed, carefree—and ravenous—self. The hearty meals she had been devouring for the past eight months—combined with an almost complete lack of physical activity—had produced the inevitable result. Always plump, she now bordered on the obese, having gained nearly fifty pounds since her last appearance in public.

As Mrs. Cash seated herself on the chair beside the prisoner's cot, Jane dug into the heaping plateful of eggs and hashed potatoes, making cheery small talk between mouthfuls. The coming events of the day seemed the last thing on her mind.

Indeed, for the past few weeks, Jane had seemed much less preoccupied with her looming trial than with her current literary undertaking. For months, she had been working on a book. It was not—as might have been expected—an autobiography or jailhouse memoir, but rather a love story. Since girlhood, Jane had been an avid reader of the cloyingly sentimental fiction of the day—books with titles like *A Noble*

Heart and *When Love Commands.* She had long as-
pired to become a writer of popular romance herself.
Even on her long watches during her student-nursing
days, she had often stolen off to a remote corner of
the hospital and worked on her writing. At Cataumet,
she was often seen "scribbling" in a notebook (as
Captain Paul Gibbs told reporters).

With so much time on her hands, Jane had set
about writing in earnest, and in recent weeks, her
novel seemed to be all she could think about. Just
the previous afternoon, when James Stuart Murphy
had come by her cell to prepare her for the trial, he
had found it difficult to get Jane to focus on the
business at hand. All she wanted to discuss was the
title of her book. She was debating among three pos-
sibilities and wanted to know which he thought was
most "catchy"—*Maude's Misery*, *Fair Fettered Florence*, or *Sweet Blue Eyes.* When Murphy had grown
impatient and reminded her that there were more
important matters at the moment, she had huffily
replied that he, of all people, should take an interest
in the book, since she planned to pay his fees with
the profits. It was, after all, destined to be a best-
seller.

Now, as Jane finished cleaning her plate, she informed Mrs. Cash that, after much consideration, she
had definitely decided on *Sweet Blue Eyes.* The jailer's
kindly wife agreed that it was the best of the three titles. Having settled the matter to her satisfaction, Jane
finally turned her attention to the trial.

By then, it was after 8:00 A.M., and she was expected in court in less than an hour.

Though her choices were extremely limited, she
spent the next thirty minutes trying to decide what to

wear. She had only two dresses and three shirtwaists (all of which had been extensively altered to accommodate her expanded girth). Still, she couldn't seem to settle on an outfit. She tried on each garment at least a dozen times. She was still having trouble making up her mind when her lawyers arrived to accompany her to the courthouse. In the end, she settled on a black dress with a white shirtwaist, a large black hat with a heavy veil and a garnish of forget-me-nots, and a white ribbon tied about her throat.

Clearly, she wanted to look her best when she appeared before the public for the first time in six months. But the crowd on the lawn outside the jail was so dense that few spectators could even glimpse her as—flanked by Jailer Cash and Deputy Sheriff Hutchins—she walked to the gray stone courthouse, less than a hundred feet away.

The heavy black veil obscured her features as Jane entered the hushed, expectant courtroom. After taking her place between the two high railings in the long prisoner's dock, she tucked the fabric over the brim of her hat and glanced around.

To one observer, her face seemed "white and strained," as though she were on the "verge of physical and mental collapse." Most people in the room, however, saw things very differently. To their eyes, Jane seemed quite relaxed throughout the proceedings. "Very often during the progress of the trial," wrote the correspondent for the *Boston Herald*, "she smiled and chatted merrily with Mrs. Cash, with her counsel, and with some lady acquaintances who sat near her."

Two weeks before the start of the proceedings,

the *Barnstable Patriot* had predicted that the Toppan trial would "not last more than three days." As it happened, that estimate was off by more than two-thirds. From the time the court opened until the jury brought in its verdict, less than eight hours elapsed.

The first order of business was the empaneling of the jury. Samuel Chapman of Dennis was the first to be called. Jane studied him closely as he strode to the juror's box, his long gray whiskers hanging all the way down to his belt. As he leaned against the railing, he calmly returned her gaze until she lowered her eyes and whispered something to Mr. Cash, who sat directly beside her. For the next half-hour, she subjected each of the prospective jurors to the same intense scrutiny. Unlike the unflappable Chapman, some flinched visibly before her penetrating gaze.

Though Jane's expression betrayed a clear distaste for several of the jurors, no challenges were made by either the prosecution or defense. Thirty-one minutes after the selection process began, the twelve "good men and true"—from various walks of life and from towns all over the Cape—had been chosen.

Smith K. Hopkins, the wizened clerk who had needed a full quarter-hour to read the indictment at the end of the Grand Jury proceedings, now took almost as long—more than twelve minutes—to read it again. According to the *Boston Post*, Jane "seemed as if she was about to faint" as she listened to Hopkins's quavering voice—though whether her reaction was the result of emotional stress or of the excruciating experience of hearing the old man stammer through the document yet again was impossible to say.

Once the indictment was read, Attorney General Parker rose to make his opening statement. He briefly set forth the circumstances in the death of Mary "Minnie" Gibbs and declared that Jane had freely admitted to the murder. As a result of her confession, the "usual issue" in such trials—i.e., whether the accused had actually committed the crime—would not be contested. "The facts known to the Commonwealth, so far as they relate to the commission of the offense, cannot and will not be controverted by the defense," he said. The only question for the jury to decide was Jane's criminal responsibility—"whether or not the defendant was morally conscious of her acts."

Having concluded his address, Parker proceeded to call a series of witnesses to establish the facts of the crime. Mrs. Gibbs's cousin, Beulah Jacobs—looking exceptionally attractive in a long black dress that emphasized her hourglass figure—told the jury that Minnie had sickened and died after drinking mineral water and cocoa wine pressed on her by Nurse Toppan. Her testimony was corroborated by Harry Gordon. The third witness—Dr. Frank Hudnut of Boston, who had been called to examine Mrs. Gibbs in consultation with the late Dr. Latter—told the jurors that Minnie's appearance was "entirely consistent" with morphine poisoning.

Other witnesses added testimony of a highly incriminating nature. Dr. James Watson of Falmouth, who had treated Minnie for a minor stomach ailment in late July 1901, asserted that she was in fundamentally sound health at the time. Certainly she had shown no sign of any condition that might have "caused her death" just a few weeks later. Mrs. Caroline Wood of Cohasset, a family friend of the Davises and mother of General Leonard Wood, revealed that Jane had been violently opposed to the suggestion that an autopsy be performed on Minnie's body. Jane's old love-object, Oramel Brigham, told the jury that he had overheard a peculiar conversation between Jane and Dr. William Lathrop the previous August. "She asked him: if a person had been poisoned with morphine and atropine and then embalmed, if those poisonous drugs would be found if they exhumed the body and had an autopsy." Lathrop himself described Jane's suicide attempts during her stay at Brigham's home in September 1901.

Druggist Benjamin Waters of Wareham testified that, during a two-week period in late July 1901, Jane had telephoned his store and ordered 120 quarter-grain morphine pills. Dr. Edward Wood of Harvard unequivocally attributed Mrs. Gibbs's death to "morphine poisoning." His examination had turned up "large amounts" of morphine in the liver, indicating that "it must have been absorbed from the stomach before death." He estimated that the poison had been taken "inside of twenty-four hours before her death."

Since the real question facing the jury was not whether Jane had committed the murder but whether she was insane, the key witness of the day was Dr. Stedman. As predicted by the press, Stedman withheld the most shocking details of Jane's confession—the voluptuous pleasure that murder provided; the excitement of holding a dying victim tight; the thrill of taking Minnie Gibbs's ten-year-old son to bed with her while his mother languished just a few feet away. Even so, Stedman's testimony left little doubt as to Jane's deeply disturbed personality.

"She told us voluntarily that she had caused the death of Mrs. Gibbs by giving her poisonous doses of atropine and morphine," he declared in response to Parker's questioning. "She stated that the drugs were in the form of tablets or pellets of atropine and morphine separately; that each pellet of morphine contained a quarter of a grain of that drug and each pellet of atropine contained a sixth of a grain of that drug; that she didn't know how many she gave; that she certainly gave over a dozen pellets, and I understood her to say she gave that amount twice."

When Parker asked the psychiatrist whether Jane had given a reason for administering the poison to Minnie Gibbs, Stedman nodded. "She did," he said.

And what was the reason?

The dispassionate tone in which Stedman delivered his reply made it all the more chilling.

"To cause death," he said simply.

Nothing more had to be said. In response to a final query from the Attorney General, Stedman confirmed his belief that Jane had been telling the full truth during her interviews with the three alienists. A few minutes later—just six hours after Parker made his opening address—the Commonwealth rested its case.

The remainder of the trial was speedily dispatched. After a brief recess, James Stuart Murphy rose to make the opening address for the defense. Acknowledging the "somewhat perfunctory manner" in which the trial had been conducted, he explained that the defense and prosecution, "after repeated conferences," had arranged "that it should be disposed of in this manner."

"Ordinarily, cases of this nature are fought out to a bitter finish," he declared. This was no ordinary case, however. Because of its "remarkable nature," the defense had agreed to abide by the conclusion of the psychiatric experts, who had found "that the defendant is and has been insane."

"We shall therefore content ourselves," said Murphy, "with presenting for your consideration the testimony of three gentlemen, the most learned and the most eminent in their profession, in their specialties, experts in mental diseases of the highest standing."

Murphy then proceeded to call each of the alienists to the stand, beginning with George F. Jelly, who testified that Jane was "suffering with a degenerative form of mental disease" characterized "by a lack of moral sense, defective self-control, and an irresistible impulse to criminal acts." Stedman—recalled as a witness—repeated his opinion that "the defendant was insane and irresponsible for the crimes with which she is charged." Hosea Quinby corroborated the opinion of his colleagues. Miss Toppan, he declared, was "incurably insane" and a "menace to society if at large."

Following Quinby's testimony, the defense rested its case. Less than an hour had elapsed since Murphy made his opening remarks.

Since the Commonwealth and defense were in perfect agreement, neither side bothered with a closing argument. In keeping with the preordained nature of the proceedings, Judge Braley then instructed the jurors that—in view of the testimony of the three psychiatric experts—only one finding was possible: "That Miss Toppan was not guilty by reason of insanity."

The jurors then retired, presumably to deliberate. Under the circumstances, it took them a surprisingly long time to arrive at a decision—more than twenty minutes.

At 5:12 P.M., they filed back to their places to deliver the verdict that they had been instructed to reach: "not guilty by reason of insanity." When Judge Braley asked the prisoner if she wished "to say anything concerning the order which the court is to make upon this verdict," Jane declined. She was then sentenced to pass the "term of her natural life" under confinement at the Taunton Insane Hospital.

The trial had been so lacking in drama or suspense that no one in the courtroom displayed the slightest surprise at the outcome. Only Jane showed any emotion at all.

"Miss Toppan heard the verdict read with a broad grin on her face," wrote the reporter for the *Boston Herald*. "When Clerk Hopkins read the order of the judges which sends her to Taunton Insane Hospital for life, she turned to her friends with a look of absolute happiness on her face and laughed aloud. When it was all over, she almost danced out of the courthouse behind Jailer Cash and a deputy sheriff to wait in the county jailhouse before being taken to Taunton on Wednesday."

The outcome of the Toppan case was a big story, covered in papers throughout the northeast, including the *New York Times* ("NURSE TOPPAN DECLARED INSANE"). Still, the trial itself had been—as James Stuart Murphy admitted—an utterly perfunctory affair. The verdict was a foregone conclusion, the testimony a dry recitation of facts already widely reported in the press. There were no sensational new disclosures. As expected, nothing had been said about

Jane's sexual pathology—about the "revolting passions" that incited her crimes. The public had heard all the lurid details of the case it ever would; there were no more shocking revelations in store.

At least, that was what everyone believed on Monday, June 23. But everyone, it turned out, was wrong.

29

—⁓—

Behind the majority of murders there lurks some sex-interest: jealousy, freedom from a discarded lover, the blood-lust of the sexual degenerate.

—HAROLD EATON, *Famous Poison Trials*

JANE'S SENIOR COUNSEL, FRED BIXBY, WAITED UNTIL the trial was over before divulging the unbelievable truth. He had heard it from Jane during his first interview with her, six months earlier.

He had arrived at the Barnstable jail back in January, intending to speak to his client about the eleven victims she was widely suspected of having murdered: her foster sister, Elizabeth Brigham; her old friend, Myra Conners; her elderly patient, Mrs. McNear of Watertown; her former Cambridge landlords, Israel and Lovey Dunham; Oramel Brigham's sister, Mrs. Edna Bannister; and his housekeeper, Florence Calkins; and the four members of the Davis family.

During that first meeting, Jane had been totally forthcoming with Bixby, freely admitting to all of these killings. She had described, in the most chillingly matter-of-fact way, how she had murdered her friends and family members with "doses of morphine and atropine tablets dissolved in mineral water and sometimes in a dilution of whiskey." Occasionally she had supplemented these lethal drinks with deadly injections. Bixby had been stunned by Jane's utter nonchalance as she recounted the grim details of her crimes.

"Have you no remorse?" he finally asked.

"None at all," Jane coolly replied. "I have never felt sorry for what I have done. Even when I poisoned my dearest friends, as the Davises were, I did not feel any regret afterwards."

She staunchly denied that she committed any of her killings out of mercenary motives. "Whatever else I have done," she insisted, "I have never stolen a cent. I did not care enough about money to steal it."

It was pleasure that drove her to kill—the "exultation" she experienced as she "kissed and caressed her helpless and insensible patients as they drew nearer and nearer to death."

It took the plump, smiling woman nearly an hour to recount all eleven killings. By then, Bixby was feeling "satiated with homicidal details" (as he later put it) and deeply relieved that she had finally reached the end of her awful confession. He was taken aback, therefore, when she suddenly added: "But that is not all."

"Why, what do you mean?" Bixby exclaimed.

It was then that Jane revealed a truth so appalling that Bixby was left breathless with amazement.

The eleven names known to the police and public were only a fraction of her victims. She had been poisoning patients for many years, beginning as a student at Cambridge Hospital and continuing throughout her career as a private nurse. Altogether, she said—counting on her fingers to make sure she was not omitting anyone—she had murdered thirty-one men and women.

Apart from the attorney general, Bixby had not shared this dreadful knowledge with anyone. When, immediately following the trial, he finally revealed the truth, even the three alienists were caught off-guard. Dr. Stedman—who was preparing a psychological study of Nurse Toppan for publication—declared that, in light of the "magnitude of the case," he intended "to consult the attending physicians of each of the twenty additional patients Miss Toppan says she poisoned to ascertain if her story is consistent with symptoms observed by the doctors."

On the following day—Tuesday, June 24—the news was trumpeted in headlines throughout the northeast. The *Boston Globe* labeled Nurse Toppan the "GREATEST CRIMINAL IN COUNTRY."

"Even if only a small part of her story is true," the story read, "Jane Toppan stands as the greatest criminal ever arraigned at the bar of the United States. It is doubtful if, as a subtle poisoner who successfully duped scores of men and women during her career, she has been equaled by anyone of homicidal mania in modern times. Certainly none of the standard medico-legal works contains a parallel case. In no volume in print have the learned authorities and investigators revealed such an inexplicable multitude of hideous offenses against law and nature."

The *Boston Traveller* went even further, branding Jane not merely the "greatest criminal" in U.S. history but—as its headline read—the "MOST HORRIBLE CASE OF DEGENERACY WORLD HAS EVER KNOWN!" That assessment was seconded by the *Post*, which ran a page-one story ranking Jane first among the most infamous female poisoners of history. Accompanied by a triptych of portraits—with Jane's image occupying the central position—the article declared that Lucretia Borgia and Catherine de Medici were rivaled, if not out-matched, by the "pleasant-faced" nurse from Massa-chusetts:

> In history's pages, the name of Jane Toppan will be written down as one of the most noted poi-soners the world has ever seen. Previous records of criminals sink into insignificance before the awful roll of victims which this smiling woman says she has hurried to untimely graves. Lucretia Borgia, Catherine de Medici, and Jane Toppan form an unholy trinity of poisoners whose doings appall the imagination. Borgia herself has evidently been outdone by Jane Toppan. Catherine de Medici had no greater fondness for the subtle poison than did this daughter of the friendly asylum. Her friends were given deadly draughts with the same indifference as strangers. It is thought that scores of people rest in their graves because of her. For 33 years, this pleasant-faced woman has led a life so horrible and re-volting that its most fearful details cannot be told in public.

It was the *Globe* that came closest to revealing the "horrible and revolting" details that the public had been receiving such tantalizing hints of. Though expressed in oblique language, the description of the ecstatic "paroxysms" Jane experienced while "fondling" her dying patients left little doubt as to the perverse sexual nature of her crimes:

> In the most decent language that can be used to describe her mania, Jane Toppan could only grat-

ify her abnormal passion by handling dying persons. So degenerate had she become that nothing short of fondling men and women in the agony of death could excite her.

These paroxysms were intermittent, she told doctors. She might nurse a patient faithfully and, being loyal to his interest, seek only to effect a cure. In the midst of this devotional attention to her duty, however, she would sometimes be overcome with a stress of passion, a craving for the satisfaction of her strange emotions. It amounted to the strongest uncontrollable impulse. When the paroxysms came, she immediately, no matter how nearly recovered her patient was, administered a poison that in a short time would make him unconscious.

As morphine generally renders a subject drowsy, the nurse reveled in the impotency of her victim, whose life was slowly being slept away. She enjoyed herself in the presence of death with the most incredible avidity. Sometimes the patient had convulsions, and then the greatest demands of that revolting passion were satisfied.

After the climax of her paroxysm came, she became normal once more.

As for the precise identity of the additional twenty people Jane claimed to have murdered in the course of her career, their names would never be made public. Asked about reports that Jane had supplied him with a complete list of her victims, James Stuart Murphy was extremely evasive, refusing to confirm or deny the story:

I have been asked several times relating to a list of supposed victims of Miss Toppan but told everyone I had nothing to say. I cannot help it if the public gets by my answers the impression that such a list exists. I have not authorized anyone to say that I had such a list, or that there was such a list in existence. Supposing there *was* a list—what is there [to] gain by its publication? Jane Toppan has been committed to an asylum for the offense with which she was charged. Further than that, I do not see how her case will interest anyone.

As one of her oldest and most loyal friends, Murphy had promised to remain by Jane's side to the very end. He proved as good as his word. Unlike his co-counsel, Fred Bixby—who, along with other participants, departed from Barnstable as soon as the trial ended—Murphy stayed in the village overnight. Early the next morning, he arrived at the jailhouse to help Jane get ready for the journey to Taunton.

She was—as usual—in a bizarrely cheerful mood. Mrs. Cash was there, and the two women chatted merrily as Jane packed up her meager possessions. After hugging Mrs. Cash's granddaughter good-bye, Jane left the jailhouse in the company of Murphy, Jailer Cash, and a pair of sheriffs and strolled the short distance to the depot, where a group of reporters was gathered.

She was dressed in mourning black, but her face—according to one of the newsmen—was "wreathed in smiles. She looked as happy as if she were bound on a shopping tour."

One reason for her blithe spirits soon became clear. Despite the court order committing her to Taunton for life, Jane seemed convinced that she would be a free woman before very long. When the reporter for the *Post* asked her how she was feeling, she smiled broadly and replied: "Oh, never better. I feel grand."

"Don't you dread your new life?" he asked.

"Not at all," said Jane. "I'll be all right again in a few years. Then they'll let me out, the way they did Freeman." The reference, of course, was to Charles Freeman, who—just eight years after being sent to the Danvers asylum for the sacrificial murder of his child—had been pronounced fully recovered and set free.

Displaying an unusual degree of compunction for a member of the press, the newspapermen then apologized for any embarrassment he and his colleagues might have caused Miss Toppan by subjecting her to such unrelenting scrutiny.

"Oh, that's all right," she said with a laugh. "I don't know but I like it." Then—to show there were no hard feelings—she shook hands all around as she boarded the 10:30 train.

As the railroad pulled out of the station, she looked out the window and shouted to the reporters: "Come and see me."

All the way to Taunton she seemed perfectly relaxed. She pored over newspaper accounts of the trial and watched the passing landscape with keen interest. When the trainman announced that passengers for Cataumet should change cars at the next station, Jane turned to Murphy and began to reminisce about the pleasant summers she had spent at that bayside resort.

It was early afternoon when the train pulled into Taunton. Jane was immediately taken by carriage to the asylum, where she was quickly checked in and assigned to Ward Six, where the less dangerous class of patients was confined. Just before disappearing into the hospital she turned to the crowd of curiosity seekers who had come to catch a glimpse of her, smiled pleasantly, and gave a last little wave.

Later that day, Jane's senior counsel, Fred Bixby, was interviewed at his summer home in Hyannis. The reporter, a young man from the *Journal*, told him that, just before boarding the train to Taunton, Nurse Toppan had expressed the utmost confidence in her eventual recovery and release.

Bixby pooh-poohed the notion. It was true, he said, that Nurse Toppan "was still not an old woman." There was always the chance that "when she approaches the middle period of life, there may be a marked change for the better in her mental condition."

Still, that possibility seemed extremely remote. If it changed at all, Jane's mental condition was only bound to get worse. That, at any rate, was the opinion of the experts. In their view, Jane was almost certainly headed for a complete lapse into madness.

Or as Bixby put it, "The physicians all thought she would become an imbecile before many years."

30

There is a mystery about me that has not been solved,
and may never be.

—FROM THE CONFESSION OF JANE TOPPAN

JANE TOPPAN'S STATUS AS A CRIMINAL CELEBRITY WAS
certified a few days after her trial when her full "terrible confession" (as it was headlined) appeared as a
special feature in the Sunday supplement of William
Randolph Hearst's *New York Journal*. Only once before had a killer's own story been accorded such lavish
treatment. Six years earlier, in March 1896, Hearst
had published, with much fanfare, the "true and accurate confession" of Dr. H. H. Holmes, the Chicago
"Arch Fiend" who had slaughtered an indeterminate
number of victims in his infamous "Castle of Horrors."

Copyrighted by Hearst, Jane's confession was prefaced with a brief introduction that touted it as nothing less than "the most remarkable and appalling
human document ever published." According to this
preface, "The confession was made just before she was
taken from the Barnstable jail to the Taunton Insane
Asylum. . . . In it, she relates with hideous glee how
she plotted and accomplished the death of one person
after another." Several illustrations accompanied the
text: a photograph of Jane at twenty-four; portraits of

four of her victims (Myra Conners, Minnie Gibbs, Alden Davis, and his wife, Mary); and a facsimile of a handwritten note in which Jane describes the poisoning of one of her patients.

It is difficult to know how much of this confession was actually written by Jane. Certainly Hearst had no scruples about tampering with facts—or even concocting them—for the sake of sensationalism. It seems likely that the confession was heavily edited, if not ghostwritten, by one of his journalists. It is clearly designed to portray Jane as a creature of sheer "malevolence" and "fiendish ingenuity" (in the words of the introduction).

Still, the facts it recounts are consistent with the truth as Jane revealed it to Dr. Stedman. And indeed, Stedman himself appears to have regarded it as a significant document, carefully preserving a copy in a scrapbook on the Toppan case that he maintained for several years. (Along with his other papers, this scrapbook now resides in the archives of the Francis A. Countway Library of Medicine at Harvard.)

The confession begins with a startling claim—that Jane *wanted* to be judged insane by the panel of alienists sent to examine her. Her professions of sanity were merely a ploy. She had completely outsmarted Stedman and his colleagues, cleverly manipulating them with reverse psychology:

I was advised to confess and plead guilty to the murder of the thirty-one persons whom I have sent out of the world by poisoning. But I thought of a better way than that.

When the famous insanity experts of Boston, Dr. Henry R. Stedman, Dr. George F. Jelly, and

Dr. Hosea N. Quinby, came down to the Barnstable jail to see if I was insane, I knew how to
fool them.

I have been a trained nurse for fifteen years
and know doctors and just how to manage
them. I know that people who are really insane
will always deny it. So I said to the alienists: "I
am not insane."

I knew I could fool them all if I wanted to,
and make myself out insane. Dr. Jelly and the
others raked me hard with questions.

They tried to play on my woman's sympathy
and asked me if I didn't think it was a terrible
thing to take those mothers, Mrs. Gibbs and
Mrs. Gordon, away from their young children.
But I knew their game and said that I just up
and killed them and didn't know why.

When I said that I killed four people in fifty-
one days and set three fires, they said: "Why,
Jane Toppan, you must have been insane to have
done such a thing." But I still insisted that I was
not insane, and did not want them to make me
out insane.

Then they went away and gave their verdict
that I was insane, which was just what I wanted.

I was too smart for the whole of them. I have
the most spunk and grit of any person living.

Having established its author as a person of diabolical cunning—capable of tricking the country's foremost "insanity experts"—the confession proceeds to
recount the murders of Mary and Alden Davis and
their younger daughter, Genevieve Gordon. In a tone
of "hideous glee" (as the paper described it) Jane re-

calls how she "made it lively for the undertakers that summer—three graves in a little over three weeks in one lot in the cemetery."

Before completing her account of her annihilation of the Davis clan, Jane pauses to explain her modus operandi. Here, too, she gloats over her ability to fool the "great" and "famous" experts:

> But I haven't told exactly how I poisoned these people. It was with morphia mostly, and sometimes with atropia.
>
> Morphia and atropia weaken the heart's action and leave very little trace behind for a doctor or a chemist to detect. They are vegetable poisons and very unlike arsenic and other mineral poisons, which are easily detected.
>
> My using morphia and atropia on Minnie Gibbs was what so puzzled Professor Wood, the famous chemist of Harvard University. He could find some traces of morphia in the parts of the body he was examining, but there [were] some complications that he was utterly at a loss to explain. It was not until I confessed that I used atropia that Professor Wood was able to apply the test for that drug and make sure of his analysis.
>
> If my poisons could so fool a great physician and chemist like Dr. Wood you can see how much easier it was to deceive general practitioners. That is how it happens that physicians have given certificates for heart disease, diabetes, fatty degeneration of the heart, prostration, anaemia, etc. in the case of the people I have killed. Almost any person in middle life, when

dosed with Hunyadi water and drugged with morphia and atropia, will show symptoms of those diseases.

After reverting to the subject of the Davises and describing the murder of Minnie Gibbs—"the crime for which I was finally arrested"—the confession travels backward in time to discuss Jane's earliest killings:

Soon after I became a nurse, fifteen years ago, when I was about thirty years old, it came into my head, I don't know how, that I could kill people just as easy as not with the very medicine that the doctors gave their patients, morphia and atropia.

After I had tried it in a few cases and it had worked well, and they didn't suspect me, I thought how easily I could put people out of the way that I wanted to.

My first victims were hospital patients. I experimented on them with what the doctors would call a "scientific interest."

I can't repeat the names of those cases—because I never knew them. They just went by numbers in the hospital ward anyway. That was when I was at the Cambridge Hospital. Perhaps it was a dozen people I experimented on in this way.

But you mustn't think I killed all the patients under my care in the hospital. I nursed back to health some very bad cases of typhoid fever.

One of the physicians at the hospital suspected me. But he dared not accuse me of poisoning. So I was simply discharged. I didn't care about that, because I had made up my mind that I could make more money and have an easier time by going out by the day in families.

The confession then returns to the recent past, briefly recounting the murders of the Dunhams, Myra Conners, Elizabeth Brigham, Florence Calkins, and Edna Bannister. "I might have killed George Nichols and his sister, too," Jane adds, "if I had stayed long enough at their home in Amherst, New Hampshire."

As for the complete tally of her victims, the confession is tantalizingly vague, suggesting that Jane murdered an even greater number than the shocking total disclosed by Fred Bixby. "I have poisoned thirty-one people as far as I can count them up and recall them. But there are more that I can't name, just hospital patients."

The confession sheds little light on her motivations. Her murders were committed "for various reasons." She makes no mention of her depraved sexual appetites, other than to say that killing "always gave me the most exquisite pleasure."

Jane admits that she is a mystery even to herself. She marvels at her own lack of remorse for the terrible things she has done. "Isn't it strange that I don't feel bad? But I can't help it. I can't cry."

Still, she insists that she is not utterly without feelings, an assertion that leads her to reminisce about the lover who jilted her in girlhood. It was this tragic event, she suggests, that was at the root of all her problems.

People say I have no heart, but I have. While I have been in jail, a friend in Lowell sent me some forget-me-nots, and I cried. They were the flowers that my first lover used to send me when I was a schoolgirl. And a forget-me-not was engraved on that precious engagement ring.

I will never tell my girlhood lover's name that is still sacred to me, even though he went back on me, and it seemed that my whole lighthearted nature changed after that. I still laughed and was jolly, but I learned how to hate, too.

If I had been a married woman, I probably would not have killed all these people. I would have had my husband, my children, and my home to take up my mind.

The confession does not dwell on Jane's life behind bars. It does, however, mention some of the books she enjoyed while in jail. Her favorites, she declares, were Dickens's *A Tale of Two Cities*—"especially those descriptions of the guillotine in the French Revolution and heads being chopped off by the score"—and the novels of Charles Reade, a popular Victorian writer of sensational fiction. One of Reade's titles had a particular relevance to this profoundly disturbed woman, whose genial facade concealed such a malevolent soul. The novel was called *Singleheart and Doubleface*.

Like all psychopaths, Jane was capable of feeling sorry only for herself. Toward the end of the confession, she voices a single regret: that her murderous career was cut short by the destruction of the Davises. "I could have worked for years longer at poisoning if I hadn't killed four people in one family almost all at once. That was the greatest mistake of my life."

In the end, Jane accepts that she "deserves to be punished for all these murders." She concludes, however, by expressing the same hope she conveyed to reporters before boarding the train to Taunton: "I've made up my mind to being sent to an insane asylum. But I have hopes of getting out in ten or fifteen years—when doctors will say I am cured of insanity."

31

The lower intestines of maniacs are usually loaded;
they should be emptied by very large enemata of
water at 90 degrees of temperature, in gallon portions
if necessary, repeated incessantly till successful.

— J. G. Rogers, *The American Journal of Insanity*

SITUATED ON A LOW, BARREN, SANDY HILL SUR-
rounded by a 140-acre wasteland of brush, bogs, and
boulders, the State Lunatic Hospital at Taunton (as it
was originally called) was opened in 1854. The central
building—three stories high and surmounted by a
seventy-foot dome—was large enough to accommodate 250 patients. In the early years of the institution,
these inmates provided a convenient supply of labor.
Under the direction of Dr. George C. S. Choate, the
first superintendent, they were made to clear the
brush, drain the swamps, and drag away the boulders,
which were then used to build an imposing wall
around the entire property.

As originally constructed, the hospital contained
forty-two so-called "strong rooms," designed to hold
the most unmanageable inmates—"violent and filthy
patients," as they were described in the First Annual
Trustees Report. Built of stone, brick, and iron, these
cells featured all the amenities of a medieval dungeon.
The walls were sixteen inches thick. Small iron-barred
slits served as windows. The iron doors were barely

wide enough to squeeze through and were secured with massive locks. In the wall beside each door was a small aperture, just big enough to permit a bowl of gruel to be passed into the cell. Since the intended inmates were raving madmen (and women) who refused to wear clothes and wallowed in their own filth, the "strong rooms" had stone floors that sloped toward the front of the cell and terminated in a gutter, "for the convenience of washing them out" (as the Trustees Report put it).

So ghastly were these tomblike cells that hospital administrators were reluctant to use them, even for the confinement of the "furiously insane." Within a few years of their construction, the strong rooms were demolished and other, less inhumane quarters built in their place.

Even with this extra space, however, the hospital soon became desperately overcrowded. By 1860, its population had swelled to close to 400. It wasn't until 1874, however, that two additional wings were added to the main building. A brief, official history of the Taunton Lunatic Hospital, published a few years later, offered a rosy picture of the recently renovated hospital:

> The new wards are very light, airy, and pleasant, with beautiful water and landscape views from the windows and veranda. Since the new wings were completed, very material changes have been made in the older portions of the hospital; some wards have been almost entirely rebuilt, which have rendered them more cheerful and pleasant, more light having been introduced and the ventilation much improved.

There are nine wards for each sex, the patients being classified into families according to their mental condition. Each ward consists of a long corridor with rooms opening from it on either side, which are occupied by the patients as sleeping rooms, the corridor having a bay-window on one side to admit light and afford a pleasant sitting room. Connected with each ward is a dining-room, a wash-room, with set wash basins, a bath-room and water-closet. The food is cooked in a large central kitchen and carried on cars through the basement, and taken to the general dining-rooms by elevators.

The hospital underwent further expansion in the 1890s. Between 1892 and 1893, two infirmary buildings were constructed, one for men, one for women, each big enough to accommodate seventy-five patients. Five years later, a 150-acre farm was purchased in the adjoining town of Raynham and made into a farming colony, where seventy-two patients lived and worked the land. By the time of Jane's arrival, there were nearly 1,000 inmates at Taunton.

From the very start (as the trustees reported), "useful employment" was regarded as "a remedial agent in the treatment of mental diseases." Besides farm work, patients were assigned various kinds of manual labor. The Superintendent's Report for 1902—the year of Jane's incarceration—described the range of jobs performed by the inmates:

About 800 patients have been employed during the year in the various departments of the hospital: upon the farm, at the barn, in the piggery, in the garden, at the greenhouse, on the lawns, at the laundry and boiler house, in the kitchen and basement, in the sewing room, at the shoe shop and brush shop, and on the wards assisting the nurses in the ward work; and the women not otherwise employed have done sewing and knitting on the wards, which is carried to them by a person who has special charge of it. The new buildings in the process of construction the present year have furnished extra work for the men. All of the grading and excavating for the buildings, the digging of the trenches for the soil pipes, water pipes, steam and gas pipes have been done by the patients, with a single attendant to direct them.

The report also includes itemized lists detailing the work accomplished in the various parts of the hospital—the Industrial Building, Upholstering Department, Sewing Room, and wards. Among the thousands of products made or repaired were 3,244 pairs of men's slippers; 1,522 bath towels; 635 mattresses; 136 gingham skirts; 82 table napkins; 74 doormats; 70 blankets; 24 overcoats; and 3 baseball mitts.

There were other, less onerous activities. On special occasions, inmates were treated to assorted entertainments. Christmas, as the trustees were pleased to report, was celebrated "by a Christmas tree in the chapel, with Christmas music and a present for each patient in the hospital." During the summer months, four picnics were held on the grounds, "enlivened with music by the home orchestra, games of ball and other athletic exercises."

Regular social dances were conducted in the

chapel, "music being furnished by the hospital orchestra." There were also educational lectures "descriptive of foreign and domestic scenery of special interest" and "illustrated by the stereopticon." As a special treat, about 350 of the most trustworthy patients were taken on a trip to the Bristol County Fair, "free admission having been given to all inmates of the hospital." As the Trustees proudly reported, "Several paroled patients were allowed to go unattended, and all safely returned with clean records, much to their credit."

In spite of the idealized depiction of asylum life contained in these authorized histories and annual reports, Taunton was, without doubt, as grim and dehumanizing as every other American mental institution of the day—places where (as Erving Goffman puts it in his classic study *Asylums*) inmates were subjected to "a series of abasements, humiliations, and profanations of self—processes by which a person's self is systematically mortified." For all the claims of enlightenment, the treatment of patients was appallingly benighted. As historian Ruth Caplan documents in her book *Psychiatry and Community in Nineteenth-Century America*, mental patients were commonly brutalized by attendants; subjected to constant purges, enemas, and primitive surgical procedures; force-fed dangerous drugs; exploited as a source of unpaid labor; immobilized with "mechanical restraints"; and in general treated as less than human— "objects to be manipulated rather than individuals to be motivated and led."

In Jane's case these dreadful circumstances were exacerbated by another factor that made her life in Taunton even more nightmarish. She was immured

within the walls of a lunatic asylum, surrounded by—
and treated no differently from—the hopelessly insane. And yet, she herself appeared to be in full possession of her rational faculties. Her grim situation was
vividly described by a reporter from the *Boston Globe*
who traveled to Taunton a few months after Jane was
committed.

It was an overcast morning in late October when
the newsman made his visit. He found Jane in the
sitting room at the far end of the third-floor corridor, in the section of the hospital known as the
"mild patient's ward." The reporter did not approach her. Rather, he studied her as unobtrusively
as possible from a short distance away. The superintendent had warned him that Jane was "very sensitive to curious stares." And indeed, when Jane realized that she was being observed by the reporter, she
"changed her seat to a more secluded part of the
room and quietly turned her chair so that she could
not be seen so easily."

Several dozen women, perhaps forty in all, were
wandering about the ward. These were the lost and
shattered souls among whom Jane now spent her
life—haggard beings with wild hair and unkempt
robes who whispered to themselves or muttered incoherently as they moved aimlessly up and down the
hallway. "Their eyes," the newsman noted, "were not
the eyes of sane people."

Amid these piteous creatures Jane Toppan, the
newsman wrote, made a "startling contrast." She was
"very neatly dressed, in a modest, dark-brown gown.
Her hair is properly combed and done up. She is
never excited. She never walks about restlessly."

At one point, the ward supervisor entered the sitting room, carrying a tray with labeled medicine glasses. Except for Jane, the patients "glared uncomprehendingly at the official or took no notice of her at all, but continued their restless walking hither and thither." Jane alone responded. She "rose quietly from the leather bench and said simply, in the voice of a perfectly sane person, 'I am Miss Toppan.' "

This small, obliging act was typical of Jane's behavior. According to the attendants, Jane had "never given the slightest trouble. She is courtesy and consideration itself. Whatever little service they do for her now and then she acknowledges with a sweet, gracious winning smile."

To the reporter's eye, Jane seemed perfectly sane. It was this very fact that made her situation so nightmarish. In many ways, she was worse off than the other inmates of her ward, who were, at least, mercifully "unconscious of their own position," and who were granted certain privileges forbidden to Jane. "Unlike the other patients," the newsman noted, "Jane Toppan cannot go out of doors and walk about on the lawn or, under the eye of a watchful attendant, wander among the cool trees of the grove. With quiet resignation, she sits hour after hour, day after day, in the spacious sitting room, whence she may look out on the grounds of the institution. Occasionally, she rises with a sigh and sits down at the end of the leather seat which runs along the side of the big room. From this vantage point, she may look upon her muttering, disheveled sister patients who ramble restlessly up and down the corridor. This may or may not be her diversion; there can be no other."

As he left the hospital, the reporter was struck with the sheer awfulness of her predicament. "An ordinary prison—or even death in the electric chair—would be wonderfully preferable to her life where she is," he wrote. For if Jane Toppan were truly as sane as she appeared, then her entombment within the walls of the sprawling lunatic asylum was nothing less than "a hell on earth."

32

Suspicion always haunts the guilty mind.
—SHAKESPEARE, *King Henry the Sixth, Part III*

IN POINT OF FACT (AND CONTRARY TO THE SPECULATIONS of the man from the *Globe*), Jane did not regard her circumstances as particularly unpleasant—not, at any rate, during her first few years at the asylum. Indeed, she adjusted quite comfortably to institutional life. According to the Medical Superintendent of the hospital, Dr. J. P. Brown, "She was, as a rule, sociable, cheerful, amiable, and spasmodically helpful, and spent much of her time reading. The change from the seclusion of the jail to the more active life of a large hospital ward interested her. In this period, she grew fat and was in excellent physical condition. . . . She soon developed a fondness for the company of the patients, in preference to that of the nurses."

That asylum life agreed with Jane was confirmed in a letter she wrote to an old friend in Lowell on the first anniversary of her commitment: "Just think, I've been here a year and find myself fond of the people and warmly attached to the place in some ways. Yes, we are well cared for, kindly and considerately."

Of course, there were certain details she withheld from her correspondent. It was not merely the "kind and considerate" treatment she received from the staff that made life in Taunton so appealing to Jane. The hospital had also proved congenial to her perverse sexual needs. In an early psychiatric report on Jane, Dr. Brown noted that she had developed a "particular fondness" for a "demented" female patient who was given to public masturbation—"open self-abuse," in Brown's Victorian terminology. On several occasions, nurses making their nightly rounds had caught Jane in bed with this patient.

In her earliest interviews with Brown, Jane seemed frank and cooperative, exhibiting a genuine curiosity about her own mental condition. She was willing to concede that she was insane, but seemed sincerely perplexed as to what her insanity consisted of. "I don't appear like these other patients," she told Roberts. "I can read a book intelligently. I don't have bad thoughts, so I don't see where moral degeneracy comes in."

If Jane seemed puzzled by the nature of her illness, Brown himself had little doubt. In a report entered into the hospital records in April 1903, he provided a ringing affirmation of the diagnosis initially given by Dr. Stedman and his colleagues. In his description of Jane's mentality and behavior, Brown sketches a portrait of a classic criminal psychopath, a serial killer who derived open pleasure from the suffering of others, and who—far from feeling any remorse for her enormities—took positive pride in her reputation as the most heinous poisoner in the annals of crime:

My study of and observation of Jane Toppan since she has been in the hospital gives me the opinion that her mental disease should be classified as moral or affective insanity. She seems to me wholly devoid of moral sense, or a clear apprehension of what is right or wrong as to her relations to other people or to society. In all my conversations with her respecting the homicides, which she freely admits, she has exhibited no remorse, regret or sorrow for any of them, but rather a sense of pride and satisfaction that the number was so large as to give her distinction above all other poisoners whose histories are known.

This lack of pity and sorrow for others in trouble or distress has been evident whenever any difficulty has occurred on the ward between patients, or between a nurse and patients. At such times, she has manifested a good deal of glee, and laughed like a silly child, but never expressed any sympathy or pity for the patient or person in distress or trouble. Trouble or pain for others seems to excite in her merriment and joy instead of sorrow.

In speaking of her homicides, she says that at the time she committed them she was not conscious of any crime or doing any wrong for which she should be punished; that the thought of doing wrong did not enter her mind and gave her no concern whatsoever; and at the present time she has apparently no comprehension that the decree of the court was right and just.

Though Brown classifies Jane's condition as a disease of her moral faculties, it wasn't long before she started to show symptoms of far more extensive mental degeneration. Indeed, even at the time of his report, she had begun to manifest increasingly erratic behavior. "During the past three or four months," Brown noted, "she has seemed more moody and emotional, either depressed or exhilarated at short intervals, and has exhibited less self-control, and with it she gives one the impression that her mind is weakening, and that she has less mental grasp of past and present events, and of her relation to the surroundings. Of this she seems to be painfully conscious herself. She has been observed to be laughing immoderately to herself, and when it is noticed by others, she blushes as though she would conceal it, and seems confused."

Her increasingly tenuous hold on reality was illustrated in a series of letters she wrote to her Lowell correspondent between May and October 1903. In the first, she strikes a note of bizarre joviality as she describes how much fun she has been having lately: "I've had a real good time in the sewing room for the past two days. I never can say that I like to [do] a thing until I get some fun out of it, and I really had quite a lot of fun. . . . Truly, I had a great, good time at the Barnstable jail after the first ten days, even then I did not have a bad time."

The next letter, written a month later, is even more manic. Referring to an unspecified incident that occurred in the sewing room, she writes: "It has left me rolling on the floor with laughter. I begin to feel like rolling on the floor now. I like to feel that way. I am having a big time, big in the sewing room."

A few weeks later, however, her tone had become far more somber: "Don't ever ask me in your letters what I mean by what I write, I don't know myself. I am talking through my hat. . . . I don't like the locality I live in, either."

Shortly after the composition of this letter, in July 1903, Jane had a wild outburst in the night, waking the entire ward with such a "violent fit of screaming for no obvious cause" (in Brown's words) that she had to be physically restrained by attendants. In the next letter written to her Lowell friend, her sense of identity has undergone a dramatic shift. She no longer refers to herself as Jane Toppan—reared since girlhood among the Unitarians of her adoptive home—but as the Boston-born Irish Catholic Honora Kelley: "I meditate and praise and pray all the time, and shall be ready at the end to take vows and become Mother Honora of the Seven Wounds."

Had it not been composed by a "moral monster" undeserving of sympathy, there would be something positively poignant about the last letter in this series, written during one of Jane's increasingly rare periods of lucidity: "I do grieve to be in this state, I do, when I have thought-force to think it out. When I am discontented, I ask myself what I want, and I don't know. A change of any kind seems torture to me even to think of, and why I want to live this way I don't know."

The process of Jane's mental deterioration was closely charted not only by the hospital's medical superintendent but by Dr. Stedman, a trustee of the asylum who visited on frequent occasions. For the eminent alienist, Jane's case offered a unique opportunity to shed light on the "intricate disorder" of moral insanity.

Stedman, along with others, had a theory about this phenomenon. It was his belief that there was "no such thing as a mental disease affecting the *moral* sphere alone." "Intellectual involvement in some form," he insisted, was an "essential feature of the disease." Those who suffered from moral insanity, he felt, frequently developed "definite delusions, especially of suspicion and persecution." In most cases, "their mental impairment advanced to noticeable dementia." In the progress of Jane's disease, Stedman found a striking confirmation of his thesis, which he eventually set forth in a published paper, "A Case of Moral Insanity with Repeated Homicides and Incendiarism, and Late Development of Delusions."

As Stedman documents in this paper, within a few years of her commitment Jane had plunged into a state of active paranoia. By early 1904, she "had become generally antagonistic towards all about her, as well as highly suspicious and irritable." In contrast to her earlier letters, praising the asylum and proclaiming how "warmly attached" she was to the place, she now "wrote voluminous tirades against the hospital and its management, treatment of patients, etc., making wholesale and absurd accusations and denunciations, some of them of an entirely delusional nature."

In one letter—addressed to her old friend from Lowell—she wrote: "Do you know, the supervisor put some poison in my tea. A patient saw her and told me and I didn't touch it. The lady heard the supervisor say she had fixed Jane Toppan this time."

In her increasingly psychotic view, it was not just the hospital staff that had it in for her. Everyone was part of the conspiracy—even her devoted correspondent from Lowell. "Sometimes it strikes me you are one of the gang," Jane wrote to this person in early 1904. "If you have fooled me also, I shall say damn you. Oh, damn you, anyway." She made a similar accusation against her lawyer and childhood friend, James Stuart Murphy, denouncing him as one of the "gang" out to "fix" her.

The sewing-room staff—for whom she had professed such affection in her earlier letters—also came in for attack. "I don't wish to associate with the low and vulgar people employed in the sewing room," she announced to Dr. Brown. "They talked about me before the other patients in a low and vulgar manner." She then proceeded to describe (as Brown told Stedman) "a revolting scene, impossible on the face of it, enacted by the two employees in charge—self-respecting, modest women—and gave an account of talk and actions on their part of the vilest kind, in a manner highly suggestive of delusions, of persecution, and hallucinations of hearing."

The real focus of her paranoia, however, was food. She became increasingly convinced that every member of the staff, from the ward nurses to Dr. Brown himself, was out to poison her.

"No, thank you, Dr. Brown," she wrote to him in early 1904, after refusing to eat the beefsteak she had been served for dinner. "I will stick to bean soup and keep safe aboveground. Some steak strikes some people right. This steak is sure death."

In another letter, dated March 1904, she wrote to James Stuart Murphy (who had recently been made her guardian):

> I am the victim of nerve paralysis, the result of food. I have to eat or I am fed with a tube with nerve-paralyzing food that I choose from the tray. Oh, I think that you and Mr. Bixby were criminals to put me through this. It was an awful thing to do to any human being, and I have my opinion of everybody who takes a hand in it. I think as the nerves of my body get more benumbed, my brain becomes clearer to the outrageous course that has been taken with me. I

suppose the next thing, something will be given to put me out of the way altogether. That would be a mercy to this.

Stedman himself received a number of similar letters from Jane. "I wish to inform you that I am alive in spite of the deleterious food which has been served to me," she wrote to him in April 1904. "Many efforts have been made to poison me in this institution, of that I am very sure. I am thin and very hungry all the time. Every nerve is calling for food. Why can't I have help? I ate a pint of ice cream and four oranges Saturday. That was all."

Another letter to Stedman (preserved among his papers at the Harvard Medical School) offers an intensely disquieting picture not only of Jane's deepening "delusional insanity" but of the kind of treatment that intractable patients were subjected to, even in mental hospitals as ostensibly humane as Taunton:

Doctor Stedman:

I wish to tell you that I am dead sick of the treatment I receive in your institution. I cannot eat this food. I do not dare to and in consequence I am held down by the head by a Dr. & by both hands and arms by an attendant and another attendant sits on my legs and another feeds me with a stomach tube. I was given a custard today and the whites of the eggs were wrong that is, bad. I don't think I shall live long and I think I shall die here soon. I had some Indian mush this noon but the attendant never puts molasses on mine as he does the others.

I am full of aches and pains from my head to
my toes and am in torture of body and mind day
and night.

Norah Kelley

In her spiraling dementia, she attempted to draw
other patients into her paranoid fantasy world, "going
so far as to shout to a melancholic whom the nurse
was trying to feed, not to eat the food as it was poison."

Jane's psychological disintegration was evident in
her physical decline. The woman who had always
taken such care with her dress—spending hours on
the morning of her trial debating which outfit to
wear—now grew utterly neglectful of her appearance,
"even having to be told to wash her face." By December 1903, Stedman writes in his paper, "her physical
condition had fallen off greatly":

She had lost fifty pounds in weight in a few
months, in consequence of her refusal of food
because of false belief in regard to it. Owing to
her weak condition she was removed to the infirmary. There she became more disturbed, as well
as destructive and dirty in habits, enraged and
somewhat violent, threatening to kill her nurses,
etc. By February, 1904, she was greatly emaciated, having lost over eighty pounds, or about
half her normal weight, and was so weak that
forced feeding with the tube was resorted to
for several days, since which time she has eaten
voluntarily, but just enough to avoid being
fed again.

In March 1904, soon after her release from the infirmary, Stedman paid her a visit. He found her "in good spirits, talking volubly and aimlessly at the nurses." No sooner did he ask about her health, however, than she launched into a bitter

tirade against the hospital, its officers, and all its belongings. She insisted that everything was "rotten," that the meat was "embalmed" beef, etc. etc. Everything was filthy, she said, even the brick walls which must be "saturated with the filth of years"; the water was "polluted with sewage"; the vegetables were "rank poison." Occasionally she would burst out unexpectedly with peculiar and piercing shrieks of laughter which would seem impossible to one in her weak condition.

Stedman left the asylum that day more convinced than ever that Jane Toppan was "weakminded" beyond cure. It seemed that Fred Bixby's prediction had come true. Jane may or may not have been clinically insane when she was committed to Taunton. But after less than two years in the lunatic asylum, she displayed the kind of symptoms that, as Stedman wrote, were "only to be found in the imbecile."

33

But they're all after me now—thirty one of them! Some want to poison me, and some come at me with their skeleton hands as if they would choke me! See! They're coming for me now! Help! MURDER!

—JANE TOPPAN, *American Journal-Examiner,*
AUGUST 7, 1904

THE SITUATION WAS EXQUISITELY IRONIC: THE WORLD'S greatest poisoner was dying of starvation, convinced that she was being poisoned herself. When the newspapers got wind of it, they had a field day.

The *Boston Daily Advertiser* broke the story on July 12, 1904. "TERROR-STRICKEN POISONER AFRAID OF DEATH BY POISON" ran the headline. Flatly asserting that "Jane Toppan has become an imbecile," the paper portrayed her awful descent into persecutory madness as an object lesson in divine retribution.

Jane, according to the story, had arrived at the Taunton asylum "cool and jaunty," convinced "that she had fooled justice." Before long, however, she began "thinking of the many people she had put out of the way" with her "black arts." Within less than two years,

Jane Toppan, who went to the asylum boasting of the way she had fooled the experts, fell a victim to her fears. Today, she shudders at what she believes is a plot to put her out of the way in an asylum, where none of the outside world knows what is going on. She whispers to herself when anyone draws near. She says that she will not touch the "poisoned" food. And, if she had her own way, she would die of slow starvation, a victim to her own evil broodings.

The moral of the story was clear. "The collapse of the woman once noted for her indomitable nerve and relentless cruelty is in itself a remarkable instance of relentless justice," the article concluded. "Not the justice of man, but of the invisible will of the gods."

Following on the heels of the *Advertiser* piece were a series of even more overwrought articles, appearing in the Sunday supplements of various newspapers. In exploiting the full, titillating potential of the story, these articles pulled out all the sensationalistic stops. Each was accompanied by a lurid illustration. In one, Jane is shown hunched over a dinner table beside an untouched bowl of porridge, recoiling in horror as a horde of black-shrouded specters closes in on her. In another, she stares fearfully out from a spider's web, as though caught in the devious strands of her own evil designs. Still a third shows her in the grasp of her ghostly victims, who are drawing her inexorably toward the grave.

Along with these drawings were before-and-after photographs, depicting Jane's transformation from the plump, matronly figure of her pretrial days into a hollow-cheeked, haunted-eyed madwoman. As for the texts of the articles, they shared the identical tone, typical of the tabloid sensibility: a kind of prurient gloating disguised as awestruck piety in the workings of God's will.

Under the headline "HER AWFUL PUNISHMENT WORSE THAN DEATH," for example, the *American Journal-Examiner* described—in language straight out of a Gothic potboiler—Jane's "terrible punishment at Nature's own hands—or God's":

> She imagines that the dead victims have come from their tombs and are trying to poison her.
>
> As the nurse brings a bowl of gruel or cup of tea to her in her narrow cell, she screams out: "It's poisoned!"
>
> She pushes it away and covers her face with her hands to hide the sight of the bony fingers of her dead patients clutching at her, and to shut out the visions of their death's heads hovering over her.
>
> It is as if the ghosts of all whom she has killed had burst loose from their coffins and come forth to torture her to death.
>
> When Jane Toppan was committed here in June, 1902, many people thought that the electric chair had been cheated of its rightful victim. Many declared that no form of execution known to law could be torturesome enough for this tigress in human form.
>
> But now Nature, through God, in its own way, is working a punishment more terrible than medieval torture could have devised upon this woman.
>
> By the progress of her disease, Jane Toppan has come [to] believe that not only every article of food that is brought to her, but every cup of

tea or coffee and every glass of water, is poisoned.

She can see the specters of her victims hovering over her and dropping the poison into these things, just as she used to do to them.

Jane Toppan is paying the penalty of her crime by Nature's or God's own law in a way that is an appalling moral lesson—that no one can take human life, even if he escapes the punishment of human law, without suffering the most awful torture to the end of his or her own wretched existence.

The intensely satisfying notion that the infamous murderess was now suffering the torments of the damned was echoed in a story that ran the following week in the Sunday Magazine section of the *New York Post*. This article—titled "Jane Toppan, Slowly Dying, Is the Victim of the Phantasies of her Murderous Work"—was written in the kind of grim, portentous voice that, thirty years later, would be a staple of radio melodramas:

> 'Twould be better that Jane Toppan was dead.
>
> 'Twould have been better, after justice had rendered its decision, that soon after that, she died.
>
> There is something more dreadful than the gallows, something more fearful than the electric chair, and that something is the human mind.
>
> During her hellish career of freedom, Jane Toppan attained the fame of being America's Lucretia Borgia. Now, her disordered mind sees in every hand extended a deadly draught, in every morsel of food offered a concealed drug.
>
> Night and day and night and day again, weeks

lengthening into years, Jane Toppan glares on,
distrustful of friendly hands, slowly but surely
starving to death.

This dreadful, self-confessed murderess is
gradually being executed by her own mind.

Clearly, this article (and others like it) was meant to
gratify a primitive passion for vengeance that had little
to do with the values of Christian mercy and forgive-
ness. Perhaps in recognition of this fact, another Sunday feature on the same subject—published in the
Boston Globe under the title "The Poison Nemesis of
Jane Toppan"—invoked pagan mythology in its
description of Jane's plight.

Prefaced with a quote from the *Eumenides* of Aeschy-
lus ("Coming to exact blood-forfeit / We appear to
work completeness"), the article imagined Jane Toppan
trapped in her "caged room" at Taunton with the

same grim, brooding Fates who sat so long ago
in the adytum of Apollo's temple and chanted
their song of vengeance to Queen Clytemnes-
tra's wretched son. Their presence in the Yankee
woman's chamber strangely reconciles ancient
mythology with New England fact. To the Massachusetts poisoner, as to the Greek matricide,
the terrible sisters have appeared to exact blood
forfeit at compound interest and to work superb
completeness in a fate woeful and inexorable beyond human power to conceive.

Whether portraying Jane's desperate fate in terms
of natural law, Old Testament retribution, or Greek
mythology, however, every article dealing with the

subject agreed on one thing: the infamous poisoner wasn't long for the world.

"Jane Toppan is today a wreck, so weak and emaciated that death is apparently not far distant," wrote the *Boston Advertiser* in September 1904.

"Her condition is such that it is not expected she will live very long," the *Globe* reported a few weeks later.

The *Post* offered the most unequivocal pronouncement of all. "She won't trouble the hospital officials or herself much longer," the paper flatly declared in its October 23 edition. "Her human destiny is nearly all in. Jane Toppan is going to die."

34

~m~

In the pleasure and excitement of crime, Jane Toppan
seemed to find the criminal's excitement of doing
artistic work, to which danger appeared to add zest.
—*Boston Daily Globe*, AUGUST 18, 1938

THE *POST* WAS RIGHT, OF COURSE—JANE TOPPAN *WAS*
going to die. But not for another thirty-four years.

She fell ill on July 1, 1938, and remained bedridden for more than a month. At 7:00 P.M. on Wednesday, August 17, she died at the age of eighty-one
years. Her death certificate, signed by Dr. Jack Oak-
man of the State Hospital at Taunton, cites broncho-
pneumonia as the primary cause of death, with
chronic myocarditis as a contributory factor.

It had been many years since the public had heard
of Jane Toppan, and it is safe to say that the once-
notorious killer—"America's Lucretia Borgia"—had
been largely, if not utterly, forgotten by the world.
Still, her passing was big news, accorded front-page
treatment in the major Boston dailies and noted with
a prominent, if not wholly accurate, obituary in the
New York Times, which misstated both her age
(eighty-four, according to the *Times*) and number of
victims ("at least 100 persons").

Exactly what Jane's life was like during the three-
and-a-half decades of her confinement at Taunton will
never be known. The hospital is still in operation, and

Jane's medical and psychiatric records have been preserved. But they are inaccessible to researchers, kept under wraps by the state's strict confidentiality laws.

According to her obituaries, Jane grew increasingly violent in the period following the onset of her delusions and "for several years was kept in a straitjacket." Eventually, however, her paranoia subsided. She regained her weight and became a generally docile patient.

Still, there were violent episodes from time to time. According to one resident of the city of Taunton, whose father was a fireman in the 1920s and '30s, Jane possessed a nearly "superhuman strength when aroused. On several occasions, she became upset over something, and several policemen had to be called to help subdue her."

In later years, however, she became—in the words of one hospital official—a "quiet old lady, just another patient who caused no trouble."

There was one story about Jane that sprang up after her death and continued to be reported by crime writers who kept her story alive in the years following her death. Given her history, it seems plausible. Perhaps it is even true.

According to the anecdote, Jane spent most of her time on the ward reading romances and writing love stories of her own. Every once in a while, however, she would beckon to one of the nurses.

"Get the morphine, dearie, and we'll go out into the ward," Jane would tell the nurse with a grin. "You and I will have a lot of fun seeing them die."

—∞—

ACKNOWLEDGMENTS

My sincerest thanks to the following people for the help they provided while I was researching Jane Toppan's story:

Karen Adler Abramson,
  State Library of Massachusetts

David Bates

Elizabeth Bouvier,
  State Library of Massachusetts

Mary Bricknell,
  State Library of Massachusetts

Mark Brown,
  John Hay Library, Brown University

Marilyn Budd,
  Brookline Hospital

Robyn Christensen,
  Bostonian Society

Marianne Conti,
  Paul Klapper Library, Queens College

Phyllis Day,
  Superior Court, Barnstable

Jack Eckert,
  Francis A. Countway Library of Medicine, Harvard

Tim Engels,
    John Hay Library, Brown University

Brian Harkins,
    Social Law Library

Stephen Jerome,
    Brookline Historical Society

Virginia Johnson,
    Taunton Public Library

James Krasnoo

Jo Ann Latimer,
    Sturgis Library, Barnstable

William Milhomme,
    Massachusetts State Archives

Elizabeth Mock,
    Healey Library, University of Massachusetts

Karin O'Connor,
    Bostonian Society

Catherine Ostlind

Ellery Sedgwick

Evelyn Silverman,
    Paul Klapper Library, Queens College

Patterson Smith

Virginia Smith,
    Massachusetts Historical Society

Doug Southard,
    Boston Historical Society

Nancy Weir,
    Superior Court, Barnstable

I owe a special debt of gratitude to Evan Albright for his generous support and assistance. Anyone interested in learning more about the rich criminal history of Jane Toppan's favorite summer resort area should consult Evan's website, www.capecodconfidential.com.

Visit
❖ Pocket Books ❖
online at

··

www.SimonSays.com

··

Keep up on the latest new
releases from your favorite
authors, as well as author
appearances, news, chats,
special offers and more.

SIMON & SCHUSTER
A VIACOM COMPANY
www.SimonSays.com

Pocket
Books

2381-01

Bela Borsodi

HAROLD SCHECHTER is a professor of American literature and culture. Renowned for his true-crime writing, he is the author of the nonfiction books *Fiend, Bestial, Deviant, Deranged, Depraved,* and, with David Everitt, *The A to Z Encyclopedia of Serial Killers.* He is also the author of *Nevermore* and *The Hum Bug,* the acclaimed historical novels featuring Edgar Allan Poe. He lives in New York State.